A new vision of the good life is creating the city of the 21st century.

Recycled from nostalgic old towns distant from major metropolitan areas, it thrives among pine-covered hills and peaceful neighborhoods. A simpler, less materialistic life beckons. We drink in the sweet air, listen to the birdsong, and know that this is where our future hangs more golden than anywhere else.

I call the new city PENT*urbia because it is the fifth since the beginning of industrialization in the 18th century. Suburbia was the fourth. Today, as suburbia is increasingly submerged in its winter of discontent, we heal our heavy hearts with the promise of something better for ourselves and our children.*

Suburbia is dying. Long live penturbia.

Jack Lessinger

Seattle, 1991

Predicting the 1990s:
Western Growth Counties*
See Appendix D for Growth in Other Regions

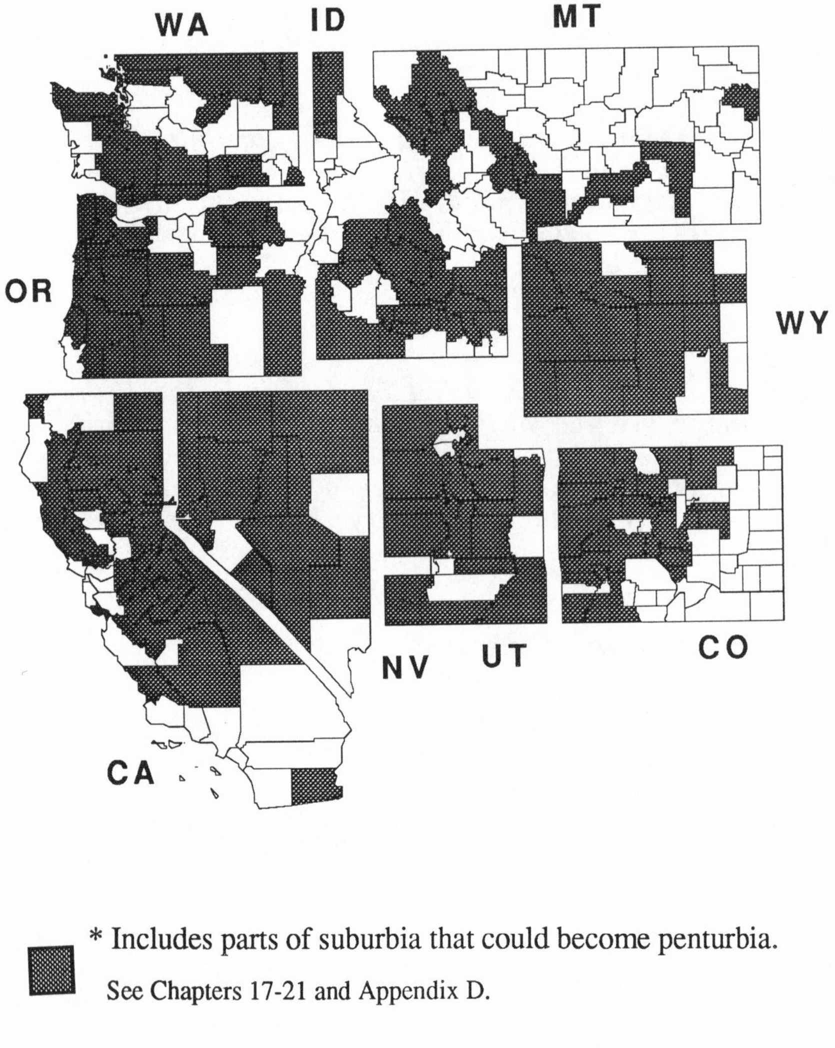

PENTURBIA

Where Real Estate Will Boom
AFTER the Crash of Suburbia

SocioEconomics, Inc.
Seattle, Washington

JACK LESSINGER, Ph.D.

Published by SocioEconomics, Inc. P.O. Box 25062, Seattle, Washington 98125-1962. This book is a sequel to *Regions of Opportunity*, Jack Lessinger, (Times Books–Random House, 1986)

Library of Congress Cataloging in Publication Data

Lessinger, Jack

Penturbia: where real estate will boom after the crash of suburbia/ by Jack Lessinger.

p. cm.

Includes index and bibliographical references.

1. Urban-rural migration—United States. 2. Suburbs—United States. 3. City and town life—United States. I.Title.

HT381.L475 1990

307.2'612'0973—dc20 89-26269

CIP

ISBN: 0-9625182-5-5

Grateful acknowledgement is made to Houghton Mifflin Company for permission to reproduce the maps, "The American Railroad System, 1870,1900," from *A History of American Democracy*, 3rd edition, p. 410, by John D. Hicks, George E. Mowry, and Robert E. Burke.

Contents

Part two

Why suburbia *must* crash and penturbia *must* boom

Part three
3,096 county predictions

Part four
Socially responsible and profitable investing in penturbia

Epilogue
Socioeconomics versus economics

Addendum

To the memory of Jascha Heifetz (1901-1987)

Acknowledgments

My wife, Natalie, was my ever-present accomplice and editor. Any lapses in clarity, logic and sparkle are due to the willfullness of the author. I am also indebted to many individuals for help with the first edition. A number of colleagues have provided useful feedback and support, from Wilbur Thomson, Wayne University, in 1962 to Benjamin E. Brewer, President of the A.I.A., in 1989. Through my years at the University of Washington, Dennis Strong, colleague and friend, was my lone support and source of encouragement. My thanks to Joanie Mackowski, Elspeth Alexander, Chad Haight and Brenda Dunford for reviews of the latest revision. The book was completed in a home designed by Robert S. Taylor, a gifted architect, who also spent many hours plowing through the underbrush of an early draft. His comments, always to the point, have undoubtedly smoothed the way for future readers. Ann Saling has once again rendered outstanding editorial assistance. Matthew Wells gave invaluable help in thinking through problems of the cover design. Leslie Jaye, master graphics designer, joyously solved numerous problems of page design. Daryl Ogden helped prepare the book for publication. My son, Harry, and daughter, Maia, helped with last-minute emergencies. The invaluable computational assistance by Amar Singh on classification of counties remains pivotal to the research. John Osborne helped with the revised classifications.

Cover illustration by Garreth Schuh.
Illustrations in Parts I and II by Christopher Mills.
Photos of Trinidad, Colorado by Dave Neligh.

Prologue

That which has been believed by everyone, always and everywhere, has every chance of being false.

Paul Valéry (1943)

What William Safire saw from an airplane window

Look out your airplane window sometime," wrote William Safire in "Wide Open Spaces," an essay for *The New York Times*, "there's plenty of room down there."[1] The North American continent is still largely empty, still beautiful. Forests extend to the far horizon, gentle slopes are interspersed with lakes and rivers, miles of flat land are free of people and hubbub.

Why, we may wonder, should Americans keep crowding into our already congested, outrageously priced, and crime-ridden cities and suburbs? Why indeed, now that new technology liberates us from the necessity of living in metropolitan areas? Computers can keep track of accounts no matter where inventories or employees are located. Teleconferencing permits face-to-face communication among people thousands of miles apart. The fax machine delivers exact reproductions without messengers or the need to fight city traffic.

The time-worn grip of the city on humanity is relaxing its hold. The country beckons. If you are going to move out from the city core, why not go *all* the way out? "You can now be close without being near," Safire argued.[2]

Suburban living was our first alternative to the congested city. Beginning around the turn of the century, the migration to suburbia reached its peak after World War II. To get a shot at one of those new tract homes, people literally camped outside the subdivision sales office. Today, that honest excitement about suburbia belongs to another age. America is moving on.

Suburbia—a leading region

Think of suburbia as a special kind of region. Call it a *leading region.*[3] Unlike a geographic region its parts are not contiguous but the sum of many, often widely separated areas. Separate suburbs throughout the nation rose at about the same time and are now, as a group, beginning to fall. This long-run cycle of rise and fall is typical of every leading region.

A leading region is where population grows faster than the national average. The elite among us come here—the rich and educated, the innovators, the avant-garde, along with the most modern and dynamic industries of our era. Property values climb in every category, from virgin forests and plains to square city blocks boasting the latest architectural designs.

Suburbia was not the first leading region to take America's fancy—it was the fourth. The first major migration, rising to a peak from 1760 to 1789, was to select middle and southern colonies. The second sent pioneers to the Mississippi and Ohio Valleys. The third filled great industrial cities such as Minneapolis, Kansas City and Chicago, and the fourth created suburbia.

Where will the nation grow in the 1990s? In the sunbelt, as is popularly believed? Not in this author's opinion. The fifth leading region will include selected small towns across the nation.

From suburbia to small towns

In the 1970s, while the fourth migration ebbed, the fifth began to flow. This migration is away from the suburbs to new and old towns distant from our great metropolitan areas. In the coming transformation, a skein of small towns within a large region will form a cosmopolitan, urban-rural complex. Its inhabitants will yield their hearts to the surrounding territory—with its ample meadows and mountains—as much as to the town.

As it is the destination of the fifth migration, I call the new region *pent*urbia.

This book is addressed:

First, to people who own homes in suburbia and are now wondering if, in the changing economic climate of the 1990s, their investment is at risk.

Second, to those who are hoping or planning to relocate but are undecided about where or how to go about it.

Third, to those seekers who would join me in my attempt to gain a clearer view of that elusive Big Picture connecting the fragments of our daily existence.

The book explains:

- why suburbia *must* crash and penturbia *must* boom
- how penturbia differs from suburbia
- when you might consider migrating to penturbia
- where you might settle among 1,708 counties of penturbia and potential penturbia
- what kind of investments will succeed in penturbia
- how the study of economics can be broadened to offer a deeper account of fundamental trends

Background of the book

Initially begun as a revision of the author's earlier book, *Regions of Opportunity* (1986), *Penturbia* has evolved into a wholly different book. Because *Regions* is now out of print, small portions of it have been recycled. *Penturbia* includes seven new county classifications to take account of demographic changes from 1980 to 1988.

All classifications are based on U.S. state and county Census data. Unless otherwise noted, the Census is the only source of data for diagrams that appear throughout the book.[4]

Metropolitan and non-metropolitan areas as defined by

the Census are unreliable predictors of growth. Some are near the end of long-run growth trends, some are near the beginning. By contrast, classifications defined in *Regions of Opportunity* have proven to be useful predictors. During the 1980s, prime penturban counties—most of them "non-metropolitan"—have grown substantially faster than the average of all counties in the nation. At the same time, mature suburban counties—most of them "metropolitan"—have continued to decline. The 1990s will see a rapid expansion of penturbia.

I discover utopia

In 1946, as a graduate student in land economics, I became fascinated by migrations. All migrations. I was as curious about Vikings "migrating" to Normandy in the 9th century as about Americans migrating to suburbia in the 20th.

Always that same burning question came to me: Why? What motivates multitudes of people to uproot their families and move to unfamiliar surroundings? Economists have invariably put their faith in the economic motive. Supposedly, people always migrate for the same reasons: better paying jobs, financial security, a higher standard of living. For the great majority, jobs are thought to be the single main attraction.

Utopia

I am convinced that conventional economic theory is betting on the wrong horse, that migrations are less the pursuit of jobs and more *the lure of utopia*. Utopia is an ancient and honorable term with a number of variations, such as Arcadia, Eden, Shangri-la, Zion or even Plato's Republic. Each variant refers to the ideals of a certain era frozen for all time, "a long lane that has no turning." It is where all men and women are happy, young, equal, educated, wealthy or wise.

In this book, utopia remains an ideal place, but the ideal is *perishable*. It lasts only for the time it takes people to change their conception of the good life. Around 1900 cities like Chicago, with its boisterous Friday-night crowds and noisy trolleys dazzled simple farmers and immigrants. *That* was utopia. Half a century later, disillusioned city-dwellers were streaming into suburbia, and *that* was utopia.

Each utopia begins life anew. It is the place of our fondest dreams, where the sky seems fairer, the people truer, the life more bountiful.

Confessions of a suburbanite

In 1935 when I was an adolescent boy, my family joined the migration to suburbia. Like millions of others in the depression era, we moved without the slightest prospect of a job. We moved from New York City, capital of the nation's job market, to Rosemead, California, where the main employment opportunities were for a few scraggly chickens. It didn't matter. We were after something else. I didn't have a name for it then. Long afterward, I knew what to call it. Utopia.

A few years later, though I didn't comprehend it at the time, I once again experienced the spell of utopia. During World War II, I was in Patton's Third Army, chasing the remnants of Hitler's Wehrmacht across the wastelands of Europe. I kept my spirits up with thoughts of raising a family in one of those glamorous new tract houses I'd been reading about in the slick magazines. (Twenty-two and naive, I never doubted that I would find and win the right girl: one who loved music, especially the violin. Somehow, it all came to pass. I found the girl in 1946, married her in 1947, and bought the house in 1948. In 1990 the girl is still the same. The house in suburbia is a distant memory.)

In the 1950s, at the University of California, Berkeley, I wrote my PhD dissertation on the migration to suburbia. I watched the conversion of the northern Santa Clara Valley from farms to suburbs.[5] I watched orchards and vegetable gardens bulldozed to make way for Silicon Valley. I also watched Karl Belser, Director of Planning for Santa Clara County, unsuccessfully attempt to stop the juggernaut. He argued that the sprawl pattern of suburbia was a voracious beast that wouldn't stop until it had consumed all the prime agricultural land of this beautiful valley, destroying greenbelts, creating traffic jams and polluting the air. Belser was 20 years too early. His brave attempts to keep subdivisions off-limits through zoning soon disappeared without a trace.

What Belser didn't realize was that this was the springtime of utopia's latest version. In the 1950s, suburbia was reaching the very apex of its popularity as the American dream. And though its social and economic costs eventually became unsustainable, I am convinced that suburbia was right for those times.

Early discoveries

After graduate school, burrowing through 200 years of history and statistics, I made what was for me an astounding discovery: the migration to suburbia was not unique. It appeared to be one cycle in a series of cycles. Each cycle rose and fell. In each, a new migration began slowly, reached a peak and then subsided. The cycle of migration was also part of a larger cycle. In each, a new kind of city and a new kind of society was created. Suburbanization appeared to be the latest of four distinct cycles since the American Revolution.

It was even more surprising to me that each rising tide of migration seemed to coincide with a long period of economic instability. *For instance, in the 1930s the Great Depression arrived during the upswing of migration to suburbia.*

I was also surprised to find that migrations continued at a rapid though declining rate throughout a long period of prosperity. The migration to big cities like Chicago, for example, slowed down in the 1920s, even as most economic indicators pointed to continuing prosperity.

My curiosity was aroused. Were my observations the result of chance? Or must migrations be cyclical and must each cycle involve depression and prosperity?

The dominant theory of migrations has little to say about cycles.[6] It has much to say about economic motivations. People move because they want to improve their standard of living and because advances in technology (especially in transportation) make improvements possible.

The economic motive has always had a certain appeal. Successive migrations are touched off by new technologies that create opportunities for economic advancement. When technology makes canal building feasible, rich land areas, formerly inaccessible, can be settled. Because they can be, they will be. *Voilà*! Canals and river boats open up the Mississippi Valley and we have a new migration. Later, railroads create the big industrial cities. Still later, autos shape suburbia. And the electronic revolution will supposedly spark the next migration.

Technology is not the cause of migration

Certainly history shows that at the time of each migration transportation technology made significant advances. But does it follow that technology *caused* the migration? Did my hand on the steering wheel cause the right turn I just made? Yes. But only superficially. The underlying cause is my *intention* to drive to a certain address.

Perhaps we, the society and economy, decide where we want to go and then technology takes us there. When we decree that cigarettes are proper and good, technology finds new and better ways to produce them. When *we* decree that cigarettes are bad, cigarette technologies languish. Perhaps, after all, we were less commanded by technology than we thought.

By the 1960s, I had assembled the rudiments of a socioeconomic theory quite different from traditional economic theories of migration. Periodically the earth rumbles with the force of social and economic change. Certainties crumple like structures sitting on a moving fault line. Amid the debris of a collapsing social and economic order, the landscape of reason is twisted out of shape. The most commonsense economic decisions are weighed differently from before. What used to be important becomes unimportant. What used to be unimportant becomes important. To migrate or not to migrate is now a question raised by people with new perceptions. Individuals by the thousands, and then the tens of thousands, get the urge to pull up stakes and move. Impelled by the different logic of an emerging social and economic order—and inspired by its potential for correcting old failures—the new migrants strike out for an updated utopia.

The 1970s proved to be a pivotal decade. In 1970 many trends died: uptrends turned down and downtrends turned up. Hundreds of suburban counties growing rapidly during the 1950s and 1960s (often with track records of growth going back to the beginning of the century) were now slowing down—like Los Angeles. Other counties, spurned before the 1970s (many with declining growth for a century or more) were suddenly hot. For them it was the rural renaissance of the 1970s, prelude to the coming boom of small towns.

Working from my theory, I became convinced that the fifth migration—to penturbia—was on the move.

Part one

Rise of a new America

Through loyalty to the past, our mind refuses to realize that tomorrow's joy is possible only if today's makes way for it...

André Gide (1928)

One

Penturbia: Emerging utopia

Every migration is a unique event. While penturbia features small towns, they are by no means the small towns of the early 19th century. Driving late-model Fords, Hondas and Mercedes, the migrants drifting in from across the nation are urban and urbane. They are a new breed of urban-rural people who are often as inclined to attend ballet or chamber music performances, as country fiddling and come-as-you-are community events.

Where is penturbia?

Look for penturbia in nearly every one of the 50 states. Find it beyond the commuting range of large industrial centers—in Whatcom County, Washington, 80 miles north of Seattle; in Greene County, New York, 100 miles north of New York City; in Adams County, Wisconsin, 65 miles northwest of Madison. Connected by major highways to the rest of the nation, the new favored areas are neither urban nor rural but urban-rural.

A cluster of nostalgic towns and villages—most are lightly populated—forms a wider regional network. Occasional historic gems like Grafton, Vermont, are cherished and preserved. A visitor attempting to describe Grafton "is left helpless before the task of distinguishing between views equally lovely, antique houses equally graceful, church steeples equally eloquent against the star-shot night sky."[7] Community centers, churches, universities, specialty shops, residential subdivisions and light industries are nestled around and among green and growing places, open spaces filled with vistas of land and water. In penturbia, no matter where you live, work or shop, nature is only a glance away.

The migration to penturbia is also going on abroad. *The Economist* reports that the "...call of the wild is stirring the breasts of the British; from Hartlepool to Hampstead they are leaving town for a leafy dream...." Western Europeans are equally fervent about putting the cities behind them. But Britain, "the first urbanised nation, is the most anti-*urbs* and the most afflicted by rural romance."[8]

In a visit to Australia in 1987, I discovered an immense stretch of penturbia along the picturesque Pacific Coast from Sydney to Melbourne. In Britain, as in America, the movement to penturbia momentarily peaked in the 1970s and subsided in the mid-1980s; at the same time many experts were predicting an enthusiastic return to metropolitan areas. Since then, and until now, the growth of penturbia has been accelerating.[9]

Location, location, location

The map of the United States in Figure 1 shows penturbia based on the logic and statistical findings presented later in this book. *Prime* penturbia is even now developing at a substantial pace. The remainder of penturbia has a potential for development in the next two to three decades. Based on the latest available data, detailed maps in Appendixes B and C show further classifications predicting growth or decline for 3,096 counties of the contiguous United States. Part III explains the classifications.

Figure 1

Penturbia and Potential Penturbia in the U.S.

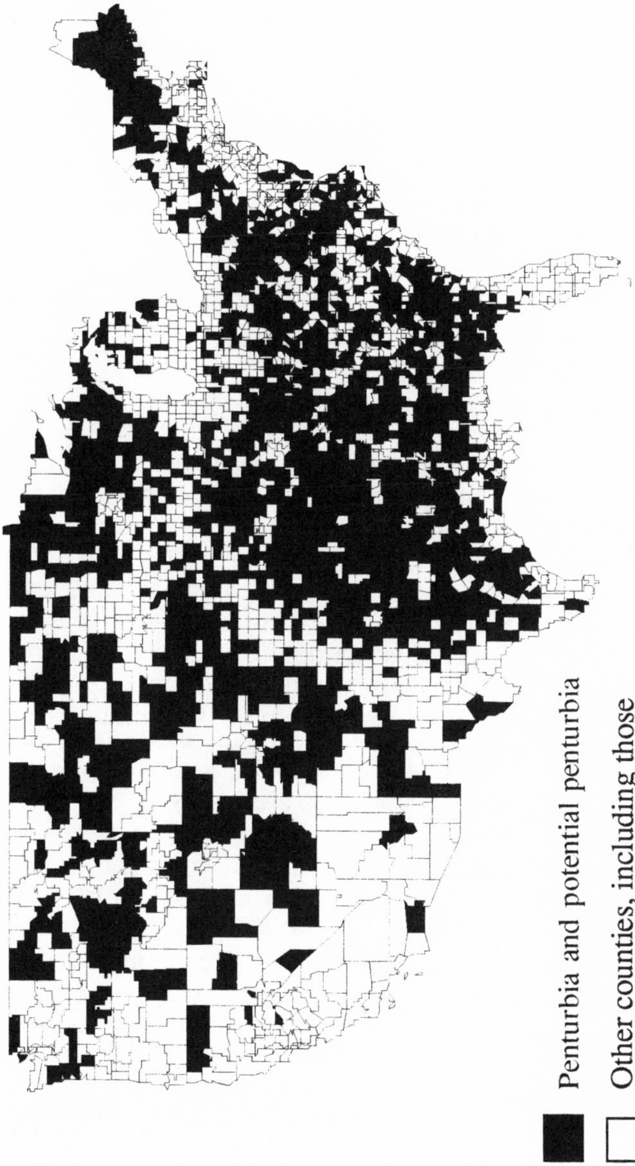

■ Penturbia and potential penturbia

□ Other counties, including those shifting from suburbia to penturbia

Two

What's driving the migration?

The squeeze on the middle class

The middle class is being squeezed out of suburbia by a pincers movement of the rich and the poor—the rich from one part of the metropolitan area, the poor from another. The middle class has nowhere to go but out.

In Los Angeles, "astronomical housing costs on the city's tony West Side—where routine homes sell for $500,000 and monthly rents commonly exceed $1,100—have forced middle-class residents to move into working-class areas."[10] But in those working-class areas the middle class faces an insuperable obstacle. It is out-competed by the poor.

The poor are relentless competitors

From near and far corners of the world comes a rush of minorities to the suburbs—our native poor plus an influx of aliens from Mexico, Central America, South America, Asia and now Eastern Europe. These are suburbia's fastest-growing populations, many with incomes below the poverty line. Los Angeles County is still a preserve for the opulent, a "land of limos and linen suits, consumerism and car phones, movie stars and million-dollar beach houses."[11] But the underclass may now constitute up to *half* the county's population.[12] The city is home for "hundreds of immigrants who congregate each morning on street corners in hopes of finding work; of thousands who live in garages, often without running water, because they can't afford apartments; of homeless who sleep in cardboard lean-tos in the shadow of downtown banks brimming with money."[13]

The poor are migrating to suburbia because they can no longer tolerate the bleakness of life and shocking conditions in our inner-cities. As described in a news report, the grandchildren of Delores Long were desperate when they "cried in fear about the rats that had chewed clear through the back of the couch in their ramshackle Chicago apartment. But they stayed until a gang of young toughs knocked Mrs. Long aside one day last winter and stole her Social Security money."[14]

Orbbia Williams and his family lived on Chicago's West side. But "...the continual gunfire and the fear that the shots might come closer one day persuaded him to move to suburban Schiller Park." According to William J. Wilson, a professor of sociology at the University of Chicago, "People are leaving the inner city because there are no opportunities left there. And they're leaving because it's not safe." [15]

The invincible poor

Poverty wields an invincible weapon, the ability to double up, and where necessary, triple and quadruple up—and not only in standard units, but in makeshift quarters. Per head, the poor pay less. Per housing unit, they can bid the price up to impossible heights—at least wherever zoning authorities are willing to wink at regulations. And because slumlords are content to mine their properties, providing minimum management and repair, occupation by the poor often results in serious damage to neighborhood quality.

"Landlords rent dilapidated apartments and barren garages in rundown sections of Hollywood, South-Central Los Angeles and the San Fernando Valley for as much as $800 a month. Struggling families crowd as many as a dozen people into one-bedroom units."[16] Why would owners allow such devastation to their property? Economists know. Ask them and they will tell you. It's the high return on investment—up to 30 percent and more. In less than five years you earn all your money back—and then some.

Suburbia attracts the underclass and alienates the middle class. There is no need to blame bigotry. *The middle class simply cannot afford to pay so much for so little.* Helpless before the onslaught of the poor, their vulnerability is rooted in the most fundamental middle-class values. They are obliged to live by those values: no doubling up, no crowding, no living in disreputable neighborhoods. Unless driven by direst necessity, each middle-class family is uncompromising in its resolve to live respectably and by itself.

Cashing in on the housing inflation

Breathing life into statistics is like filling a ghost with blood. At times, however, a statistical trend so violates normal expectations it fairly leaps from its chart and shrieks. Consider the national trend in home prices. Since 1950, they have risen far more rapidly than inflation. From 1950 to 1986 the consumer price index rose over four times,[17] family incomes over six times.[18] During the same period *prices of new homes increased almost 11 times*![19]

Pounded by nearly a century of steady growth, home prices are substantially higher in suburbia than in penturbia. In 1980 the median home price in suburban Alameda County, California, was 47 percent higher than in the typically penturban Whatcom County, Washington, even though average household incomes were nearly comparable.[20]

As suburban prices soar above those in penturbia, there is a corresponding incentive to sell out. That's what Lou and Mildred H. did. In 1958 they bought a lot and built a home for $75,000 in Encino, a suburb near Los Angeles.

Lou's building skills and Mildred's talent for design added to the value of the property. In early 1988, after 30 years of uninterrupted use, the couple was delighted to find that their house could be sold for $475,000. They sold it, bought another house in Eugene, Oregon, for $150,000 and, after paying the capital-gains tax, invested the difference in government bonds. Now they have a house they like even better, with more land (something they've always wanted), congenial neighbors (urban-rural types), an unpolluted environment (that is also more scenic). And best of all, they earn over $20,000 a year in secure income from Treasury bonds.

Because the H's bought early in the boom, they reaped a very large capital gain. The steepest rise occurred during the 1970s. Families that bought before the rise are now able to take advantage of the price difference between homes in suburbia and homes in penturbia. Buy cheap and sell dear. Never was that axiom of business more fully realized.

Jobs, jobs, jobs

Hold on, says conventional wisdom. It's all very well to talk about life in the country, but can people expect to make a living so far away from our economic centers? Aren't the jobs in the cities and suburbs, along with the people, the markets, the industrial might of the nation?

For almost two decades, penturbia has been growing faster than the national average, in some places a good deal faster. That growth could not have been sustained without a commensurate growth in employment opportunities.

Maury County? Never heard of it

In the 1980s, big industry was discovering penturbia. Making its high-tech response to the Japanese challenge, General Motors put over $3 billion into its Saturn plant in Maury County, Tennessee. Billions more were invested by subcontractors and service industries.

General Motor's choice of obscure little Maury County was the result of a long, drawn out search. Hundreds of counties competed for that prize, most of them from old-established metropolitan areas. Distinguished civic leaders delegated to lobby the company, came bedecked with credentials. They sought to prove their superiority with a long track record of growth, accessibility to gigantic markets, and the latest production facilities. By contrast, Maury County was lightest of the lightweights. In 1970 Maury County numbered 43,376 rural inhabitants. And before 1970 it had been declining for a century.

But in 1970—long before General Motors put the Saturn plant on their agenda—the first migrants to Maury County were already responding to the new cycle. Their decisions to reverse a century of decline were duly recorded in *Regions of Opportunity*. Maury County is listed there as Class II—in the second rank of penturbia.

Choosing Maury County was no accident. Saturn had an urgent, perhaps desperate, mission. Faced with a ruinous loss of market share, the company was ready for a complete transformation—in labor relations, management, technology, and in the nuts and bolts of manufacturing. Saturn was to be the example that "will teach the rest of GM how to reform its own ponderous culture."[21] The task was deemed nearly impossible. As one company executive put it, "To take a company that has 800,000 people worldwide and try to change the culture, that's kind of like trying to parallel-park the Queen Mary."[22] The desired transformation could develop only in a totally fresh, unspoiled environment. What the company needed—and got—was a blank slate on which to write its future.

GM needed a piece of penturbia. It would be followed by other innovative companies.

Electronic workplaces in the home

A particularly fast-growing group of penturbanites is served by the electronic marketplace. Personal computers in mere seconds can connect with headquarter offices anywhere in the country or the world. All that is required to merge office with home is a separate room with good lighting, and, one hopes, a view. Nothing to get in the way of birds and trees and the smell of new-mown grass. As for equipment, essentials include a personal computer, printer, modem, a photocopier, a fax machine, perhaps two phone lines, and a cordless telephone.[23] Gone is the age-old necessity to live within an easy commute to work; one authority estimates that 24 million now sleep and work at the same location.[24]

In tiny Effie, Minnesota (population 135), attorney

Barry Feld writes of his reliance on the technological revolution: "I can do everything here that I could do in in my office at the law school [in Minneapolis]."[25] Many professionals can tolerate a longish commute, so long as it is less than five days a week. The number of occupations that are fully functional outside the metropolis is now impressive. Among the ranks of the self-employed—and getting along just fine from a distance—are craftsmen, artists, writers, composers, musicians, sales representatives and entrepreneurs of every type, including those earning a livelihood in cottage industries like dress-making and light manufacturing.

Retirement: The starter industry

Old-timers in search of a delightful and economical retirement are likely to be among the first arrivals in penturbia. Their Social Security dollars and other outside income are pure adrenaline for the local business community, creating wholesale, retail and service-related jobs. More jobs will be contributed by the snowballing growth of tourists, vacationers and "second-homers."

"Oh, but it's just a retirement community," people say disdainfully. What continues to go unrecognized is the fact that retirees have always been and will continue to be an indispensable vanguard building that all-important economic base.

In the 1930s, Los Angeles was deeply beholden to its retirement industry. There was deep skepticism about a young person's future in Los Angeles. "How will you make a living there?" people asked prospective migrants. Los Angeles was about as far from the center of U.S. industry as it was possible to be. If you were serious about wanting a job you'd go to Chicago, New York, or Philadelphia. That's where the jobs were, and the markets and the infrastructure.

Los Angeles? Sure, for retired people. And so it was, for a while. But on that platform all the rest was built.

Penturbia's economic base

People are penturbia's leading resource, hard-working, loyal, know-what-they-want kind of people. Bob Goodner in

Broken Bow, Nebraska (population 3,800) was featured in a *Wall Street Journal* report.[26] Having discovered a flair for working with wood, Goodner now designs and sells a range of wood items. He and his wife now market their *Fine Wood* products in 30 states. Goodner claims that 85 percent of his estimated $200,000 in annual sales will come from outside Nebraska. Nor is he the only one in town creating an economic base. Other residents are expanding the town's economic potential with a variety of sewn toys, ceramics and other crafts.

Broken Bow refuses to die. Like other small towns, it competes with metropolitan areas by dint of talent, low costs, a willing work force and entrepreneurial skills.[27]

As penturbia continues to grow, its job market will grow with it. Like a coral reef that deposits layer on layer, penturbia's economic base will gradually build a future that everyone can believe in.

The lure of utopia

Silicon Valley: Utopia passe´

A reporter explained why many firms are leaving Silicon Valley. The "freeways filled with cars, the hills grew hazy behind the smog, and the driving time of some six-mile commutes lengthened to 45 minutes." Toxic chemicals were found in the public drinking water, white-collar crime had become the order of the day. Employees were stealing chips and circuit designs and selling them on the high-tech black market.[28]

The price of raw land was becoming ridiculously uncompetitive—between $8 and $12 a square foot in Santa Clara, compared with 20 cents in Austin and 65 cents in Colorado Springs. Moreover, raw land in Silicon Valley was virtually nonexistent. An official of the Rolm Corporation reported that in 1981 his company could not find the 125 acres it needed for a new plant in south San Jose.

Has anything improved? Not to the naked eye. We're still multiplying congestion on the freeways, still creating deadly anonymity in our residential districts, still bulldozing open spaces to make way for shopping malls and subdivisions. But we have a deeper complaint: suburbia has become like a B movie we've seen too many times. We are ready for a new life that is less edgy and gluttonous. Utopia beckons, where spiritual deficits can be addressed and life can proceed at a more humane, less hurried pace.

Stevens County, Washington

Stevens County, Washington is one corner of the new utopia. Why do people come here, clear across the state from Seattle and the other older population centers? asked Bill Dietrich of the *Seattle Times*. To find out, he tells us, breathe the air and contemplate the scenery. This is spectacular mountain country. Lakes and streams abound and the water is pure. The only congestion is from roaming deer. Nearby Ferry County has a single traffic light, and it's a yellow blinker. Olaf Heintz, a recent migrant to the area, recalled, "I came over the hill down into Chewelah. The sky was totally clear. The hills were beautifully green. The farms were green, gold and brown. I knew I'd found it."[29]

Amador County, California

In the 1960s Susan Woods, model and part-time actress, was an exemplary member of the 20th century consumer society.[30] Somewhat richer than most, she was able to buy what others could only dream about. The bedroom of her Manhattan Beach home near Los Angeles flaunted a Pacific view. Her dresses came from Beverly Hills. On weekends she sailed a 30-foot sloop. She often visited posh night spots.

Early in the 1970s Woods fell out of love with her lifestyle. "I needed to get away from the condo people in Gucci shoes who kept asking, 'Where did you buy that?' at every cocktail party... The yachts near us in the marina were only used for cocktail parties. My 10-minute walk to the beach just put me closer to drugs. I knew it was time to leave when two of my neighbors hired attorneys and went into court over a 6-inch property dispute."

In 1976 Susan Woods sold her sloop and headed for Amador County, a piece of penturbia in the Sierra foothills 400 miles north of Los Angeles. Today she lives in a smaller house fronting an evergreen forest. She's 20 miles from the nearest supermarket and gets her haute cuisine at community picnics. But, she affirms, she has "never been happier."

To Woods, happiness is being aware of the "nowness" of things—the feel of the day, the temperature, the people next door and the people passing by, catching the splendor of sun at midmorning, indulging the itch to take a footpath or to linger at a waterfall. These are values indigenous to penturbia.

Another value indigenous to penturbia is its freedom from suburbia's fatal flaw.

Three

Suburbia's fatal flaw

Reader: Remember suburbia before World War II? Clean air, cows and chickens, a serene countryside. People penned up in the cities couldn't wait to move out there. After the war they arrived in an endless stream. And then came the calamity, creeping at first, then rushing along. A family thinks it's moving to the country and ends up with a 90-unit subdivision for a neighbor. We've seen it happen in Long Island, Los Angeles, Phoenix. Won't penturbia suffer the same fate?

Author: No, because penturbia will be planned. Planning will channel growth, tame it, make it serve rather than sabotage the community.

Reader: You think suburbia isn't planned? Every suburb has its planners, planning board, master plan, zoning regulations, building codes and all the rest.

Author: Oh, I have no doubt that planners can zone sheltering plants out of residential neighborhoods. They can also deal with many other neighborhood-size problems. It's the block-buster problems affecting the metropolitan area as a whole that make them throw up their hands. You know them—congestion, gridlock on the freeways, pollution, deterioration of the environment...The list is long.

Reader: Why blame the planners? The problem is growth—decades of sustained, irrepressible growth. Growth on that scale can defeat the best-laid plans.

Author: I too hold the planners blameless. But there we part company. I don't believe that growth is the problem.

Reader: You don't? If the problem isn't growth, what is it?

Author: Let me answer that by telling you something that will surprise you.

Reader: Feel free. Surprise me.

Author: The first glimmerings of what we know as suburbia appeared around the turn of this century. At the time, it seemed a normal-enough birth, and it was. But all beginnings have within them a unique vulnerability, a fatal flaw ensuring that what begins must end. Suburbia's fatal flaw sealed the limit on its potential for growth.

Fragmentation

Reader: And what was suburbia's fatal flaw?

Author: A quirk in its nature made the failure of *comprehensive* planning inevitable—as inevitable as death in a Greek tragedy. Allow me to explain. Early in the 20th century, the metropolitan area was splintered into hundreds of separate and sovereign jurisdictions—suburbs, we called them—with each suburb going its own way, following its own agenda. Metropolitan areas were turned into confederations of separate municipalities. At the time, the change seemed vital and wholesome. It was the wave of the future.

Reader: It *was* the wave of the future. We were desperate to get out of the big cities. Do you see something wrong about our moving to the suburbs?

Author: Not wrong for 1900. In 1900 moving to suburbia was a very good thing. It permitted us to

escape the offensive atmosphere of the big industrial cities. The bad thing came later. The metropolitan areas had become *unplannable*. There was no mechanism in place to prevent them from being overwhelmed by the torrent of growth that hit them in the 1950s and 1960s. What we didn't understand then—or perhaps even now—is that a metropolitan area is an indivisible whole, as indivisible as you or I. Pinch it in one place and it cries "ouch" somewhere else.

Reader: I would argue that a metropolitan area is not an indivisible whole but a community of neighbors, together and yet separate.

Author: You'd be right if the "neighbors" were truly separate, if you as an individual lived and worked in the same suburb. But you don't. You live in one suburb, work in another and pass through several others on the way.

Let me ask you something. For the average suburbanite, what is the single activity that uses up more time and causes more aggravation than any other? I'll tell you: it's the daily commute, from home to work and back again. To make that commute most efficient, both destinations should be planned for at the same time.

But commuting isn't the only issue. Just as the congestion in one suburb depends on the traffic generated by another, the quality of air in one suburb depends on the kinds of industries in another. The quality of water in one suburb depends on how sewage is treated in another. The enjoyment of nature by residents of one suburb depends on planning in another. By opting for independent communities—by dividing the indivisible—we've opted for inept planning.

Reader: Maybe you're complaining about the way the roads were planned. We could have handled the commuting problem by developing a more intelligent road system. We should have known that building a freeway in one location would encourage growth in another. By clever forecasting, we could have accommodated commuters more efficiently. Is that what you have in mind?

Author: Better transportation planning would have helped. But the problem goes deeper. It's in the haphazard arrangement of homes, jobs and shopping facilities. Essential functions are scattered willy-nilly throughout the metropolitan area. Do you know that from 1959 to 1970 more than 13,000 shopping centers were strewn throughout the nation? And scattered among them are subdivisions, factories, office complexes and countless commercial outlets.

The result is that jobs are everywhere,

shopping is everywhere,

autos are everywhere,

and congestion is everywhere.

Commuters driving through different suburbs at peak hours create dense knots of traffic. Pollution spreads like smoke that seeps under all doors and through all cracks. Why does it happen? **Because every little suburb makes its own decisions about what should go where.** The effects of this chaotic arrangement became apparent in 1989 when the San Francisco earthquake disrupted the local economy: "No fewer than twenty-three public transit agencies had to attempt last-minute coordination of the area's commuters, who, it should be noted, are addicted to their cars, in part because of the disorganization and inefficiency of public transportation."[31]

Reader: There's nothing to stop any individual suburb from consulting and cooperating with any others.

Author: But there is. Start with the sheer numbers of separate municipalities. Robert Wood reported that the 22-county metropolitan area of New York was split into 1,467 taxing and spending jurisdictions.[32] Imagine the representatives of 1,467 jurisdictions sitting around a table to hash out detailed plans on a comprehensive metropolitan plan!

But the bigger problem is competition—inappropriate competition. Each suburb is scrupulously for itself, at liberty to "beggar its neighbor" via municipal mercantilism. By zoning lots as large as an acre or more, suburbs fob off the poor on their neighbors. Most counties would compete to win high tax-paying industries, even if some other location would better serve the wider metropolitan area. If forced to surrender, an army whose battalions had that much autonomy would be too disorganized to deliver itself to the enemy.

Perhaps nowhere is the problem of fragmentation more severe than in Los Angeles. The L.A. 2000 Committee appointed by Mayor Bradley depicted Los Angeles as a "Balkanized landscape of political fortresses, each guarding its own resources in the midst of divisiveness, overcrowded freeways, antiquated sewers, ineffective schools, inadequate human services and a polluted environment."[33]

Let me reiterate. Fragmentation is the ultimate mischief-maker and suburbia's fatal flaw.

Putting the author on the spot

Reader: If you don't mind, I'd like to propose a little fantasy. Let's say that the Almighty sends down a bolt of lightning as a sign to all the suburbs in the Los Angeles metropolitan area. They *must* join in amiable cooperation—or else. It is 1990 and they ask *you* to search the bulging files of your mind for the best transportation plan you can devise. What do you do?

Author: A very nice offer and I thank you but unfortunately, there's nothing I can do. It's too late. The damage is done and it's irreversible. Perhaps you'd like to ask what I *might* have done had your offer arrived 30 years ago, before growth got out of hand.

Reader: Very well. Set the clock back 30 years.

Author: I'd concentrate all industrial and commercial activities in a few major centers that occupy 5 percent of the metropolitan area. Within and close to that 5 percent, to facilitate an easy commute, I'd reserve land for future access roads, widen the arteries leading to all major centers and create elaborate connections for funneling traffic to plenty of park-and-ride lots.

Above all, I'd make provision for mass transit—which now becomes a more feasible alternative for the daily commuters. All of these measures would reduce congestion, as well as the cost of building and maintainence for the entire transportation system.

Reader: But you've only dealt with 5 percent of the metropolitan area. Aren't you going to do something about the 95 percent that's left?

Author: I've already done it. By concentrating employment in 5 percent of the metropolitan area, I've immediately freed 95 percent from future congestion.

Reader: As usual, hindsight is most helpful. But aren't you forgetting something? You might have made mass transit more feasible, even more attractive to commuters, but they wouldn't have bought it. In the 1950s, Americans were as intoxicated with automobiles as they were in 1927 when Ford announced he would come out with a new car. On opening day, a hundred thousand people rushed into the Ford showrooms in Detroit. Mounted police were called out to control the mobs in Cleveland. For months afterward, a new Ford on the streets invariably drew crowds.[34]

Author: You're point is worth pursuing. Why was the auto so fascinating to people during the first half of the century? They were fed up with 19th-century mass transit—

the great subway and elevated systems in New York, Chicago and other big cities. Hanging on those straps at rush hour, jammed in like sardines in a can, was what Americans now wanted to escape. Our disinclination to plan for mass transit in the 1950s brings us closer to what made suburbia the new utopia.

Reader: What was that?

Author: The mindset of the 20th century.

Four

The mindset of the 20th century

Do the Japanese save their money? Do they bow to authority and work as a team? There's a collective mind at work, a system of values. *A mindset.* Are Americans big spenders? Are they competitive and impatient to get what they want? A collective mind is at work there too. A different mindset.

Mindset changes. You think that the Japanese are thrifty by inheritance and that Americans have always been improvident? Not true. Americans of 1900 worked just as long and hard as the Japanese today. And they too were ardent savers. Our great grandfathers would not have bought a Model T on credit. They would have saved up for it. Borrowing money for anything but productive investments was unthinkable.

The unthinkable turns thinkable in the next mindset. "Until the French Revolution...," says Ivan Illich, "it was simply not thinkable that a king could be beheaded. Then suddenly, the king was beheaded and a dramatically new image of the common person's role in society emerged."[35]

Early directions

In the first decade of the 20th century we sped away from the Victorian era. Where were we headed? Nobody knew. It was the decade when the Wright brothers flew their fragile craft at Kitty Hawk, Ford manufactured his Model T, Freud electrified American audiences with his theory of the unconscious, Bracque and Picasso launched their cubist art, Schoenberg developed his twelve-tone scale, Einstein announced his special theory of relativity, and middle-class Americans—not only the very rich and privileged—were beginning to migrate out of big cities to former farmlands that everyone would come to know as suburbia.

Arching above all these innovations, linking them in a common outlook, was the awakening of a new mindset. Its aim: liberation from Victorian certitudes. (See Chapters 12 and 13.) Top-hatted industrial tycoons advising a stiff upper lip, iron will, and hard work were dethroned from positions of eminence. Average Americans would no longer hang reverentially on their every word of advice.

In the 1910s, Charlie Chaplin dramatized the little guy's revolt. What made Chaplin one of Hollywood's brightest stars? His baggy pants, bumbling misadventures and fiercely independent spirit (watch him twirl that cane) became firmly implanted inside the psyches of our great-grandparents. The Little Tramp was Mr. Everyman, personifying a widespread antagonism toward 19th-century subservience. His mischievous bumbling *tripped up the big shots*. Audiences loved him for that.

New lessons were being taught, assimilated and propagated. We were all paying close attention as one stupendous idea broke like a sun through a skin of clouds. Not only would we ditch the old authorities, we'd also get rid of their insistence that we pay now for a glorious future. We turned the old formula on its ear. *Get it now and pay later*

Our rambunctious ancestors

Get-it-now became the liberating theme, overthrowing a lifetime of rankling constraints and eventually redirecting all social and economic behavior. Although an older generation lived for a golden future that might never come, the new mindset instructed Americans to live for a present that would never die. And as nearsightedness magnifies what is close and

Why am I popular? It's not that I'm jocular

blurs the distance, the emerging mindset magnified the present and blurred the future. It still does.

In describing the 1980s, Richard G. Darman, President Bush's budget director, referred to "'now-now-ism,'...our collective short-sightedness, our obsession with the here and now, our reluctance to adequately address the future."[36]

Listen to me you people of the '90s
The fun began in the roaring '20s

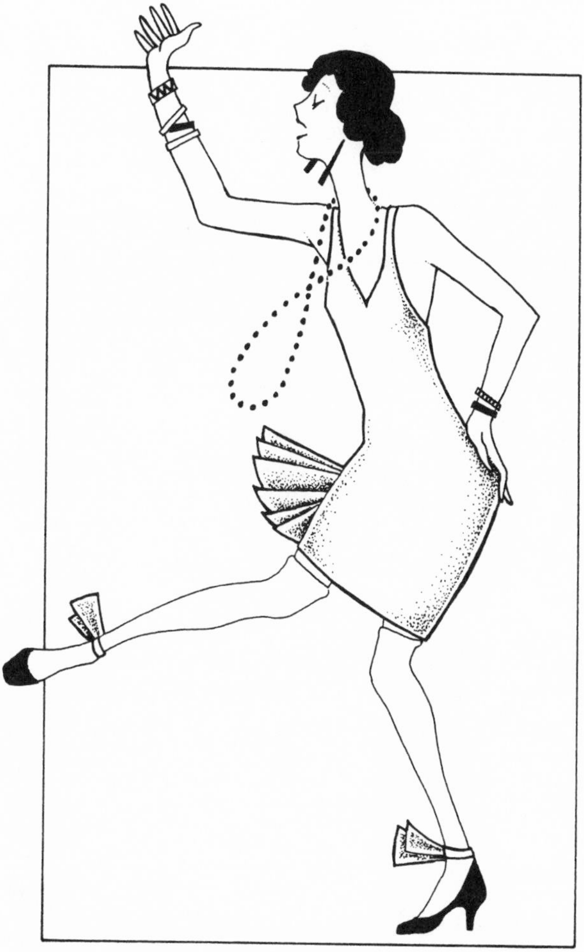

A mindset is cyclical; it rises and falls. By the 1920s, the emerging mindset was in early adolescence. We were fast becoming a people of impatience with a rage to live in the present. Throw off the yoke, kick up those heels. Not even the law would interfere with our pleasures. Average Americans thumbed their noses at Prohibition. Speakeasies became downright popular. Under the sway of a new mindset, it all seemed right and good.

Young ladies racing toward modernity wrenched free from their stern-faced parents to exchange toe-length dresses and layers of petticoats for daringly short skirts. No need to wait for marriage either. Love affairs could be negotiated from a rumble seat. The prevailing mood yielded a swashbuckling self-indulgence with a clear directive: whatever it is you want, get it now—this month, this day, this hour. And to bolster the exhilaration of getting it *now*, get it *new*. People trashed yesterday's newspapers, last month's dresses, last season's shoes and later in the century, last year's husbands and wives.

The importance of being a consumer

People of impatience whipped up a prodigious appetite to consume, along with a well-developed indifference to produce. Economists make a fundamental distinction between production and consumption. Consumption is immediate. Production takes patience. The apple consumed in minutes takes years of preparation and dollars of sacrifice for pesticides, fertilizer and water. Prudence dictates a fine balance between consumption and production, the short run and the long run. The 20th-century mind remains indifferent to that balance.

Impatience in the 1990s

In business

Our sights remain fixed on the short run. The world of business prizes the quick killing. A new breed of privateers turns great corporations into quick cash, saddling their long-run futures with enormous debts (junk bonds). To flaunt quick profits at the next stockholders meeting, CEOs often prune budgets for research and development. R&D requires too many years of patient effort for uncertain results. Nicholas Brady, Secretary of the Treasury in the Bush Administration, "has agonized over what he sees as Corporate America's vulgar obsession with fast-buck deals, pyramiding debt, and mindless takeovers—an unseemly culture of greed that makes his patrician blood boil."[37] As he puts it, "We've developed a fly-now, pay-later mentality, and I've got this gnawing feeling that sooner or later it's going to bite us."[38]

In suburbia

Suburbia is the citadel of impatience, temple of the short run. It specializes in wait-lessness. Once, average Americans worked and waited their lives away, scrimping to save for a home of their own. That idea is almost incomprehensible today. Whatever for? asks the real estate salesman from deep in the heart of suburbia. You can buy mile after mile of brand-new houses on credit. All you need is $10,000 down for a $100,000 home. You don't have ten thousand? Not to worry. Someone will lend it to you.

On the freeways

The same impatience is even now corrupting our environment. We look the other way as the daily armada of suburban cars belches tons of pollution into the air. We love those comfortable cars with their four-speaker stereos and cellular phones. They give us personal transportation—on demand—free of bus schedules and waiting in the rain. Of course we hate traffic, and pollution makes us sick. But the tiny daily damage to our long-suffering lungs may show up in only twenty years. We'd rather choke on foul air than undergo a lengthy sacrifice to get rid of it. Imagine the uproar if every owner of a single-passenger car had to pay $5 for the privilege of using a busy freeway. We can live with it for now, we say. So we push the costs into the less visible long run. Some day there'll be hell to pay. Some day....

On drugs

The same impatience empowers the purveyors of drugs.

Where do the annual billions come from to pay the drug dealers? The inner city is notorious for its record on drugs. But suburbia is where the money is—and the craving. Suburbia craves drugs for the same reason it craves unaffordable houses and unaffordable cars and for the same reason it slides easily into unaffordable debt to pay for them. Drugs provide instant happiness. One jab of the needle and the future doesn't matter. So my liver won't last forever, shrugs the tuned-out druggie. Today it's okay. Right?

With children

By providing an inferior education, the same impatience wastes the potential of our children. Children are our future. But the get-it-now mindset doesn't value the future. So, even though billboards proclaim that a mind is a terrible thing to waste, minds *are* wasted. Children emerge from a decade of public education (if they don't drop out) with little to show for their time. The waste is two-fold: what these children could have contributed and the cost levied on society. The neglected, abused and poorly educated children are those most likely to enter our public hospitals as adult patients and our prisons as inmates. The bill is incalculable.

In creative potential

To empty our warehouses burgeoning with stock goods, we stifle creative potential and develop stock personas perfectly attuned to mass consumption.We delight in standard shopping centers where standard goods are sold at standard prices to customers capable of savoring the same fastfoods, the same bestsellers, the same advertised headache remedies. Conformity is the fast track for people impatient to get-it-now.

In competitiveness and economic base

The same impatience is responsible for our most immediate economic problem—capital shortages. It limits our disposition to save, to leave some income unspent. Saving generates capital, and capital insures our future. For lack of capital, much of our economy is literally crumbling, flooding, silting, or blowing away. The Associated General Contractors of America, the largest organization of construction firms, puts the cost of needed infrastructure in the U.S. at $3.3 trillion, which includes $1.6 trillion for highways, $53 billion for bridges and $142 billion for water supplies.[39] Nor is infrastructure the only or even the most serious "capital" problem facing us. America's industrial technology is no longer first in the world; our work force is equipped for defeat by a second-rate education. America's industrial base is being bought up a piece at a time by eager Europeans and Asians with abundant capital. Economist Leonard Silk observes that "...the United States has been compelled to sell assets to foreigners to maintain its existing level of consumption and investment...How long can this go on?"[40]

We are like the bankrupt playboy portrayed by Walter Matthau in the 1970s movie, *Falling Leaf.* One memorable scene went something like this: Matthau nods impatiently while his accountant explains that he cannot possibly buy a very expensive Ferrari...because...*he has no more money.* Matthau seems not to understand. The accountant struggles to make his point. He expounds principles. He gives examples. He reviews. He agonizes. He shouts. Finally, slowly forming each word, he says, "There is nothing left. Absolutely nothing. You have no money in the bank. *You are broke.*" To which the irascible playboy responds, "All right, all right, I heard you. Now quit fooling around. Write me a check. I want that Ferrari."

In this caricature of contemporary life, we see an exaggerated but accurate portrayal of the current mindset. We can also see the underlying reason for suburbia's fragmentation.

Five

The reason for fragmention

There's one and only one reason for fragmentation, suburbia's fatal flaw—*the mindset of the 20th century.*

Start with a simple fact: the vote. It is a fact that Americans voted for fragmentation. When the time came for decision, the good people of North Hollywood opted for an independent local government. So did the good people in all the other suburbs of the San Fernando Valley. Had they all annexed themselves to the city of Los Angeles, they would have formed one integrated metropolitan area. But they didn't. That much is well known.

Suburbia, a tax haven

Here's more that is well known. In the big city, taxes paid by middle class families reflect the presence of the poor. A sizeable portion of the tax base must pay for the inevitable effects of poverty (welfare and low-income housing); and crime (an increased number of jails, police, judges and probation officers). In suburbia the middle class escape many of these public costs. Taxes can be lower or spent on more libraries, better schools, a new civic center. As late as 1989, the county executive of suburban Westchester, New York decried the $64 million the county spent on the homeless, "Think of the other services—parks, programs for the elderly, the arts, day care—$64 million could buy."[41]

Who could fault the middle class for leaving the cities and

removing their share of the tax base? We give free people a choice and trust self interest to do the rest. Economics predicts that in a free market people will always choose the better alternative, the one that maximizes benefits over costs. For middle class families, autonomous suburbs were simply the better choice.

What is *better* depends on how you weigh specific costs and benefits. You can come to any conclusion you wish. Want a decentralized metropolis? Then give little weight to its costs.

The costs we ignored

The exodus of the middle class from the cities created our inner city ghettoes and their anguishing long-run costs to the nation. But we chose to give them little weight. We also slighted the long-run costs of permitting a haphazard metropolitan land-use pattern. Those costs weren't invisible either. We all saw the growth—developers rushing in and spaces filling up. By the 1960s almost anyone could have predicted the inevitable—the pile-up of automobiles, congestion, pollution and all the rest. Had we given those costs more weight, the outcome would have been different.

The benefits we didn't ignore

So much for the cost side. On the benefit side—in addition to the exceptional buy in public services—the middle class reaped a further advantage of fragmentation less apparent to the naked eye. Nobody said so, but for the advancement of economic growth, fragmentation was a catalyst extraordinaire.

How do you make the quickest, hottest fire? Do you put a match to a single log or do you cut the log into kindling? Kindling draws far more oxygen. Each exposed sliver of wood will burn, causing the fire to blaze up with intensity. Cutting the metropolitan "log" into slivers energized the fires of suburban growth.

To lower its costs and increase its tax base, each suburb competed for growth. To grow—the way Phoenix, Los Angeles, Miami and San Jose grew—many surrounding suburbs extended their boundaries. They gladly issued permits for housing tracts, shopping centers and office parks. From local administrative offices the invitation went forth: "Annex your tracts to Suburb X or Suburb Y. We want you. We need you. Sign up. We'll help with sewer and water lines. Apply now for attractive government benefits." Few developers could resist such an appeal.

The benefits of fragmentation were enormous. They created a new urban land supply to fuel the prosperity of the whole post-World War II era.

Inventing the suburban land supply

Suburbia began as an ingenious invention. According to U.S. patent rules a patentable invention must pass three tests. It must be *useful*. It must be *novel*. And it must be a *surprise*—unlikely to be conceived and implemented by ordinary reasonable individuals. On all counts, suburbia qualified as an authentic invention.

As elegant as anything created by Leonardo da Vinci, the suburban invention was as simple as it was unique, valuable as it was bold. What the get-it-now mindset accomplished was to break the monopolistic grip of the central cities on the urban land supply. How? By chopping the metropolis into fragmented independent fiefdoms thereby *rearranging the urban landscape*. In suburbia, employment, shopping, and public centers no longer converged in an orderly manner around a single point as in cities of the past. Now, as though conceived by some mad planner, those destination points were deposited here and there, apparently in chaotic abandon, throughout a huge domain.

Cutting out the center

But if the planner was mad, there was genius in that madness. While the old city radiated its beneficence on a tiny circle of urban land a few miles from the center, suburbia created a vast supply of urban land in and around the random archipelago of shopping malls, factories and subdivisions.

For the rampaging horde of expatriates from Chicago, New York and Philadelphia, accessible land was suddenly cheap. Gloriously cheap. Blessedly cheap. Every sliver of meadow and forest flat enough to be bulldozed into subdivisions and shopping malls became another potential competitor to the big city. The old downtown, with its astronomical land values, once monopolized all opportunities to shop at a Woolworth's or a Macy's, to attend a first-rate theatrical performance or to seek legal advice. No more. Districts within a trolley commute of downtown were where we raised our families and relaxed between daily stints at the factory. Again, no more. Suburbia came to the rescue with an abundance of *affordable* land.

The blessings of fragmentation

Now serious consumers could afford the houses they needed for a lifestyle dedicated to consumption. They had places to put those thousands of articles made cheap by everyone's commitment to buy them. Urban land in staggering abundance changed everything. To hell with apartment living. There would be no more of that. It was like moving out of a coffin. Now there was room, plenty of room. Everything would fit—automobiles, all the furniture you could wish for, even large private gardens. Such was suburbia, invention of the get-it-now mindset.

Cheap land whooshed the fires of growth. People who wanted houses found them inexpensive enough to buy. And every house sucked in a truckload of appliances and furniture. The torrent of consumption spending brought spiraling prosperity to the nation.

What would Freud say?

Was it our conscious design to cut up the metropolis in the name of growth and prosperity? Did even one economist announce a discovery with a cunning little kink in it? "Fellow citizens, to achieve growth and prosperity, let's chop our metropolitan areas into small competing snippets."

No, of course not. Nothing so conscious as all that. Led by Sigmund Freud, social science has long ago glimpsed the subterranean flow beneath the surface of rational thought. We *know* more than we can explain. Author Isaac Bashevis Singer was asked if he really believed in the dybbuks and demons that figure so prominently in his short stories. "I don't know if I believe in them," Singer answered, "I only know that I am afraid of them."

When doing nothing is doing something

Like an individual, a society also knows more than it can explain. It's not so much how people *talked* about metropolitan areas. It's what they *did* about them. On the surface it *seemed* that we had no knowledge of our implication in the long-run disasters that followed from fragmentation. It *seemed* that we acted in perfectly normal, rational ways. To cut short-run costs and secure better services from local government, we moved away from the central cities to the suburbs. Some critics blamed the middle class for this. But nobody was accused of purposely fragmenting the metropolitan area in order to stimulate the economy. Nobody knew that it was *possible*. Not explicitly anyway.

Yet we *did* know. Beneath the surface of rational thought we *liked* what was happening. And it showed. How? By doing nothing. At any point, had we wished, we could have stopped the train. But we didn't. There seemed to be no compelling reason to do so. Not even economists— darkly reputed to be practitioners of the "dismal science"—could bring themselves to worry very much about the long-run future. They saw the humming economy, the steeply rising GNP—and they ascribed it to the accumulating wisdom of contemporary Western economics.

Wasn't fragmentation perfectly shaped to the specifications of the get-it-now mindset? We saw the splintering of the metropolis and ignored its long-run costs. We valued the immense short-run benefits of competition among suburbs—the expanding urban land supply, accelerating new home construction, snowballing sales of consumer durables and sharply rising GNP. So far as we were concerned, fragmented suburbia was making an indispensable contribution to our ability to "get-it-now." All of it.

We are now feeling the ebb-tide of the suburban expansion. The great American buffet began to pall in the 1960s and to sour in the 1970s. Suburbs springing out of farms in remote areas soon filled in the countryside to become part of vast metropolitan areas. People who believed they had escaped the city found the city crowding into their backyards.

A new and opposing mindset is now emerging. Penturbia, unfragmented and beckoning, will spring from that soil.

Six

Penturbia and the mindset of social responsibility

The 20th century gave us suburbia.

The 21st will shift the nation's center of gravity in a massive swerve, from fragmentation to consolidation— from suburbia to penturbia.

Penturban consolidation will arise from a popular revulsion against get-it-now attitudes of neglect. Along with the war against a century of environmental pollution, the fight to defeat fragmentation will be powered by the emerging mindset of social responsibility.

Great change must always spring from the people. One mindset caused the problem. Another will solve it. Activist Curtis W. Johnson put it right: Government can't do much to "change our fundamental condition. It can only do what citizens—citizens—empower it to do. Only citizens can make safe ground for different decisions than the ones we're getting now."[42] People are the seat of change: not Democrats, not Republicans, not a more efficient rapid transit, not the coming electronic age.

Logic suggests that our neglect has exceeded reasonable limits. We cannot allow things to keep getting worse. The erosion of our productive capacities is now invading healthy tissue at an alarming rate. But are there any signs of the needed turnaround? Have we, in fact, moved at all from the get-it-now mindset?

On the road to penturbia

You can discover the answer by taking a simple test. Ask yourself:

• Are *you* willing to make sacrifices for a healthier, cleaner environment?

• Have *you* adopted a more healthful lifestyle: less fatty diet and more exercise?

• Would *you* accept a lower dollar income for a more meaningful life?

• Can *you* imagine taking a more active part to assure a better future for your own community?

• Would *you* volunteer your services to help others in your community—hospices, ambulance services, food banks, big brothers and sisters, teachers aides, etc.?

Millions who might have answered "no" to these questions in 1970 (the first year of "Earth Day") answered "yes" twenty years later. In 1990 a New York Times/CBS poll revealed that 71 percent of the respondents agreed with the statement, "We must protect the environment, even if it means increased government spending and higher taxes." 56 percent agreed with even the more extreme statement that "We must protect the environment, even if it means jobs in the local community are lost."[43]

We are turning into activists and environmentalists. After every oil spill a dozen organizations rise up to combat it. New beginnings are opening up like buds in the springtime—"green" politics, socially responsible investing, bio-regionalism, right and left-wing environmentalism, even Christian ecology. A plethora of organizations are mandated to protect natural and environmental resources—the Sierra Club, the North American Bioregional Congress, the Institute for Security and Cooperation in Outer Space, Planet Drum Foundation, Clean Water Action Project, Earth First, the Environmental Defense Fund, Nature Conservancy, World Watch Institute, etc.

No trend goes straight to the mark.The most bullish market on Wall Street has its daily fluctuations, its dips and valleys. We can expect many and large lapses in our progress towards social responsibility. No day passes when developers aren't bulldozing land that should be left to open space. Wheeler-dealers go on milking corporations instead of strengthening them for the long pull. Cities keep piling up solid waste without a thought for tomorrow. Oil spills continue to poison our coastal areas. Public infrastructure is poorly maintained. In Oakland, California (November, 1989) people killed by the failure of a section of the Nimitz Freeway paid the bitter price of our neglectful attitudes. The California earthquake of 1971 had sent an alarm. Engineers warned that the ground under the eventually-collapsed section was "spongy-soft." But no one took effective action.[44]

A century of unconcern for the future will not yield in a moment. But it *will* yield. It must.

Conglomerate municipalities

Reliance on big national government and small municipalities will be transmuted into the new politics of the 21st century. Interdependent municipalities will learn to cooperate. Eager to avoid the transgressions of suburbia—counties, cities and towns will form *conglomerates* of local power.[45] Oh, we'll still enjoy home rule in the design of neighborhood streets, parks and playgrounds. But to the conglomerates will fall the task of limiting sprawl, maximizing accessibility, minimizing damage to the environment, and assuring its affiliates that there will be an abundant supply of urban land with plenty of open space for all.

Social responsibility in business

Concerned for its long-run future, business itself will have a selfish interest in being unselfish. More accurately, it will practice *enlightened* self-interest.

To attract and hold a highly skilled and educated staff, business *must* ensure environmental excellence. It must take a stand on issues of local planning—land use, public infrastructure, open space, ecological conservation. And it *must* be concerned with educational excellence. To bolster our eroding ability to compete in international markets, it is imperative that many of our disadvantaged—including women—upgrade their skills to fit the rising labor market. An increasing number of employees are now attending company-provided "schools," often with childcare thrown in as part of the package. Though progress is evident, there is much much left to be done.

Business leaders will show themselves to be community leaders as well. No longer purely economic men and women, millionaire executives will increasingly find that they *want* to go public, *want* to assume activist positions. The townspeople will expect no less. So speaks the increasingly influential mindset of social responsibility.

A conversation with an economist

Economist: If we become more socially responsible, I assume we'll be spending less and saving more. The implication is clear—fewer trips, older cars, fewer houses—less of everything. In other words, a lower standard of living. Do you take this to be good news?

Author: Absolutely. We'll be getting more from less. Quantity of "stuff" consumed has been what interested most of us in the past. What the *new* mindset finds missing here is a capacity to savor what we buy, to dream in non-commercial terms, to distill adventure and enlightenment out of ordinary materials and experience. Call it a flair for self-fulfillment.[46]

Economist: I suppose a few people can convince themselves to get more from less. But I don't see this as any kind of solution to the problem of overconsumption—which is what I thought you were trying to tackle.

Author: Self-fulfillment is our perfect weapon in the battle against overconsumption. We can win that battle because the enemy is ourselves. You economists assume that *preferences* are beyond the limits of economic calculation and that it is impossible to count on changing preferences as a solution to an economic problem. "People are what they are," you say. "It's their preference, and that's that."

Let me point to a major difference between our two approaches. Consider the hypothetical case of Jones and Smith. With interest rates at 7 percent, Bob Jones has little incentive to save. (To Jones, future needs are much less urgent than the claims of the present.) We both agree that if interest rates increase to 15 percent, Jones will be glad to save. The size of the reward overcomes the size of the sacrifice. Mind you, Jones hasn't changed—he still puts the present far above the future—the higher interest has merely twisted his arm.

At 7 percent interest, Warren Smith has no more incentive to save than Jones. But lately he has been increasingly disconsolate about life in America. One evening, after seeing the movie, *How I found Utopia and Escaped the Rat Race,* he experiences an awakening. Henceforth, he is a changed man. He has shaken off the compulsion to compete with the Joneses, no longer hungers to buy everything he can imagine, and is beginning to enjoy the fragrance of a forest as much as the smell of upholstery in a new car. He has also become more concerned about the homeless and the environment and now saves to give them sizeable contributions. Of course, he still prefers more to less. Even in his new state of mind he'd prefer 15 to 7 percent interest. But because it is no longer such a great sacrifice, he is now willing to save even if all he could earn was 7 percent.

In various degrees, we are all undergoing a conversion similar to Smith's, and it is pushing us to *prefer* things that are inexpensive yet are still able to yield profound satisfactions. Perhaps you will see in this the alchemist's magic. Things perceived as near-worthless are presto! converted into purest gold.

Economist: What in your opinion was nearly worthless that is now imbued with value?

Author: *Penturbia.* Twenty years ago it was the "sticks." Now it is precisely where people want to live. Perhaps self-fulfillment comes more easily at the foot of a blue-gray mountain, where spending less is not "cheap" but downright commendable. Here, low-cost or no-cost activities win commendation from the community. "It's creative," people say and nod approvingly. The new values de-emphasize the importance of money. Consider too that every dollar saved is a contribution to the nation—to infrastructure, welfare, education as well as to the individual's quality of life.

By enhancing the quality of life, penturbia helps to address the larger social and economic problem of overconsumption. It substitutes for urban extravagances that drain our savings and consume our capital. Here are some examples.

"Free" scenery

Sumptuous scenery and sheer space substitute for expensive goods and services made necessary by the artificialities of urban life.

The underground economy

Penturbia is the natural milieu of the underground economy. Bartering is commonplace here. Productivity and savings multiply as people use "spare" time and "free" land to make things otherwise expensively produced, transported, brokered, and retailed in metropolitan areas. By trading skills, material, and labor, penturbanites can get a house built, fill a wardrobe, and enjoy all the organic fruits and vegetables needed to feed a family. In health costs alone, the savings are incalculable.

Conservation of old buildings

Decrepit 19th-century structures rich in nostalgia (plentiful in many rural counties) are joyfully restored and substituted for costlier new buildings. In Stevens County, Washington, Sarah Lee Pilley, wife of a retired Marine Corps colonel, bought a 1900s-era farmhouse overlooking the Colville Valley: "It was horribly rundown.... The interior was derelict, the porch crumbling.... We all worked night and day, for five months." Pilley converted the upstairs into their family home and the downstairs into what reporter Bill Dietrich calls the "valley's best restaurant."[47]

Lower transportation costs

Working at home or in neighboring towns is commonplace. For the individual as well as the nation there is a direct benefit from savings in fuel and infrastructure.[48]

Volunteering

New York City cannot depend on volunteers. Greene County, NY, (population under 50,000) can—and does. Dynamic Gail Appel—a certified K–9 teacher and a recent migrant from a suburb of New York—is typical of the new breed. She's one of the "14-karat, 100-hours-a-week volunteers" working as an emergency medical technician with the county's ambulance corps. "All the people who run ambulance also volunteer for the local rescue squad of the local fire department," she points out, "And they can't do it without training....They love to take training.... The university medical-technican-training-program is at night. And it's six months long, not an easy thing to do."[49]

Whereas penturbia holds no monopoly on the spirit of cooperation, its friendly, small-town environment seems to yield a better fit for volunteer activities. Greene County is not remarkable in this respect. Throughout penturbia you will find a similarly cooperative spirit. Volunteers substitute for a spectrum of expensive services in schools, hospitals and public functions.

Economist: Suburbia is dying and penturbia is taking its place?

Author: Yes, and many will be affected: owners (who imagine that their homes will provide retirement income), bankers (with their vast collateral in suburban real estate), economists (who aim to preserve prosperity), business persons (interested in knowing where to locate and where to market products). And of course, politicians, who we depend on to steer us all to safe harbors.

Seven

Obsolescence: Land value goes *down* as well as up

Ancient wisdom speaks: everything in this world eventually dies—people, possessions, cultures, and societies—but not the land. Land is space on the planet. For millions of years to come, barring some rare astronomical incident, the planet will persist in its orbit around the sun. Land is indestructible. A car can be written off in eight years, a computer in twelve, a building in eighteen. It takes an eternity to write off land. Popular wisdom and the IRS say that land does not depreciate.

How land depreciates

Except for the special world of the IRS, land can and does depreciate, as does the real estate in which it is embodied. The cause of depreciation? Obsolescence. A particular piece of land can become as obsolete as a three-year-old computer. At the end of three years the computer is still intact. Its circuits still whirl electric currents with unerring aim. But it is superseded by later, smaller, faster, more sophisticated computers. A leading region becomes obsolete too, and is eventually superseded.

A region of obsolescence is like a faithful servant trained to serve one master. When a new master with a very different temperament and needs takes over, the servant, whose habits have crystallized, cannot be more than second-rate. That servant will be replaced.

Obsolescence could be mitigated if adjustments were

made rapidly enough to match the pace of change, if changing social and economic relationships were welcomed and incorporated into the current stream of life. In the case of mature real estate, this does not happen. Adjustment is neither easy nor rapid, for it is in the nature of real estate to resist change. When change is denied, obsolescence is inexorable.

In the 19th century the Cockerill steel plants of southern Belgium were the most modern and productive in the world. Their location—inland and close to the coal fields— was ideal for the 1800s, but not for the 1990s. Yet they still stand: monstrous structures partly sleeping, partly functioning, partly crumbling, an enormous patch of obsolescence casting a pall upon a wide area. It is a discouraging environment for industrialists who might consider locating there. The community suffers from chronically high levels of unemployment, innumerable dissatisfactions, and a foundering local economy.

Must suburbia go the way of the Cockerill steel plants? Nothing is impossible. But the rehabilitation of suburbia is most unlikely. Consider the case of greater Seattle in 1990, whose thriving suburban areas are still attracting hordes of migrants from the rest of the nation.

Greater Seattle: The nation's most livable urban area?

In 1989, to unclog Seattle's freeways, environmentally conscious planners proposed a light-rail system. But the plan had to be derailed. In the daily tangle of trips going every which way, workers and shoppers travel from suburb to suburb rather than efficiently in a single direction—from suburb to downtown. Under these circumstances, light rail requires too many tracks, carrying too few riders per track.

As one Seattle pundit wrote, "By even the most optimistic estimates from most experts, light rail is not a realistic option anytime soon. Far more urgent are the problems of local travel on an overwhelmed network of city, county and regional roads—mostly the kind of trips that do not lend themselves to light-rail technology."[50]

Federal funds, freeways

Another obstacle to improved transportation in Seattle (as elsewhere) is the Federal budget deficit and the increasing difficulty of obtaining immense federal grants for public works. Another is the improbability of building new freeways through suburbia. Assume that a mile of metropolitan freeway takes 50 acres of land.[51] A conservative estimate of fifteen dispossessed voters per acre comes to 750 dispossessed voters per mile. A 100-mile freeway could send 75,000 angry voters to the polls.

But surely, the reader presses on, there must be times when the motivation to find a solution is great enough to overcome all obstacles.

Is Los Angeles fixable?

Few problems are more serious than choking on bad air. And few places are more likely to make you choke than the Los Angeles basin. It is widely recognized that Los Angeles has the nation's worst air quality. To end the problem, a newly organized agency has proposed the first phase of a twenty-year plan. It contains 123 separate controls.[52]

The L.A. air pollution proposal attempts to activate plans deadlocked by individual municipalities where decisive action is continually postponed. Yet even if a definite plan of action were to be enacted, would it work or would it, as one observer wondered, be rendered impotent by "local prerogatives, parochialism and pettiness."[53] Here is one observer's reaction to the L.A. plan: "...since each rule has to be adopted individually, the political heat from the business community can be expected to rise in the future. Stay tuned."

Regional obsolescence

The greatest resource of new land is its blankness, its freedom from the dated styles and building types popular in the last wave of growth. New land provides release from three shackles limiting adjustment in old settlements:

1. Immobility

Obsolete buildings infect the land on which they stand with an epidemic of decrepitude. Why? Every building is virtually anchored to the spot on which it is built. When mindset shifts and habits change, a building cannot readily be moved to a more desirable location.

The ideal city would be completely mobile. Imagine a city built on barges. A skyscraper on a barge? Yes, also houses, factories, shopping malls. One structure to a barge. Now suppose mindset changes. Habits shift. The old downtown becomes obsolete because customers prefer new kinds of buildings in different locations? No problem. The old downtown is simply towed away to secondary, less important locations. Other barges are towed in to take their place.

2. Durability

Usually designed for permanence, a structure is expected to endure. And in most cases it does endure. A building may fail in its plumbing and wiring, its floors may buckle and its plaster disintegrate, but until a more profitable use can be found for the site, it will escape the wrecking ball.

Of course, partial adjustments can be made. A structure uneconomical in its original use can be consigned to other uses. A school is converted into a factory, a warehouse into a theatre, a millionaire's mansion into low-income apartments. But these "make-do" arrangements are rarely ideal. The original structure always intrudes, always prevents total adjustment to changing circumstances.

3. Interdependence

Real-estate units are not independent entities. As an investor during the 1990s, I would be ill-advised to plan an industrial campus for high-tech firms in a city that does not offer the right environment to attract highly educated professionals—neighborhoods, schools, galleries, shopping centers, concert halls.

Suppose I own a property that is potentially suitable for

industrialization. Furthermore, suppose that potential depends on substantial improvements being made in the rest of the city. *Unfortunately, the improvements are not made.*

What do I do? *Wait.* That's the bitter truth. The others, for whom I am waiting, are also waiting. *They're waiting for me.* Everybody waits. The result is stagnation for long periods of time.

It is the tangle of countless interdependencies that makes change so painful and slow. If we could somehow eliminate them, we could speed the pace of change. But we can't. Interdependence is the essence of economic life.

Immobility, durability and interdependence explain the slow and protracted decline in regions of impending obsolescence. Note, for example, what happened to the counties participating in the industrial revolution of the 19th century. After peaking in 1910, their percentages of U.S. population swept steadily downward. (See Chapter 12, Figure 2.)

Once an area is gripped by obsolescence, decline is sustained long enough to dissipate old patterns, divest vested interests, reduce its population and its desirability. In the distant future a new order will eventually give the old real estate a comparative advantage and a more honored place in contemporary life. Every leading region is eventually recycled. But it may take a century or more.

Developed in response to a passing era of short-run gain, most of suburbia is now past all hope of rescue. Yet while hobbled by its past, it will not be abandoned. Competition will merely push it off America's growing edge. Except for limited successes here and there, nothing is going to rehabilitate it—at least not in the next half-century.

Eight

The crash of suburbia

Homeowner: All the capital I own is tied up in my home, so you will understand why the failure of the S&Ls makes me nervous. The foreclosures are more widespread than I thought. They are not confined to Texas, Oklahoma and Louisiana as I had assumed.

Author: It was when the world price of oil tumbled in 1986 that the drama first unfolded. Because our domestic oil industry couldn't make a profit at $12 to $18 a barrel, many companies went belly up, wildcatters and oil rigs suspended operations, people were thrown out of work. Thus, when mortgage payments couldn't be met or rent paid, hundreds of billions in real estate values began a free fall. Many a high-rolling oil man was ruined. John Connally, former Texas governor and former millionaire, lost so heavily he had to auction off his household furniture.

Homeowner: Corruption is also playing a part, isn't it? John K. Galbraith blames the S&L mess on bureaucratic "inadequacy and incompetence, perverse ideology, money in large amounts for the political protection of flagrant rascality, public lack of interest, and (for a long while) neglect by the press and the triumph of a hands-off administration...."[54] Reprehensible behavior, but certainly correctable.

Deflation in real estate?

Author: Unfortunately there's something rather more ominous in the background of the S&L crisis. Let me draw your attention to a slackening in the price of real estate—all types of real estate in almost every area of the nation—and not just for one or two years. Since 1980 U.S. home prices (adjusted for inflation) show a decided leveling off.

Figure 1

Prices: Existing Homes (adjusted for inflation)[55]

Median Prices in the U.S. (1967=100)

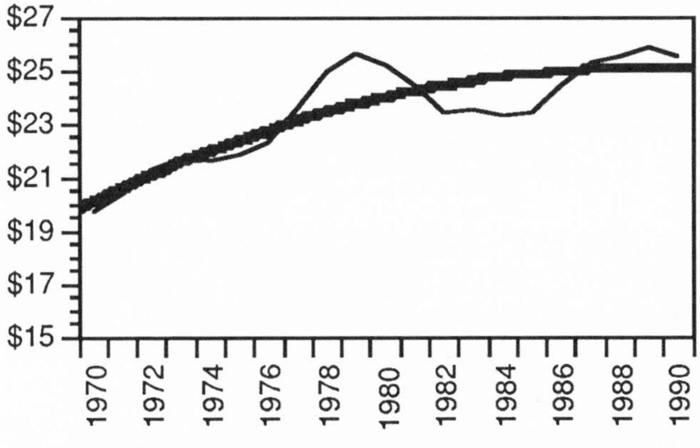

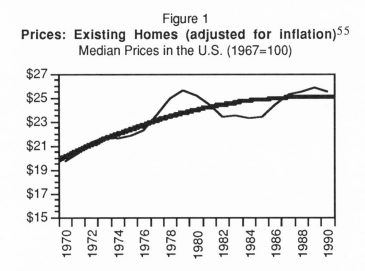

Have you seen *The New York Times* report on April 13th, 1990, entitled "Collapse in Region's Housing Market Is Taking a Toll on Owners' Emotions?" It cites the case of one buyer, June Richardson, who in 1987 paid $260,000 for a town house in Bridgeport, Connecticut. Now she doubts that she could get as much as $160,000 for it. Yet mortgage payments are $2,050 a month. "I'm frustrated and I'm angry," she said. "I felt this would be a secure place to put my money. Now I feel like I've lost my shirt, and that terrifies me."[56]

Homeowner: Everybody knows that the main reason for weakness in real estate prices is the shortage of young adults 25–34 years of age—the most eager home buyers of all. The post World War II baby-boom swelled between 1940–1970. Now those "babies" are 20–50 years old. Our reserves of first-time home buyers are drying up. Lower demand has resulted in lower prices.[57]

Author: The young adult factor is much overrated.[58] Numbers in the 25-34 age group actually increased by 15 percent during 1980–86. Furthermore, by historical standards, 15 percent is more than enough of an increase to sustain a steep rise. From 1950–1970 those in the 25–34 age group increased by only 5.4 percent. Yet home prices (adjusted for inflation) nearly *doubled*!—from $10,264 to $20,124 in 1967 dollars.[59] (See Figure 2.) There's no doubt that the number of people in the 25–34 age group will decline in the 1990s, but it won't make a lot of difference. Factors other than the young adult population are clearly at work.

Figure 2
Home Prices vs. Young Adults
Percent Changes

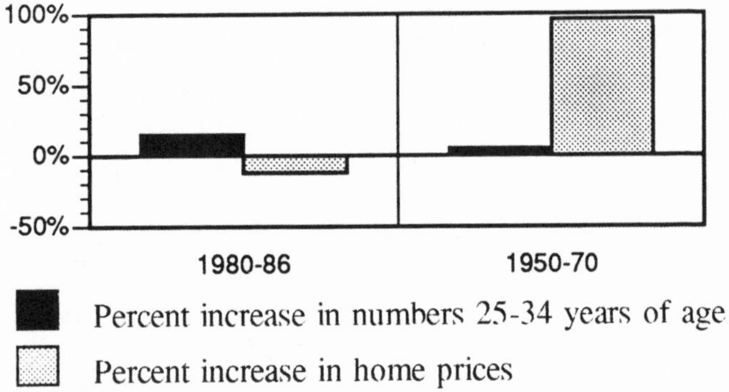

Why don't variations in the number of young adults explain variations in home prices? *It's because people don't necessarily buy houses to live in.* Since 1950 another reason for home purchase has become at least as important. Speculation. (See section on speculation below.)

Homeowner: If not first-home buyers, it must be the long-continued inflation in home prices that has made homes unaffordable.

Author: Affordability is important in extreme cases,[60] but largely irrelevant. Why worry about whether you could afford a house or not? *House purchases were not meant to be paid for out of regular income.* They were costless. Better than costless. You could count on reselling at a profit.

Homeowner: What about high interest rates? Wouldn't that explain the cooling of demand?

Author: On the average, interest rates were lower in the 1980s than in the 1970s. In 1990 interest rates on home mortgages are at least 3 percentage points *lower* than they were in the late 1970s. And yet the rate of building starts was greater in the 1970s than they were ten years later.

Homeowner: Perhaps too many homes have been built.

Author: The market *is* glutted, but not because many houses have been built. (See Figure 3.)

Figure 3
Private Housing Starts
in thousands

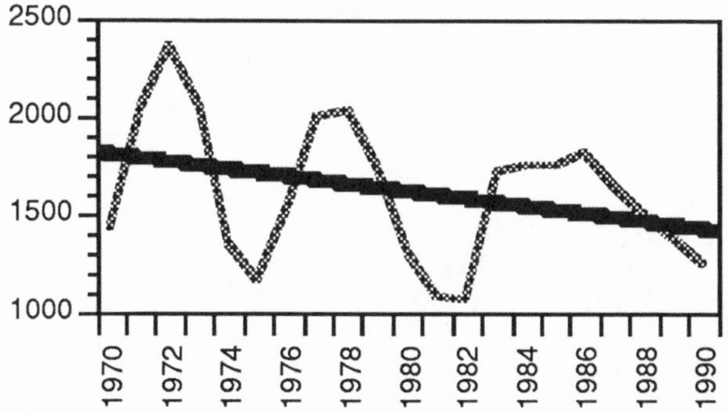

Homeowner: I give up. How do *you* explain the falling home market?

Author: The answer is in Figure 4.

Figure 4
Metropolitan Population
Percent of U.S. Population

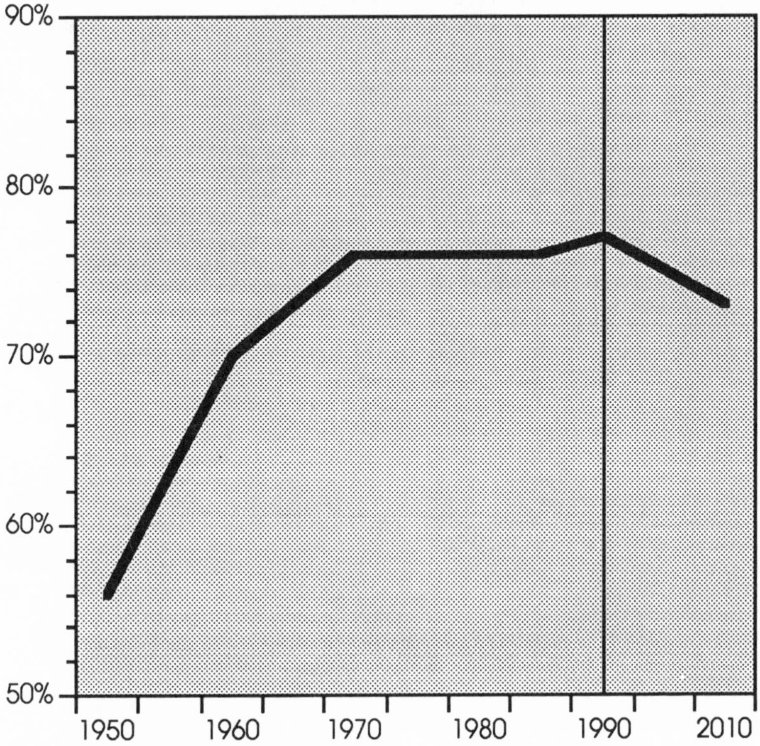

In the 1950s metropolitan populations (city cores and surrounding suburbs) expanded every year by a large and predictable amount. That growth put a tremendous pressure on the supply of suburban homes. The trend eased a little in the 1960s and flattened in the 1970s. Migration to the metropolitan areas no longer grew faster than the US. A slight gain in the 1980s was largely due to foreign immigration. If penturbs are not added to the roster of metropolitan areas, we can expect the curve to decline in coming decades.

Slackening metropolitan growth reflects the decline of the American passion for home and car in suburbia. Although masked during the 1970s by speculation, declining demand now plays a major role in the decline of home prices. In the 1990s, even prices unadjusted for inflation have fallen.

As there are many reasons to expect the slowing to continue, in fact to become more pronounced, I am predicting a further fall in the price of homes.

Our vulnerable economy in the 1990s

Homeowner: Are you suggesting that Americans are deciding to leave our metropolitan areas?

Author: That's very nearly accurate. Allowing for foreigners, metropolitan Americans are barely keeping ahead of the natural increase in population. In fact, if the chart were based on better data, you'd see an actual decline. The data reflects a certain ambiguity in defining the term *metropolitan*. That definition has been stretched in recent years.

Every little county *wants* the label "metropolitan" because it's worth big money in federal handouts. Many counties identified as metropolitan in the 1980s were actually fast-growing, semi-rural penturbs, bearing little resemblance to cities like Yonkers, New York or Bellevue, Washington. In 1980, for example, rural Greene County, New York (site of Rip Van Winkle's twenty-year-long nap in the Catskills) was declared *metropolitan*. Had Greene County and others like it not been classified as metropolitan in recent census reports, the chart of metropolitan growth would show an even more pronounced change after 1979—a drop instead of a plateau.

Homeowner: A drop? We're talking about America's major industrial and market centers, the financial base propping up the whole national economy. It's not only the S&Ls that own mortgages on metropolitan real estate. Commercial banks own them too.

Author: It's true. Commercial banks have been rapidly increasing their portfolio of real estate loans. (See Figure 5.)

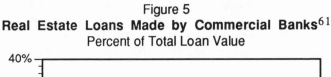

Figure 5
Real Estate Loans Made by Commercial Banks[61]
Percent of Total Loan Value

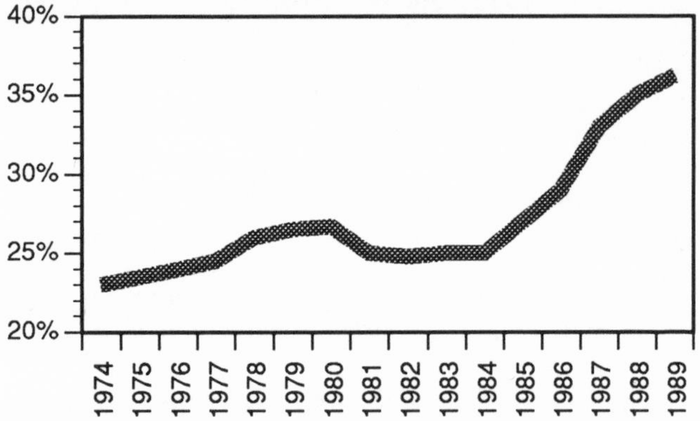

Homeowner: That helps explain why major banks have been running into a spate of non-performing loans. According to *Business Week*, "For the first half of 1989, nonperforming real estate assets, including loans and foreclosed properties, were up 50% at the Bank of Boston. They almost doubled at the Bank of New England [and]... rose 70% at Suntrust Banks Inc. a superregional based in Atlanta. And at Citicorp, the largest U.S. real estate lender, the total was nearly $2.6 billion, up 80% from the end of 1988."[62]

Author: The decline of stock prices in Real Estate Investment Trusts (REITs) shows that Wall Street is worried, too.

Homeowner: We don't know if the weakness of real estate will soon blow over, or if it's a long-run problem that will spread and threaten the whole economy.

The power of competition

Author: In my opinion, there's really very little mystery about what is happening. We're seeing something we've known about all along. It's the age-old power of competition—the ruling force of capitalism. Competition is always the impartial purveyor of change. Its "invisible" hand sweeps out the inefficient, the irrelevant, the obsolete. What metropolitan areas lose in population, a competitor gains.

Demand is now shifting to the competition. We're "selling" suburbia and "buying" penturbia. Yesterday, we headed for the Levittowns of suburbia. Tomorrow the roads will be gorged with people relocating in penturbia. That competition between yesterday and tomorrow will bring on the crash of suburbia.

Homeowner: I can see why the slowing of metropolitan growth would eventually damp down the boom in suburban real estate. But why expect a crash?

Author: The answer is *speculation.* Speculation will play a crucial role in the coming crash.

Some thoughts on speculation

In the age of the short-run and the fast-track, we've become a nation of speculators, and not only in cattle, pork bellies, gold, art treasures, old Italian violins, and ancient Roman coins. We speculate on *the homes we live in.* Profit, big profit, can be made from buying and selling our homes—as average Americans in every walk of life have learned.

In bygone days, a home was a place to eat, sleep and raise a family. A home was "shelter." That included architecture and furnishings that advertised our flamboyance or dullness, poverty or affluence.

Shelter used to be a good reason for buying a home. Speculation was not a good reason. As late as 1950, to buy a home for speculation verged on idiocy. From 1940 to 1950, the price of a typical American home jumped from $2,377 to $7,400. But our thinking remained stuck in the 1930s. We could not imagine steady, unrelenting appreciation. DE-preciation seemed the more likely possibility. In those days homes aged, got used up, fell out of fashion—like old cars or refrigerators.

Old houses never die. Neither do they fade away. They keep on appreciating?

After 1950, with inflation continuing year after year, the right side of our brains began to glimmer with the new idea. "Home" could be two things at once: shelter *plus* speculative opportunity. If a home selling for $100,000 requires $35,000 down with a mortgage of $65,000, and two years later fetches $150,000, the seller profits by $50,000. Subtract about $15,000 for costs and the seller nets $35,000. A 100 percent return on a $35,000 investment. Not bad. If the purchaser is lucky enough to acquire the house with only 10 percent down, he or she nets the same $35,000 with only a $10,000 investment. Figure it out—a 350 percent return in two years!

David and Amandine[63]

A couple I know is typical of today's real estate scene. David works for the telephone company. Amandine is a psychologist. Since 1975 they've bought, lived in, and sold five different homes. Each time they made "improvements," waited for the market to rise another notch, sold at a profit, enjoyed a lavish vacation, and started hunting for another house. Their cheerful motto: "Buy high, sell higher."

Countless buyers are willing to pay for the chance to swing a handsome profit on a "sure thing." What they pay is a premium for the opportunity to speculate—like the price paid for a stock option. The premium becomes incorporated into home value. Each additional sale deposits another layer of speculative value.

How to estimate the speculative component

Author: No one knows the precise size of the speculative component in home prices. But we can estimate it. The method is simple. Find what a house would rent for (rent has no speculation in it). Divide the rent by the monthly cost of owning the home. The result is the non-speculative portion of value. The speculative part is the remainder.

In 1990 a $250,000 home in Seattle rents for roughly $1,250 a month. How does that compare with the cost of ownership? The rule of thumb is that the monthly cost of owning a home—including the cost of keeping your equity tied up in the home—is something like one percent of the home's value. By that rule—and it is very rough—a home worth $250,000 costs $2,500 a month to own. So the speculative component is about 50 percent of the home's value ($1250 divided by $2500.) If you make allowances for tax advantages and other benefits of home ownership, *the speculative component is perhaps one-third the current value.*

Why would anyone pay such a large sum over and above rent? There can be only one answer. Inflation in home prices. That inflationary rise is the "profit" on the speculative premium. Now ask further, what dampens the inflationary rise created by speculation?

Homeowner: Anything that slows down the rise of home prices. No rise, no gain, no incentive to speculate.

Vestibule of the coming crash

Author: Slowing the rise is precisely what happened in the 1980s. You will recall that the median price of homes (corrected for inflation) was lower in 1989 than in 1979. In other words, in most areas of the U.S., for the past decade, speculation in housing has been an increasingly poor investment .[64]

Homeowner: But Mr. Author, a slight lowering of prices over 10 years isn't exactly a crash. A slow leak maybe, but not a crash.

Author: That's right. It hasn't happened yet. The crash will not come so long as the market still expects a resumption of the old housing inflation. It will come the moment that expectation dies. It has already happened in isolated areas. In January 1990, prices of distressed real estate in Colorado Springs, Colorado, a formerly flourishing metropolitan area, sank to half the levels existing earlier in the decade.[65]

Homeowner: I understand your argument, and in the very long run you may be right. On the other hand, my concern is with the short run. To reverse years of experience can't be easy. I for one don't feel pessimistic enough to imagine that the housing inflation is really over.

Author: You're not alone. That's precisely the attitude explaining why the crash hasn't occurred yet. But I believe you and the general public are getting closer to that precipice of belief that will bring it on. Listen to five market authorities quoted in 1989 by *The Wall Street Journal*.[66] They all reveal a hardening conservatism.

Five Wall Street voices

- What is changing is the willingness of investors to assume risk. What is disappearing is the airy confidence that levitated markets in the 1980s.

- In the 1990s, safety and liquidity will be at a premium. People will be glad to hang on to what they have, rather than reach for the highest yield.

- If the 1980s were about anything, it was optimism, but in the 1990s, optimism toward marginal borrowers is giving way to a Big Chill in credit. Solvency and growth will be prized commodities.

- Credit in the latter half of the 1980s inflated real estate and financial assets but did nothing for the economy's nuts and bolts. What happens as the cycle unwinds? The value of those assets [become] more tenuous.

- The golden era has ended. Many of its excesses flowed from the open spigot of credit.

Homeowner: What happens when we *reach* that precipice of belief?

The crash

Author: In an atmosphere of lowered confidence, current home prices will suddenly seem ludicrous, out of scale and out of reason. In that time of revised expectations, speculative value falls away like a shadow, shorn of substance. The price of a home bumps down not by some small increment, *but by the full speculative premium* (on the order of one-third the current value). Whammo! Bulls become bears. Everybody wants to sell. Nobody wants to buy. Everybody lunges for a buyer who is no longer there and prices plummet.

Homeowner: You're turning out to be quite a doomsayer.

Author: Not at all. I'm mainly interested in what happens *after* the crash. My message is one of optimism. I see the 1990s brimming with opportunity. For many counties a century of decline will come to an end.

Homeowner: How can you be so sure?

Author: This is not the first time one migration has been eclipsed by another. It is the fifth. Read on.

Part two

Why suburbia *must* crash and penturbia *must* boom

In facing America's promising future, one caution deserves major emphasis: Do not extrapolate trends from one decade to the next. Not in this decade. There are times when current trends seem limitless. They shoot into the social and economic stratosphere as though born to remain in flight, conquering all restraints. Eventually, however, every trend reverses. An up trend turns down. A down trend turns up. In such moments of reversal, one decade does not foretell the next.

In the decade of the 1990s, a century of migration to suburbia will come to an end. And, in an economic environment of chronic depression, suburban real estate values will crash. At the same time, the migration to penturbia, launched in the 1960s, will accelerate.

Must these reversals occur? Part II sets forth a theory of socioeconomic cycles which explain why they must. It also shows how the theory is supported by two centuries of American history.

Nine

The theory of socioeconomic cycles

Five planners discover the need for a theory

Author: Look at this population graph of "County A." Would you say that this is where the U.S. Department of Housing and Urban Development should be spending money on public works—roads, utility systems, etc.?

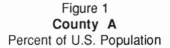

Figure 1
County A
Percent of U.S. Population

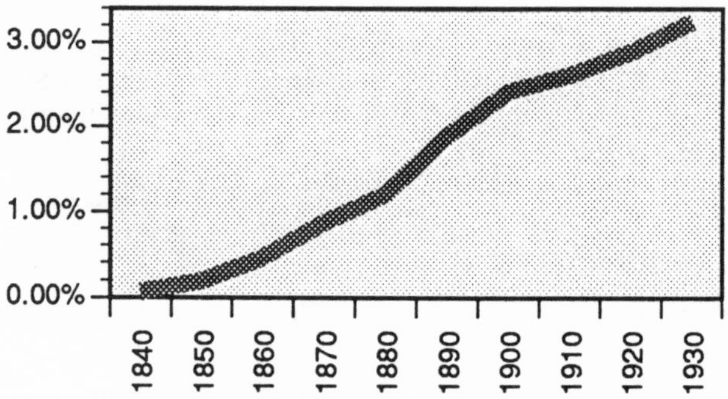

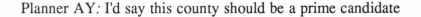

Planner AY: I'd say this county should be a prime candidate

for *any* kind of investment—public or private.

Author: No hesitation?

Planner AY: Obviously people are pouring into this county. That's what the graph shows quite clearly. I wouldn't hesitate. Invest by all means.

Author: Now I'm going to widen the choices to include "County B." In which of the two counties would you now invest HUD's millions—County A or County B?

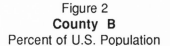

Figure 2

County B

Percent of U.S. Population

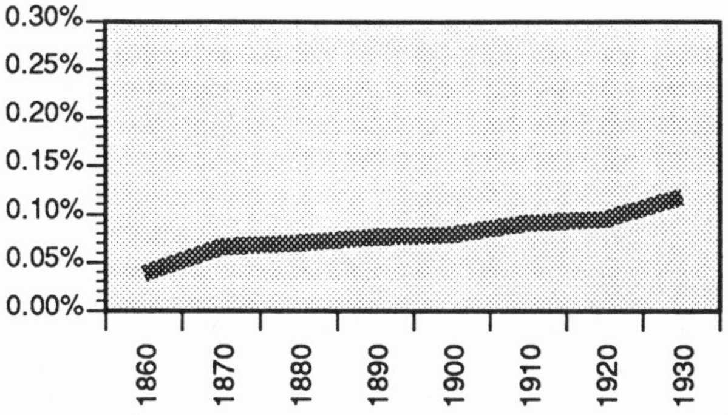

Planner AY: County A, of course. That seventy-year rise is decisive.

Planner QD: County A.

Planner TK: County A.

Planner EC: County A.

Planner ECC: County A.

Author: Let me show you what actually happened to each of these counties after 1930.

Figure 3
County A
Percent of U.S. Population

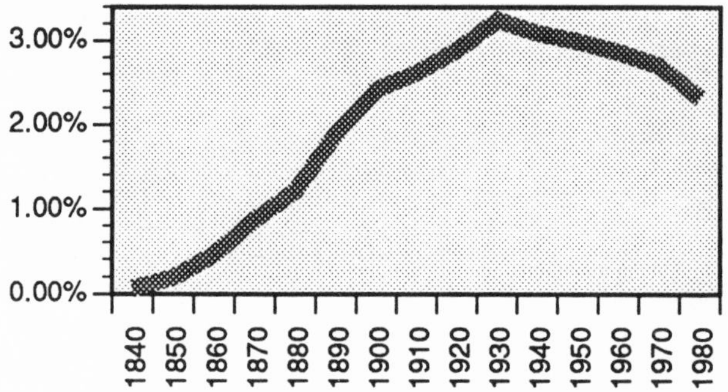

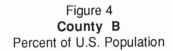

Figure 4
County B
Percent of U.S. Population

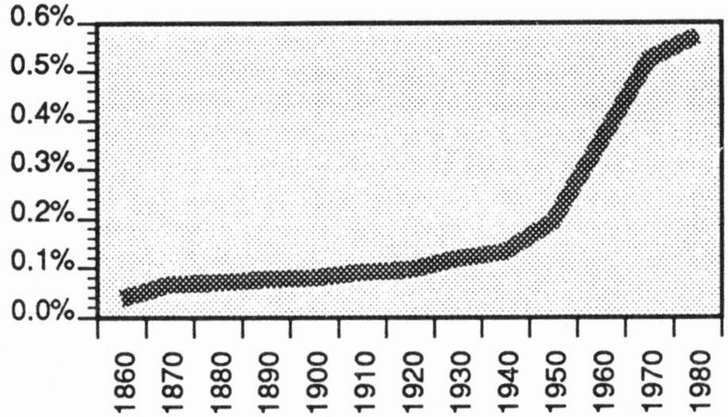

Author: I hear your groans and sympathize. County A is Cook

County, Illinois (which includes Chicago). As you see, it began a long decline after 1930. County B is Solano County, California, a suburban county in the San Francisco-Oakland metropolitan area. Solano, along with many other suburban counties, was just beginning a spectacular rise. (See Figures 3 and 4.) You would have provided immense capital sums where people were leaving and denied them where they were arriving.

Planner QD: Why didn't you tell us that County A had Chicago in it and County B was suburban?

Author: You didn't ask. You were convinced by a seventy-year trend.

Planner TK: Had you given us more complete information we could have made a better decision. Everyone knows that the great migration into the suburbs started in earnest during the 1920s, and that industrial cities like Chicago would soon decline.

Author: You know that now, *after* the fact. What you would have known *then* is the track record I showed you—growth and more growth for Chicago. Going by track record alone, the future for Solano looked flat and unpromising.

Planner QD: Economists would have known.

Author: How? By the prevailing theory? Economic theory even now assures us that large cities—because of their markets, infrastructure and jobs—are the most likely to grow. In the 1920s it was more than theoretical. It was common sense. *Of course* Chicago would grow—probably into the world's largest city. As for counties like Solano, little was expected of them. They were suburban, that is, rural—hardly a land of promise. In the 1920s suburbia was no more recognized or understood than penturbia is today.

Planner TK: I suppose you think we should be wary of today's fast-growing suburban counties—like those close to Los

Angeles, Houston and Phoenix. But if we can't foresee a turnaround, how are we supposed to make rational decisions?

Author: By relying on a theory able to predict cyclical turns in the long run.

Planner *QD*: And you, I suppose, happen to have such a theory?

Author: I do.

Planner *TK*: Can your theory help us predict *changes* in migration?

Author: Judge for yourselves.

Mindset and the socioeconomic cycle

A thousand men prostrate themselves in the mud at the feet of an all-powerful Pharaoh. Is this an instance of naked force? Not likely. Those men of ancient Egypt believe in the Pharaoh. They do not dispute his potency, his divinity, his right to govern. Ask them. In prosperous periods they will give the Pharaoh a high confidence rating, and not in spite of his authoritarian manner. *Because* of it. What we are witnessing is a venerable and venerated shared belief, a mindset.

Every new mindset creates a world in its own image. It establishes two main guidelines for action: what is worth striving for and how individuals should organize to attain it—by what social controls (pecking order).

In the sweep of reform, a drastically altered society and economy emerges to support the new mindset. New laws, organizations, products, arts, sciences, technologies, even new utopias spring to life. Get-it-now people found their way to suburbia where the life of consumption could best be played out. (See Chapter 4.) They also built a social and economic environment unified around the great enterprise of facilitating consumption. In the 1990s, we are seeing the next turn of the cycle, as the social and economic environment created for one mindset yields to another.

The socioeconomy

A mindset and all its creations form a self-contained system of countless interacting parts unlike any other in all time. I call it a *socioeconomy.*

The socioeconomy consists of a single mindset and everything it creates to realize its fullest expression. Mindset is the socioeconomy's spiritual core, defining its identity and directing its destiny; it is the scaffolding around which all social and economic changes are made. All the contrivances, plans and maneuvers, all the trends, propensities and preferences—all the institutions, land, capital and other resources, everything that summarizes, characterizes or describes what a socioeconomy is and what it is trying to become—all of this is regulated by the socioeconomy's *mindset.*

If mindset is the rudder of the socioeconomic structure, what are the rules by which it periodically transforms the society and economy? Here I would ask the reader to extend a short line of "credit." Accept six major propositions on faith for the duration of this chapter, after which the "loan" will be repaid. The six propositions will be demonstrated in the sequence of socioeconomies appearing in America since 1735.

> 1. At any time, *the* society and *the* economy can be separated into two overlapping socioeconomies. No one socioeconomy can represent the whole society and the whole economy. It always takes two. Both are ever-present.
>
> 2. The two overlapping socioeconomies are perishable. As one rises to a peak of integration, the other falls and is eventually replaced.
>
> 3. A socioeconomy falls as a result of its cumulating and *unpreventable* excesses. The result is a single, problem it cannot solve, the "key" problem.
>
> 4. A new socioeconomy rises to solve the key prob-

lem. That is its *mission.* And its mission determines its mindset, its institutions, its industries and its leading region.

5. The overlapping socioeconomies are always in opposition to each other.

6. The opposition of socioeconomies is never exact—each socioeconomy is unique, never to be repeated again.

A socioeconomy begins

When *we the people* become convinced that our current social and economic life can no longer be endured, when we no longer see our values as good, our beliefs as true, our lifestyle as desirable, another socioeconomy is born and the old one eventually perishes.

Once the inertia of the past is overcome, every familiar landmark is swept away in the current of comprehensive change. Like an earthquake that resolves pent-up tensions in the earth's shifting strata, a transition from one socioeconomy to another resolves pent-up pressures for social and economic accommodation. In the process we alter who we are as a people, what we hope for, how we live, and—of special importance to the predictor of migrations—*where* we live.

A new socioeconomy begins when the old socioeconomy no longer serves the public interest. At first everyone seems to be asking: How did we get into this mess, and how can we get out of it? At this stage we see little agreement, only an abundance of conflicting interpretations on social and economic issues. Then, gradually, in public reactions, outcries, agreements and disagreements on the great events of the day we discern a definite direction of change. Without conscious design or awareness of the increasing break with the past, a new mindset begins to coalesce.

Integration

All living systems aim at perfect integration. The baby's arms and legs flail, its digestive system is rudimentary. Gradually coordination improves as integration of body and mind increases. A new socioeconomy too is born poorly coordinated, weak and imperfect. In thousands of successive steps each socioeconomy perfects its integration.

Can the degree of integration be measured? Not at present. But we can speculate on a theoretical model. (See Figure 5—representing the socioeconomy rising during the late 19th century.) To change the world in its image, a mindset calls for a telephone book full of distinctive social and economic connections. The rise of every socioeconomy is the story of its attempts to create those connections. But total integration—100 percent—is clearly impossible. Say that 50 percent is the likely maximum—represented here as the *peak integration.* After the peak, integration declines.

Figure 5
The Cycle of a Socioeconomy
Percent of Integration

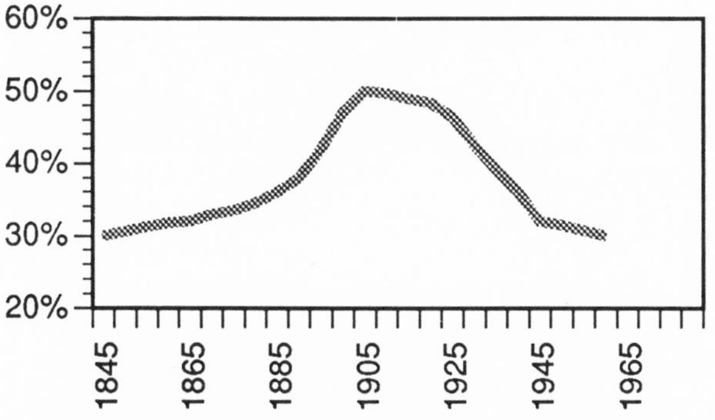

But integration never falls to zero. There are always irreducible connections which remain as a residue from past socioeconomies. For present purposes, we will arbitrarily set the likely minimum at 20 percent. Elements of the early 19th century socioeconomy can still be observed in any major city of the nation. Walk a few blocks off Market Street in San Francisco and you'll see old-fashioned Mom and Pop stores reminiscent of its '49er days. A visitor to the Catskills in the upper Hudson Valley of New York can feel the presence of pioneers first drawn to the area in the early 1800s. A stroll through town reveals evidence of Greek-revival architecture.

Editorials in the local newspapers still show a preference for small-scale government along with a passion for independence from outside "interference"—poignant reminders of life here in the early 19th century.

On the way to peak integration

Whatever contributes to the integration is readily adopted—whether it be works of art and literature or science and technology. Whatever does not contribute is rejected. Little by little integration grows, becomes larger, more distinct, more coherent.

The favored lifestyles are pushed in magazines, books, television, and newspapers. People experiment with the new modes. In one era they wear trench coats, slouch, and smoke like Humphrey Bogart. In another, they exercise, breathe deeply, and eat healthy foods like Jane Fonda.

Experimentation and development go beyond the creation of new lifestyles to trial and error experiments in the expansion of a new *leading region.* That region grows more than any other. The value of its real estate increases. Energies of the mindset spill out in still wider circles. Laws favorable to the mindset are passed. New industries and new technologies—under the aegis of a favorable mindset—appear as though by invitation.

Peak integration

At peak integration, the mindset is supported by a smooth-running social and economic machinery. The socioeconomy becomes a veritable bulldozer programmed to scoop out, heap up, and reshape the world in its own image. Laws of the land now require us to perform almost precisely what the mindset prescribes. Demand is universal for products the mindset deems valuable. Industry gears up to meet those demands. Plants and commercial outlets will locate or relocate in regions best able to facilitate the new priorities. Writers, artists, musicians, and philosophers congeal the mindset into "spiritual realities" every bit as substantial as mountains and rivers.

Economists might call peak integration "equilibrium," biologists, "maturity." Whatever the label, optimism is high at this time, agreements are many, and disagreements are few. There is little controversy on the nature of the good life or how to achieve it. This is the comprehensive achievement after decades of development.

In this moment of maximum influence, the socioeconomy easily dispatches the last vestiges of its former opposition, the preceding socioeconomy. The 19th century taught children to be frugal. By the 1950s those teachings were completely forgotten by the new majority—all of them avid consumers.

Excess and decline

A socioeconomy's limited vision makes it insensitive to damage caused by the *momentum* of its growth. Therein lies its tendency to excess. The relentless rush of people into the leading region drives real estate values to outrageous heights. Favored industries overexpand to a point where they are constrained by scarcities. Favored lifestyles are pursued until they become both unaffordable and less satisfying. Governments—no less vulnerable to a fixed mindset than individuals—become too small or too big or too decentralized. The socioeconomy nurtures whatever advances its mission. It rides roughshod over other concerns.

Having completed its mission, the socioeconomy has lost its *raison d'être*. Ideally, it should wither away, for it serves no further function as a guide to future social and economic progress.

Yet the mindset does not and cannot change. Fixated by habit, vested interests—and especially by a history of past successes—it continues to solve the already solved problem. That blind persistence gives rise to a single new problem that the socioeconomy can never solve— its key problem.

The key problem and the next socioeconomy

Why can't a socioeconomy solve its own key problem? Its mindset is programmed to reject all adjustments that violate a predetermined direction. The sole hope for rational change lies in the birth of a new socioeconomy whose mission it is to end those excesses, thereby solving the key problem.

Every excess signals an opposing response. As a key is shaped to open a lock, the new socioeconomy shapes its identity to reverse every tenet of the old mindset. If there is a predilection for smallness in business and government, it will be opposed by a preference for bigness. A stand for centralization will be followed by another for decentralization. An indifference to waste will be challenged by a commitment to conservation. These oppositions are always effective. They eventually end the old socioeconomy's excesses—and the old socioeconomy as well.

Cycles of migration

Under the spur of its unique mindset, every rising socioeconomy sends people on a migration to a new utopia.

In John Steinbeck's *The Red Pony*, an old pioneer gravely explains to his small grandson that the westward migration has ended. "No place to go, Jody. Every place is taken. But that's not the worst—no, not the worst. Westering has died out of the people. Westering isn't a hunger any more. It's all done.... It is finished."[67]

Hungering for the pioneer frontier of the 19th century does seem to be "done." But the yearning to be on the move is not done, will never be done. New hungers and new migrations periodically capture the imagination of a nation, often engaging the passionate commitment of our brightest and most enterprising citizens. Each migration creates unique opportunities for launching new homes, businesses, lifestyles.

Five migrations

There never was a true "westering," one long gulp from

the shores of the Atlantic to the shores of the Pacific.

There have been, in fact, five distinct migrations. The first (during the colonial period) drove settlers southward rather than westward. The second (early in the 19th century) deposited migrants in farms, plantations and villages of the Mississippi and Ohio Valleys. The third (late in the 19th century) completed the conquest of the enormous American continent. It created great industrial cities and, to supply them with raw materials, vast rural hinterlands throughout the length and breadth of the nation. A fourth migration (after 1900) brought us to suburbia. The fifth (beginning in the late 1950s) is bringing us to penturbia.

Leading regions

Each of the five migrations created a new *leading region.* Here, sweat and capital were stirred into inspiring dreams. (See Prologue, page 4.) What joins these counties into a single region is not contiguity but *timing* of rise and fall. In its upswing, an entire *region* is targeted all at once. In the earliest flush of suburban growth, the environs of New York, Chicago, New Orleans, and Los Angeles grew and flourished in the same decades.

After reaching its peak percentage of U.S. population, a county declines for many decades—often for a century or more—before it is able to grow again. Its social, economic and geographic assets are no longer prized by the national community. It has been dated by the kinds of people, structures and industries acquired during its period of sustained growth.

The rise of a leading region begins at about the same time as the rise of the socioeconomic cycle to which the region belongs. Both rise to a peak at approximately the same time then both decline as a new socioeconomy and a new migration begin. (See Figure 6.) (Counties that have passed their peak can be said to join an emerging *region of obsolescence.*) At its peak, each leading region included about half the total U.S. population. If the same pattern continues, the fifth region will attain its peak share of U.S. population some time after the year 2020.[68]

Figure 6
Development of a Leading Region
Percent of U.S. Population

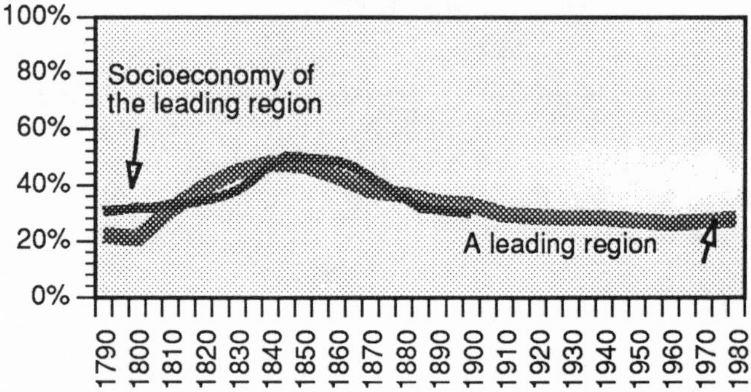

Figure 7
Economic Seasons and Socioeconomies

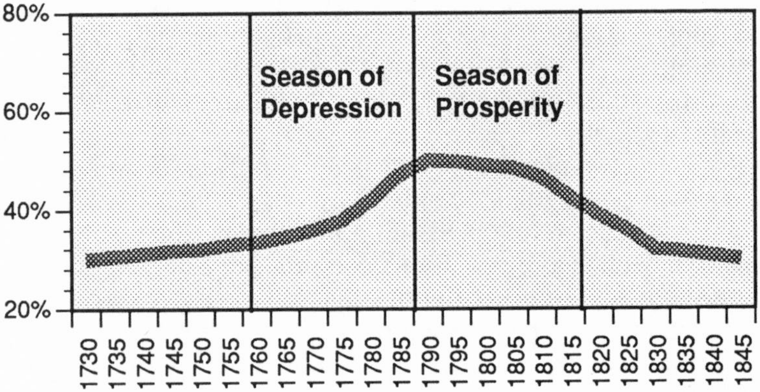

Economic cycles: Seasons of prosperity and depression

Every socioeconomic cycle sets off two economic seasons—a season of prosperity and a season of depression.[69] Unlike annual seasons, *decades* will pass before economic winter passes into economic summer, and still more decades before summer passes into winter. See Figure 7.

Economic winter showers discontent on both co-existing socioeconomies. Economic summer favors both.

Annual summers bring a variety of temperatures, most of them warmer and more equable than winter. But even summer may include some violent storms. The season of prosperity offers generally more prosperous times than the season of depression, but may also suffer some minor or even major recessions. The generally good times are reflected by rising demands and general inflation.

No season of prosperity has been free of recessions. But recessions occurring during economic summer have not led to depression, and government policies undertaken to relieve crises at this time—long before Keynes—have almost invariably been effective. Abnormal rates of unemployment have not extended beyond two years.

While enjoying a momentum of rapid growth, the socioeconomy becomes increasingly subject to *socioeconomic* decline induced by accumulating excesses. As the summer days grow shorter, there is an increasing probability of storms. As the socioeconomy's excesses accumulate, there is a low but increasing probability of depression.

Winter months are not uniformly harsh. Some days will be bright, clear, and mild. During a season of depression we can expect fits and spells of prosperous periods. Economic "winter" displays a greater range of variations than economic summer—from deepest depression (with declining demand, increasing unemployment, mounting bankruptcies, falling standards of living), to bursts of prosperity. The long-run outlook is a generally falling price level—deflation.

The probability of depression is far higher in economic winter than in economic summer. Nevertheless there may be several consecutive years of relief from high unemployment, though seldom more than three consecutive years of boom. Except for war or the threat of war, in "winter," government actions to ameliorate depression are rarely successful and recessions almost invariably lead to depression.

Economic seasons coincide with "Kondratieff Waves" discovered by Nicolai Kondratieff in the 1920s. Economists have rightly remained skeptical of his findings. Without a credible theory, his supporting data was too meager. Any statistician would laugh at a sample of five cycles based on the uncertain fluctuation of prices. Kondratieff's claims, however, are validated by my socioeconomic theory. We can now draw logical connections between prosperity, depression, inflation, deflation, migrations to and from leading regions, shifts in mindset and the integration and disintegration of vast socio-economic systems—all borne out by two centuries of history.

Paying back the "loan" (See page 80.)

A succession of unique socioeconomies can be discerned between 1735 and 1990, each with its own leading region—each rising, reaching a peak, developing excesses and declining, each with distinct seasons of prosperity and depression. Five socioeconomies are examined in the next five chapters. Two additional chapters, 15 and 16, explain *why* the economic seasons *must* appear when they do.

Ten

Cycle 1—*The Mercantile Aristocrat;* Opening curtain

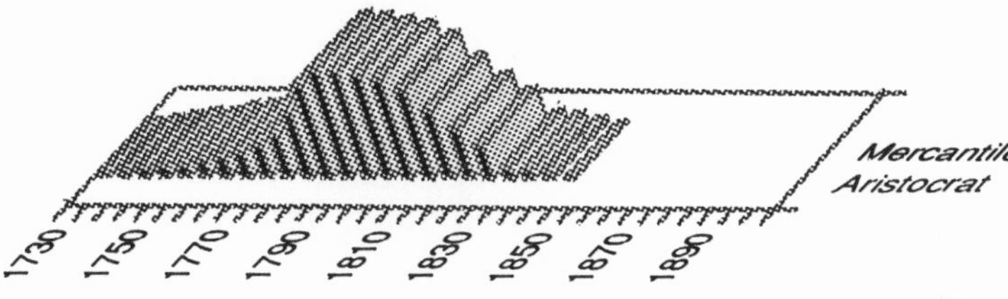

Figure 1
The Rise and Fall of the Mercantile Aristocrat
Percent of Integration

To understand the nature of any socioeconomy, *cherchez la predecessor*. To understand socioeconomy M we need to go back to L; for L we need K; for K, J... Must we then cycle back to the very dawn of history? Perhaps. But this book is less ambitious. We begin with one socioeconomy as a launching pad for all the rest and waive all questions concerning its origins. As a starting point, our interest centers on its mindset, its main institutions, its migrations and (as the bridge to the next socioeconomy) its excesses.

Because it brackets the incubation period of the modern industrial era, I define the socioeconomy existing between 1735 and 1846 as the first. It is also the first socioeconomy of the new U.S. republic. I call it *the Mercantile Aristocrat.*

On the way to peak integration

After 1735, the American colonies were increasingly bound within a mercantile system, a centralized state apparatus for the support of England, the dominant mother country. The reigning aristocracy in both England and America exerted a firm command over that system.

Four assumptions were bred into the mindset of the Mercantile Aristocrat: *centralization* (an economic system centralized around an elite aristocracy)*; big business* (large-scale enterprises and government-sponsored monopolies); *the rule of law* (stable laws permitting greater predictability of economic decisions); and *inequality* (acceptance of a steep social pyramid). Up to 1789 these four precepts were the socioeconomy's pillars of strength.

In England, as in its American colonies, the indigent poor no less than the landed aristocracy embraced the proposition that what the common man did best was to labor at menial tasks, while he who stood on the pedestal of birth and breeding could better lead the nation, direct large enterprises, and ensure prosperity.

Thomas Jefferson described English society of 1814:

> The population of England is composed of three descriptions of persons.... These are, 1. The aristocracy, comprehending the nobility, the wealthy commoners, the high grades of priesthood, and the officers of government, 2. The laboring class, 3. The...paupers, who are about one-fifth of the whole.

"The aristocracy," he adds, "...have the laws and government in their hands...." They "have so managed them as to reduce the third description below the means of supporting life, even by labor; and to force the second...to the maximum of labor which the...human body can endure, and to the minimum of food...."[70]

I'm the very best
People jump at my behest

While Jefferson accurately pointed out the unfortunate effects on the poor during later phases of the socioeconomy, its early influences were much more salutary. The impetus to entrepreneurship which marked the beginning of the modern industrial era could be seen in a pronounced shift of 18th century "megatrends."

The existence and progress of the Mercantile Aristocrat can be measured by an unexpectedly rapid growth of population. British population had long been stagnant or declining. But when the new socioeconomy emerged, population began an astonishing climb. (See Figure 2.) A similar shift was observed throughout most of Europe.

Figure 2
Population of England[71]
in millions

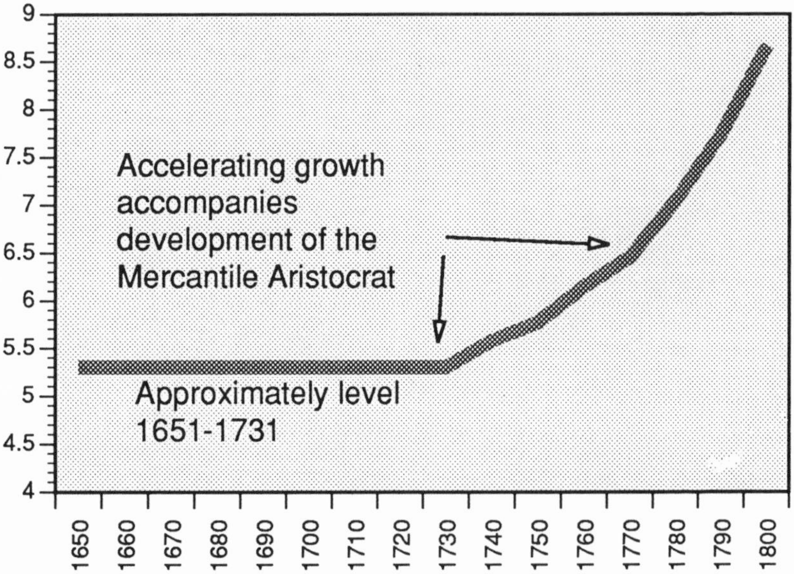

There can be little doubt that the growth of population was due to the socioeconomy's beneficial effect on the death rate. With increasing national wealth, substantial funds were allocated to medical schools and medical research, to clinics and dispensaries. Newly-built hospitals received the sick. Drainage of omnipresent swamps curbed the spread of insects and disease. The building of vermin-resistant brick houses further minimized health hazards. There was also a change in attitudes toward personal hygiene. Soap graduated from luxury to necessity.

Peak of integration

Jefferson saw America as a kind of paradise on earth where the common man could resist the onslaught of aristocratic rule. (In the 1990s Americans are little aware of the colonial aristocracy of the late 18th century.) But in 1790—and in spite of having won the Revolutionary War with Great Britain—the aristocratic mindset prevailed in America as in England. This fact was brought home to Jefferson when he returned to the New World after a six-year absence as special envoy to France: "When I arrived in New York in 1790...I found a state of things, in the general society of the place, which I could not have supposed possible." It was "the prevalence of monarchical sentiments" in the new republic that so astonished Jefferson. At a number of large dinner parties, he found his own to be the only voice speaking out for democracy. The others were solidly in support of aristocratic ideals.[72]

Jefferson should not have been surprised. It was, in fact, the moment of the Mercantile Aristocrat's peak integration. A form of privileged capitalism, based on a mindset unequivocally supporting aristocracy, accorded opportunities to aristocrats rather than to commoners. Federalist leaders like Alexander Hamilton, who favored highly centralized (undemocratic) government, also played leading roles in government. In 1787, Hamilton made no effort to hide his anti-democratic sentiments. During debates on the Federal Constitution he argued:

> All communities divide themselves into the few and the many. The first are the rich and wellborn, the other the mass of the people....The people are turbulent and changing; they seldom judge or determine right. Give therefore to the first class a distinct, permanent share in the government. They will check the unsteadiness of the second, and as they cannot receive any advantage by a change, they therefore will ever maintain good government.[73]

A letter written by Jefferson in 1797 is consistent with the proposition that the Mercantile Aristocrat's peak integration arrived around 1790. Referring to the still mighty influence of Hamilton's "rich and well-born," Jefferson wrote: "Hitherto, their influence and their system have been irresistible, and they have raised up an executive power which is too strong for the Legislature. But I flatter myself they have *passed their zenith.*"[74] (emphasis added.)

History proved him right. By 1800, Jefferson was elected President, and before two decades had passed, the Federalist party had withered away. However, *at least* until Andrew Jackson's administration in the 1830s, the aristocracy remained a powerful force .

The first leading region

To support its mercantilist policies, Britain depended on the colonies for raw materials—tobacco, lumber, fish, and grains. This dependence created a burgeoning demand for agricultural land in the New World—not for a scattering of thin-soiled parcels but for immense stretches of lush, virgin acres, permitting the huge estates preferred by aristocrats.

The region best able to serve these requirements would be located near the Atlantic Ocean, the most accessible waterway from which to conduct large-scale commerce. Selected areas within Pennsylvania, Virginia and North and South Carolina proved best able to meet these requirements.[75] Due to lack of suitable county data, the first leading region was approximated here by total populations in the four colonies. (See Figure 3.)

Figure 3
First Leading Region in America
Location

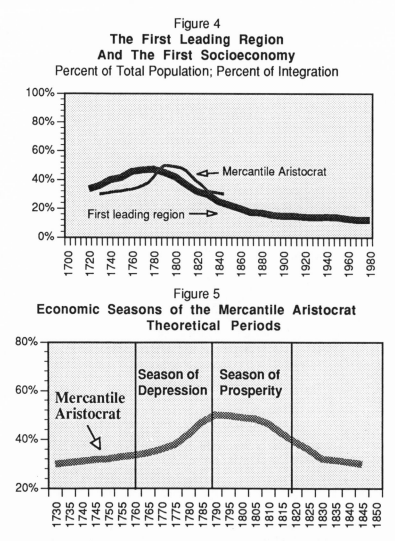

Figure 4
The First Leading Region
And The First Socioeconomy
Percent of Total Population; Percent of Integration

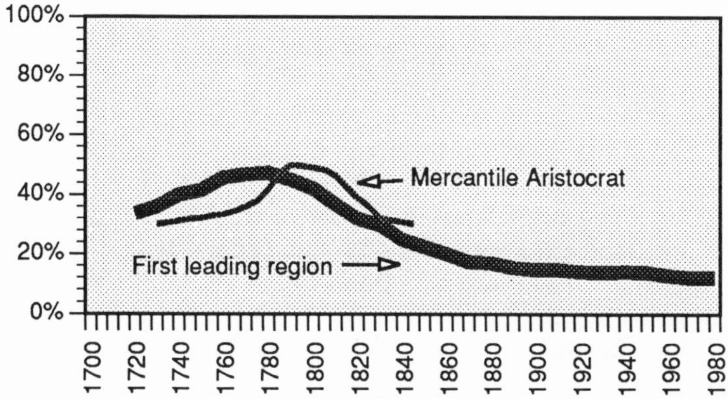

Figure 5
Economic Seasons of the Mercantile Aristocrat
Theoretical Periods

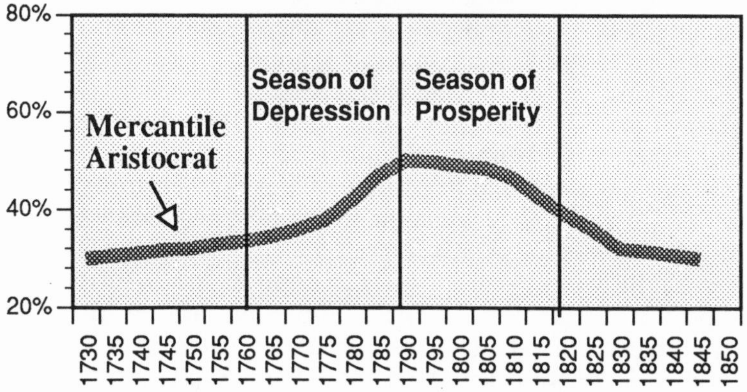

Figure 4 shows how the first migration coordinated with the rise and fall of the socioeconomy.[76] As the socioeconomy peaked around 1789, the region should have peaked in 1789 or later. It actually peaked around 1780, *at which time it contained nearly half the total population of the American colonies.* The slightly premature peak may well be due to the Revolutionary War (1776-1782). Operations by British and

American armies throughout the coastal states undoubtedly stimulated premature relocation to the more-inland, less-vulnerable second leading region. As predicted by my socio-economic theory, in every subsequent decade, the region's percentage fell.

The first season of depression 1760–1789

Depression hit many areas of the world during the first season of depression, 1760–1789. Figure 5 shows the timing of economic seasons during the Mercantile Aristocrat's reign.

England experienced a crisis in 1763 which soon spread to Europe. The failure of a brokerage firm "...in Amsterdam carried with it eighteen important Dutch houses and many merchants in Hamburg. The shock was so great that for some time business was transacted for cash only."[77]

On February 2, 1764, the *New York Post-Boy* reported that "There are more Houses to be let in this City, than there have been at any time for 7 years past. The commerce of the continent is in a languishing condition; our Debt in Europe increases; our Power to pay it off decreases." From another contemporary observer came this report: "If creditors sue, and take out executions, the lands and personal estate...are sold for a small part of what they were worth when the debts were contracted. The debtors are ruined. The creditors get but part of their debts and that ruins them. Thus the consumers break the shopkeepers; they break the merchants; and the shock must be felt as far as London."

Eight years later, in 1772, another credit crisis was exported by England: "The number of failures that year reached 525, the greatest since the memorable year 1720." A serious depression followed, noted by Adam Smith in his epochal *Wealth of Nations*.[78]

The year 1783 brought still another alarm: "British consols fell to 63-1/4, the lowest on record." Large extensions of international trade had produced a strain on the gold reserves and finances of the country.[79]

According to one historian, the depression of 1785–89 was "...the gravest crisis in American history. Both the government and the people were bankrupt. There was no money to pay the ministers to foreign countries, and they actually had to beg the foreign governments for funds."[80]

*The first season of prosperity 1789–1817**

The general prosperity after 1789 is consistent with the rising price level during the period.(See Figure 6.) After the Mercantile Aristocrat's peak integration around 1789, a few recessions occurred, but none lasted longer than two years.

Figure 6
Wholesale Price Index of All Commodities, 1789-1817

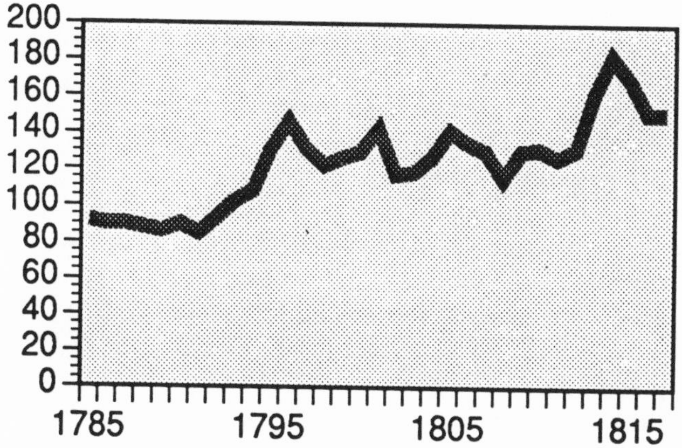

For a time the system of economic privilege worked exceedingly well. It launched the first wave of Western industrialization. In Great Britain (including America, its vassal colony), the Mercantile elite accumulated the capital, brains and markets permitting an industrial blast-off. Cities expanded as people flocked to areas of plentiful employment. English families migrated from small villages to cities like London, Manchester and Birmingham.

Key problem of the Mercantile Aristocrat—Overpopulation

As predicted by my theory, prosperity at this time was accompanied by a worsening key problem. The flood of population washing over the face of Europe and the New World could not be turned off. As a matter of fact, increasing population stimulated demands for goods and services, which generated business activity, which led to improved health conditions, which brought the death rate lower still. The curve of population growth kept rising.

Concern grew over the consequences of this inexhaustible human torrent. An entire generation was horror-struck by the possibility that the world would soon be inundated by famines, wars and epidemics. To the common sense of the time, it seemed that population, by its very nature, must always expand faster than the food supply.

The most famous statement on the problem was written by the Reverend Thomas Malthus in his 1798 *Essay on the Principle of Population*. In a world impressed by the mathematical proofs of Isaac Newton, Malthus made a splash with his mathematical *proof* of a dismal future (a proof withdrawn in later editions). Population grows exponentially, he said. In successive periods a population of 2 grows to 4, to 16, to 256, etc. On the other hand, the food supply (and other means of subsistence) can grow only arithmetically—2 to 3, to 4, to 5....A population of 2 can be fed by a food supply of 2. But tragedy awaits a population of 256 faced with a food supply of 5. Malthus launched economics as the dismal science.

***Socioeconomics* offers a very different interpretation of the Malthusian dilemma. The crisis of overpopulation was not due to an excess of population. It was due to excesses arising out of the aristocratic mindset.**

Overpopulation was the key problem of the Mercantile Aristocrat. Each new person added to the population required an addition to the world's supply of capital. *The aristocrats could not and would not supply it.* Inevitably there would be a shortage of capital needed to produce food, clothing, and shelter required by the growing poor. To survive, the poor would have to create their own capital. But how? The system barred the way.

The key problem was a mindset that denied both respect or property to a huge surplus of people at the bottom of the social pyramid. Common people were supposedly lazy and ineffectual. *Nature* made them that way. This was the premise studied and believed by both rich and poor throughout a lifetime. Absurd, said economist Adam Smith in 1776, "A person who can acquire no property, can have no other interest but to eat as much, and to labour as little as possible. Whatever work he does beyond what is sufficient to purchase his own maintenance can be squeezed out of him by violence only and not by any interest of his own."[81]

The problem went even deeper. Brainwashed by the prevailing mindset, the unprivileged masses imagined their very survival depended on the aristocratic elite.

Progress was sabotaged in yet another way. Not only did the poor produce too little, what they did produce was appropriated by the aristocratic world for its own purposes—creating sumptuous estates and multiplying personal wealth and leisure. It was an age of conspicuous consumption for aristocrats. A great land owner was not much concerned with developing new land to raise food for the masses. As described by Adam Smith, the

> ...elegance of his dress,of his equipage, of house and household furniture, are objects which from his infancy he has been accustomed to have some anxiety about. The turn of mind which this habit naturally formed, follows him when he comes to think of the improvement of land. He embellishes perhaps four or five hundred acres in the neighborhood of his house at ten times the expense which the land is worth after all his improvements; and finds that if he was to improve his whole estate in the same manner, and he has little taste for any other, he would be a bankrupt before he had finished the tenth part of it.[82]

In 1797, Jefferson depicted the aristocracy as enemies of democracy who "...are enriching themselves to the ruin of our country and swaying the government by their possession of the printing presses, which their wealth commands, and by other means not always honorable to the character of our countrymen."[83]

While Hamilton promoted the Mercantilist strategy of centralization, Jefferson's dissenting voice argued against "...the consolidation of the government; the giving to the federal member of the government...a control over all the functions of the States, "[84]

Had Hamilton and the Federalists won their campaign to keep the price of public land high and the terms of sale exacting and beset with obstacles, potential settlers would have had little chance to own their own land. They would have been nailed to their jobs in the East—in Boston, New York, and Philadelphia—trapped by the necessity to survive.

For their wealthy employers, however, things would have been quite different. Potential settlers would have provided cheap labor as well as large and accessible markets, and America would have taken its place as a proper mercantilist power. The traditional formula of the Mercantile Aristocrat would have been maintained: aristocrats contributing money and influence, the common man patience and brawn. That formula grew increasingly unacceptable—not only to the common man but to the aristocrats as well.

The social pyramid was upside down, balanced on its tiny apex, rather than its broad base.

People born into the primitive world of the industrial revolution were indeed vulnerable to starvation. Yet not because of a "natural" imbalance, as Malthus believed.

The shortage of capital for the poor was directly due to the mindset of the Mercantile Aristocrat. It prevented the common man and woman from exerting their best efforts. And it diverted capital to conspicuous consumption for the rich. The key problem of the Mercantile Aristocrat was deeply felt in the 1790s. Those Mercantile Aristocrats "knew" that any change in their

accustomed attitudes was unthinkable.

In the United States, Jefferson (along with Madison, Monroe, Franklin and others) was one of the leaders storming those barricades of the mind. Jefferson saw the need for shifting the balance—to respect the rich less and the poor more. With indignation bursting all bonds he promised that his presidency would ring in the "revolution of 1800." He would fight for "those who labor in the earth...the chosen people of God." Jefferson helped usher in an idea lying dormant since the ancient Greeks—that nations could thrive on the wits and efforts of the common man.

As the democratic mindset increasingly took hold, Americans and Europeans poured into the second leading region and the second socioeconomy began to write itself into the pages of history.

Eleven

Cycle 2—*The Bantam Capitalist;* David kills Goliath

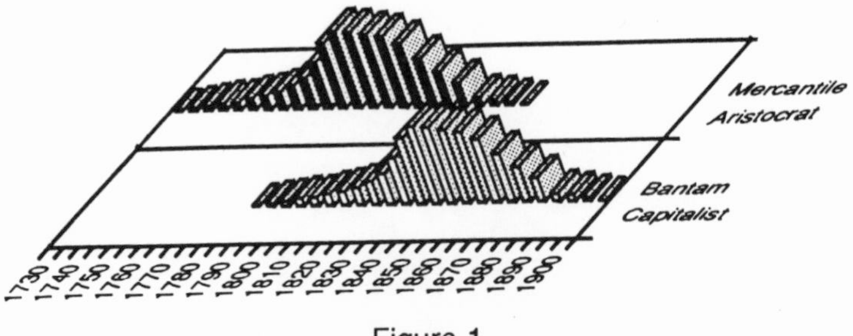

Figure 1
Rise and Fall of the Bantam Capitalist
Percent of Integration

I call the second socioeconomy the *Bantam Capitalist* because its mindset aimed at a proliferation of very small-scale capitalists drawn from the ranks of the common man.

It may seem that small scale was dictated by the practical necessities of those pioneering times. It wasn't. It was decided by excesses of the Mercantile Aristocrat. If the Mercantile Aristocrat had continued its influence, if it had not been driven off the stage of history by its excesses, the early 19th century would have told a different story. The privileged capitalism of rich aristocrats would have continued to dominate the country. In cities like New York, Philadelphia, and Boston, large enterprises would have grown still larger.

On the way to peak integration

Signalling the rise of new democratic trends worldwide, the Bantam Capitalist took off around 1789, coincident with the French Revolution and the American Constitution. Peak integration arrived in the 1840s. (See Figure 1.)

Half-way between 1789 and the 1840s, America became aware that it had changed forever. Architect-historian Talbot Hamlin observed: "It was as if man in America, around 1820, had rediscovered his five senses, had suddenly, like one breaking through from the forest to sun-drenched, sea-bordered downs, all at once become conscious of bright sun and distance and freedom; had suddenly...[awakened] from a nightmare."[85]

Had an opinion poll been taken around 1817, it would undoubtedly have shown a spectacular collapse of respect for the still dominant aristocracy. Hereditary landholders (the rich and mighty who formed the privileged class of the 18th century) were shoved from their places of eminence. Now ordinary laborers earning a scant $150 a year were newly esteemed and encouraged to swim in the capitalist stream. Many did. They became farmer-entrepreneurs who bought land, developed it as quickly as they could, and, if possible, sold it at a profit. Posterity celebrates them as "the pioneers." Here was the effective antidote to the Malthusian dilemma—a bull market of laborers turned businessmen.

Malthus counseled sexual restraint as the solution to overpopulation. The world pointedly ignored his advice. The actual historical solution to the Malthusian dilemma was one no Mercantile Aristocrat could have imagined: to infuse society's wretched masses with a *will to make money*. An English visitor to America in the 1820s was quoted as saying that "he had never heard Americans converse without mentioning the word dollar." Another said that "in snatches of conversation caught in the streets, the restaurants, and the cars, the continual cry is always, 'Dollars—dollars—dollars.'"[86]

In the 1820s and 1830s the masses set out with a passion

to become rich, to acquire farms, animals, houses, gardens, and, above all, respectability. Money was freedom. Money was security. Money was independence.

Opportunities to make money fired up the commoner with the energy of achievable goals. Every man and woman—no matter how common—could now become an effective generator of capital. The "trickle-down" philosophy was abandoned. Instead of depending on aristocrats to dispense charity, those little capitalists would make their own way.

In 1818 a British author attested to the ability of Americans to work hard and long. "An *ax* is their tool, and with that tool, at *cutting down* trees or *cutting them up*, they will do *ten times* as much in a day as any other men that I ever saw. Set one of these men...upon a wood of timber trees, and his slaughter will astonish you."[87]

States rights, county rights, city rights—even neighborhood rights?

The new socioeconomy reinforced all barriers against any resurgence of the privileged class. The new mindset intended those dollars to circulate among the common people: "The Jacksonian enterprisers simply wanted more capital for themselves rather than for such as the Lowells, the Astors, the Girards, who had hitherto controlled and wielded the bulk of it."[88]

Because the federal government was the seat of centralized power and essential to big business (Mercantile Aristocrat style) the Bantam Capitalists vowed to reduce federal power. Their principal tactic was "states rights." Redistribute power to lower levels of government—states, counties, cities—where it could be controlled by the common people. They'd see to it that small business would prevail over big business.

It happened. The resulting hodge-podge of laws and infrastructure throughout the land, and the difficulties of navigating poorly maintained roads, effectively quashed the potential for national markets. In the late 1830s a British traveler described his four mile an hour journey on the "great high road from the Capital of Virginia to the seat of the Federal Government."

> It is needless to dwell on the horror of that night....Under [the driver's] experimental guidance we certainly did receive such a jolting as I had never supposed a carriage capable of enduring; and the courage with which he led it on to charge stumps and trees, and to plunge into mud-holes, in the dark, excited my admiration.... The description here given of this road is not overdrawn. I will defy pen, pencil, or malice to do it...[89]

Had the electorate desired, important roads could easily have been kept in good repair. But the states rights mentality would not permit it. As someone told de Tocqueville in the early 1830s, "In general our roads are very badly kept up: we have no central authority that can force the counties to do their duty. Supervision being local, it is partial and without energy."[90]

Were bad roads an accident of history? Perhaps. But they certainly helped the socioeconomy realize its anti-aristocratic mission. They helped deal the desired death-blow to the privileged capitalism of the Mercantile Aristocrats. Within the multiplicity of small, isolated markets, local manufacturers could easily produce at lower costs than could larger competitors.

Sabotaged by the states-rights mentality and the local obstacles it produced, an aspiring corporate giant was as helpless as a whale in a fishpond.

Bantam Everything

Small was never more beautiful than in the socioeconomy of the Bantam Capitalist. It welcomed bantam manufacturers, bantam retailers, bantam wholesalers. Thousands of small producers coexisted in an era when iron mills were often no larger than an eight-by-ten-foot room attached to the blacksmith's house. Tiny family-run flour and lumber mills supplied customers who lived no more than a few miles away. That's the way it was "supposed to be." No one fretted that the scale of production was inefficient. It was the scale everyone wanted.

Five little capitalists are we
No more bending of the knee

In 1815, with a population of 500, Mt. Pleasant, Ohio boasted 3 saddlers, 3 hatters, 4 blacksmiths, 4 weavers, 6 boot and shoemakers, 8 carpenters, 3 tailors, 3 cabinet makers, 1 baker, 1 apothecary, 2 wagon makers, 2 tanneries, 1 shop to make wool carding machines. Within 6 miles of town were 9 merchant mills, 2 grist mills, 12 saw mills, 1 paper mill with 2 vats, 1 woolen factory and 2 fulling mills. **(Niles National Register)**

Peak of integration

In the 1830s, during Andrew Jackson's administration, the Bantam Capitalist neared the peak of its integration. Jackson was the national hero vowing to crush the aristocrats once and for all. He would stop them from controlling "...the political conduct of the many by first acquiring...control over the labor and earnings of the great body of the people."[92]

Jackson saw the Second Bank of the United States as the enemy personified. He wrote, "The bank is, in fact, but one of the fruits of a system at war with the genius of all our institutions—a system founded upon ...distrust of the popular will as a safe regulator of political power." Jackson's victory over the Bank in the 1830s revealed the enormous edge of the Bantam Capitalist over the declining Mercantile Aristocrat.

For the most part, Whigs and Democrats had represented opposing sides of the leading issues—Whigs for the Mercantile Aristocrat, Democrats for the Bantam Capitalist. Finally, the struggle over "privileged capitalism" was over. By

1846 (the socioeconomy's peak integration) the long controversy had run its course. Within a decade, the Whig party was dead and government intervention on behalf of privileged capitalism locked into history.[93] The Bantam Capitalist reigned unchallenged.

The second leading region

The new leading region contained scattered counties favored by good land and ports on the Mississippi, and Missouri rivers, and eventually, canals like the Erie, Wabash, Illinois and Michigan. Geography united with mindset to provide an environment favorable to small towns and small markets. Soon there was a profusion of isolated village-ports, each filling its hinterland with farmer-entrepreneurs. Land was fertile and abundant. Bulky crops could be cheaply "shipped" to overseas markets.

Figure 2
The Second Leading Region

Because the migration was localized within the Mississippi and Ohio Valleys, this new leading region has been approximated by adding relevant state populations—Louisiana, Alabama, Georgia, Mississippi, Tennessee, Kentucky, Ohio and Indiana. The state of New York was also included. It was connected to the Mississippi economy via the Great Lakes and the Erie Canal.[94] (See Figure 2.)

At its peak in the 1840s, the second leading region contained around 50 percent of the national population.[95]

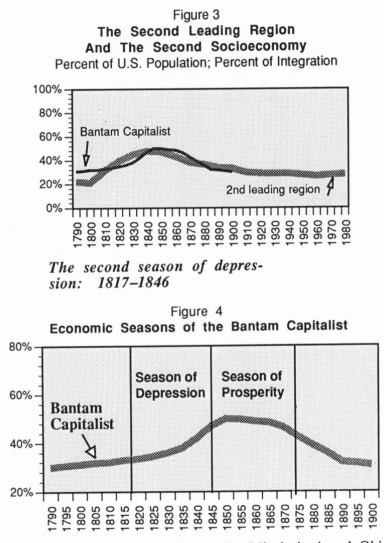

Figure 3
The Second Leading Region And The Second Socioeconomy
Percent of U.S. Population; Percent of Integration

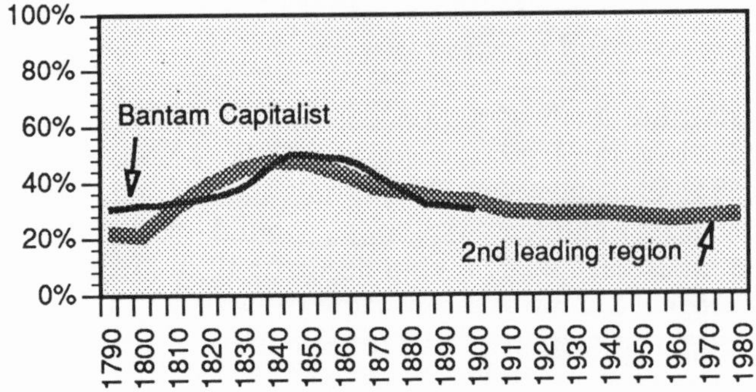

The second season of depression: 1817–1846

Figure 4
Economic Seasons of the Bantam Capitalist

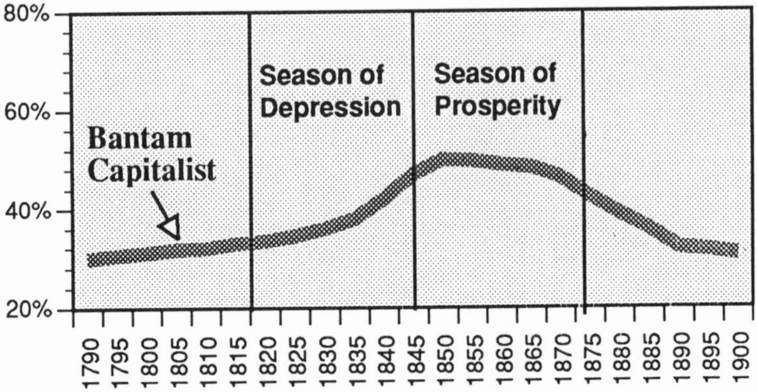

Accelerating migration to the Mississippi and Ohio Valleys was accompanied by a season of depression. It began around 1817, between the peaks of the Mercantile Aristocrat and the Bantam Capitalist. It ended at the second peak—around 1846. (See Figure 4.)

That the economy was chronically depressed is supported by the generally declining price level during the period. (See Figure 5.)

Figure 5
Wholesale Price Index of All Commodities, 1815-1845

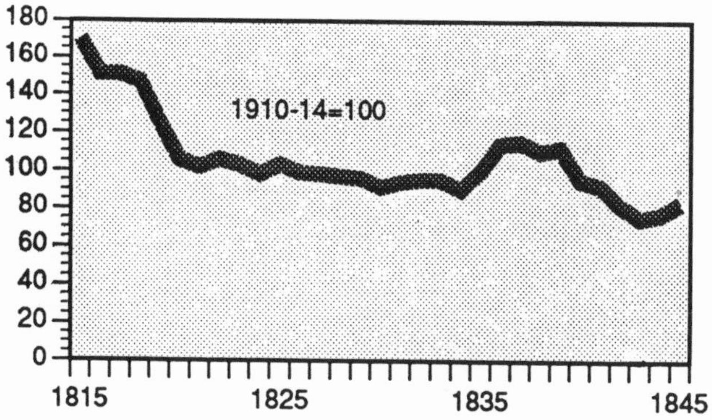

Except for 1828 to 1836—one brief interlude when gray skies cleared— the twenty-six years between 1817 and 1843 were chronically depressed: "By 1828 the postwar depression in the West [Mississippi-Ohio Valley] as well as the South was already ten years old with no relief in sight," writes economic historican Howard R. Smith.[96] The first urban soup kitchens in the New World appeared in 1820.

Henry Clay, a leading American statesman of the time, gives us an eyewitness account of the U.S. economy in 1824:

> In casting our eyes around us, the most prominent circumstance which fixes our attention and challenges our deepest regret is the general distress which pervades the whole country....It is indicated by the diminished exports of native produce; by the depressed and reduced state of our foreign navigation; by our diminished commerce; by successive unthrashed crops of grain, perishing in our barns and barn-yards for want of a market; by the alarming diminution of the circulating medium; by the numerous bankruptcies, not limited to the trading classes, but extending to all orders of society; by a universal

complaint of the want of employment and the consequent reduction of the wages of labor...[97]

After the economic boom, 1828–1836, came a disastrous bust. "There is abundant evidence," wrote economic historian Douglass North, "that the depression from 1839–1843 was one of the most severe in our history."[98]

The second season of prosperity: 1846–1873

Once again, the rising level of prices helps attest to the period's general prosperity. (See Figure 6.)

Figure 6
Wholesale Price Index of All Commodities, 1844-1873

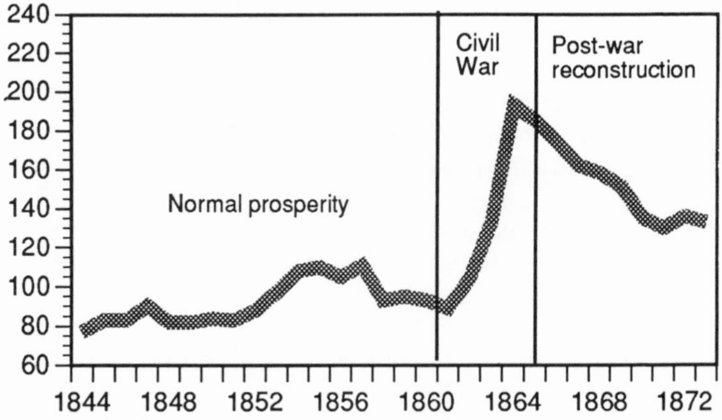

Following the lead of John Maynard Keynes and his theories of governmental management of the economy, 20th-century economists have often taken credit for the long prosperity after World War II. With allowances for the artificial stimulation of hot and cold wars, the Bantam Capitalist prosperity, 1846–1873, was approximately as long. Several recessions intervened, but no depressions.

Again we witness the paradox of economic prosperity, and high but slowing growth of the leading region. As usual, the facts belied popular beliefs. The French consul at New

Orleans told Alexis de Toqueville that in "... fifty years the Mississippi valley will hold the mass of American population..."[99] As usual, the leading region was only an accommodation to a single perishable socioeconomy. After 1846 the world was moving on. The tendency toward excess was visibly on the rise. The Bantam Capitalist began to choke on its characteristic "improvements."

The second key problem: Overtaxing small-scale capacities

The golden age for the river town had been in the 1840s—at the peak of integration. That was when and where Mark Twain was raised. He remembered

> ...the white town drowsing in the sunshine of a summer's morning, the streets empty, or pretty nearly so; one or two clerks sitting in front of the Water Street stores, with their splint-bottomed chairs tilted back against the wall, chins on breasts, hats slouched over their faces, asleep—with single shavings enough around to show what broke them down; a sow and a litter of pigs loafing along the sidewalk, doing a good business in water-melon rinds and seeds; two or three lonely little freight piles scattered about the levee, the fragrant town drunkard asleep in the shadown of them; two or three wood flats at the head of the wharf, but nobody to listen to the peaceful lapping of the wavelets against them; the great Mississippi, the majestic, the magnificent Mississippi, rolling its mile-wide tide along, shining in the sun....

In towns like that people behaved themselves. They could hardly do otherwise. Each and every man, woman and child was personally known by the whole community. Social control was achieved by looking into each other's eyes. But after the 1840s, with prosperity and growth, the towns were increasingly jam packed with strangers.

Small-scale urban capacities were becoming overtaxed. Without professional management and a full-time police force, municipal crime and corruption grew at an alarming rate. The towns had no way to control the depredations of gangsters, gamblers, holdup men, prostitutes, arsonists and other undesirables—endlessly depicted in the Wild West movies of a later era. Other urban problems also begged for professional services. The rutted, muddy roads and poor sanitary facilities (smelly open cesspools were not uncommon) made urban life frustrating and perilous.

The Bantam Capitalists' fascination with decentralization introduced layers of costly duplications. Travel by rail was a nightmare of transfers to different rail lines with different-gauge tracks and different rates and rules. Factories, machinery, and all the nuts and bolts of industrial civilization were a hodge-podge of sizes and descriptions conjured up by millions of small, independent improvisers. "Yankee ingenuity" they called it. Unnecessary layers of middlemen made prices both variable and unduly high.

The dilemmas resulting from small-scale could never be resolved by those with profound Bantam loyalties. Any initiatives they'd recommend would only worsen the problem. In the 1840s an opposing mindset waited in the wings to be born.

A chasm gaped between the world that was and the world that would be. As the utopian appeal of the second leading region dried up, Americans began streaming into the third.

Twelve

Cycle 3—*The Colossus;* Goliath kills David

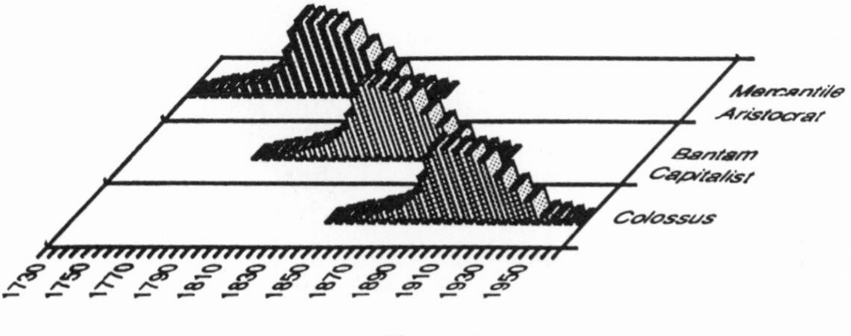

Figure 1
The Rise and Fall of the Colossus
Percent of Integration

The third socioeconomy I call the Colossus because its mindset aimed at a spectacular scale of industrialization—enormous factories, giant corporations, mighty cities, vast commercial farms. Above all, it aimed for Colossal nationalistic power. Every industrialized country in the world sought to be Number One—one powerful nation *über alles*.

The Colossus was everything the Bantam Capitalist was not. Whereas the Bantam Capitalist distributed power far and wide in an orgy of democratic equality, the Colossus conferred power on a few millionaire captains of industry—the Rockefellers, the Vanderbilts, the Carnegies. Whereas the Bantam Capitalist opposed centralization with Jeffersonian ardor, the Colossus gave centralization its highest priority. Whereas the Bantam Capitalist conceived a passion for small independent business, the Colossus was stirred by giant corporate structures. Whereas Bantam Capitalists were ferociously individualistic, people of the Colossus were inclined to see themselves as wheels and pulleys in a massive and magnificent industrial machine.

On the way to peak integration

Beginning around the middle of the 19th century, a groundswell of changing beliefs united national and personal goals. Nationally, Americans sought to outdo the world in industrial achievements. They took pride in America's might, its superior technology, its coast-to-coast railroads, its giant factories, its enormous cities.

The Colossal philosophy

The crucial battles of the advancing socioeconomy were spearheaded in the arena of the mind. The heavy artillery was manned by philosophers like Herbert Spencer, William Graham Sumner, John Fiske, and others who called themselves "Social Darwinists."

Drawing on Charles Darwin's theory of natural selection, the Social Darwinists recommended the study of Nature as a means of understanding society. For them, society was a biological mechanism, like a plant or animal, governed by similar laws of organization, growth, and change. If people would study Nature, said the Social Darwinists, they would find that society's wholesome path of development lay in its increasing differentiation, specialization, and control by a central organ. These philosophers "proved" that the target of an evolving universe is centralization. And from that, they insisted that hierarchy and authority are the essence of civilization.

The Social Darwinists arrived at that conclusion by their analysis of evolution. At the bottom of the evolutionary ladder were protozoa in which all functions were managed by a single cell. Progress meant organizing specialized cells around a dominant organ—such as the brain—to ensure that all functions were coordinated in the service of the whole organism.

The paradigm for society was military organization. A commanding *center* ruled, its regime authoritarian and absolute. Indeed, said the Social Darwinists, it is the duty of society to centralize. "Higher" nations had a responsibility—the so-called "white man's burden"—to colonize nations "lower" on the evolutionary scale. And they did. Imperialistic nations—England, Belgium, France, Russia, and later, Japan, Italy and Germany—acquired colonies, and with good conscience dominated them. America too, joined in the ideology of expansionism. It fought and won its war with Mexico, acquiring Texas, California and other valuable real estate. It fought again in the Spanish-American War of 1898, winning the right to command the territories of Cuba, Guam, and the Philippines.

Just as powerful nations dominated weaker peoples, big corporations swallowed smaller businesses. Big cities dominated little cities. Autocratic husbands presided over docile wives and children. Whites felt superior to blacks. Christians felt superior to Jews. And the rich could believe that they were not only more fortunate but "better."

While the Colossus is considered here as an American phenomenon, the socioeconomy extended throughout the civilized world. Men and women of the Colossus celebrated hierarchy by evoking heroic Wagnerian themes and the pomp of a Bismarck and his Kaiser inspecting legions of goose-stepping *Teutons*. They welcomed fraternal organizations such as the Masons with their thirty-three steps to the dizzy heights of Grand Inspector Inquisitor, Knight of the Sun, and Sovereign Grand Inspector General. Knights of Labor conferred titles like Venerable Sage and Unknown Knight upon its distinguished members. The years 1845–1900 saw a proliferation of these hierarchical organizations—like the American Order of the Hibernians, the Knights of Pythias, the Elks, the Ancient Order of United Workmen, the Knights of Columbus.

It was no accident that after 1860 fragmented nations broke out of their Bantam Capitalist shells. Germany consolidated its separate states into a powerful nation. So did Italy, though it never achieved Germany's stature. And through the agonies of the Civil War, America's status as a pre-eminent center of Colossal power was achieved by *preventing* its dissolution. In a celebrated letter to Horace Greeley, Lincoln wrote: "...my paramount object in this struggle is to save the Union, and is not either to save or destroy slavery. If I could save it by freeing all the slaves, I would do it; and if I could save it by freeing some and leaving others alone I would also do that...."

Colossal dreams of the future

The Colossus built cities. Big cities. Dense cities. Giant corporations attracted swarms of migrants who pressed into cities like Chicago expecting to make their fortunes. While waiting for their fortunes to materialize, the new migrants fertilized the economy with cheap labor and then obligingly bought back what they had produced. Their tolerance of crowded conditions, back-breaking work, and hand-to-mouth penury allowed savings needed by the socioeconomy for reinvestment.

Mindset, urged on by an optimistic Horatio Alger outlook, wrung from the migrants the great personal sacrifices needed to build this industrial Gargantua of the late 19th century. (Half a century later, in Communist Russia, Stalin relied on the repressions of the KGB to win similar sacrifices. Still later, modern Japan faithfully reproduced the winning formulas of late 19th century America.)

On the personal level, flesh-and-blood models like John D. Rockefeller, Andrew Carnegie, and Edward Harriman were inspiring proof that the rags-to-riches dream could come true. In an age when the average laborer earned a dollar a day, to become another "Rockefeller" was an outsized dream but not an impossibility. A man might not make it. But he had a chance. Everybody had a chance.

Starting from near poverty, people of the Colossus expected to emulate the millionaires who now lived off the cream at the top of the bottle. Why not? Weren't they once poor themselves? Rockefeller began as a $4-a-week clerk in a commission merchant's house. In 1892 his fortune was estimated to be $815,647,796.89.[100] Andrew Carnegie started out at the age of thirteen as a bobbin boy in a cotton mill at $1.20 a week and became the largest steel manufacturer in the world. From 1889 to 1899 the profits from Carnegie's industrial empire averaged $7,500,000 a year. And in 1900 that figure spiralled to $40,000,000.[101] According to popular opinion they "made it" by patience, initiative, punctuality, reliability, will power, discipline, an iron sense of purpose—plus a bit of luck. *Above all, they made it by saving their money.*

A new dress? I'll never
acquiesce.
Save. Save for later. Time's
an incubator.

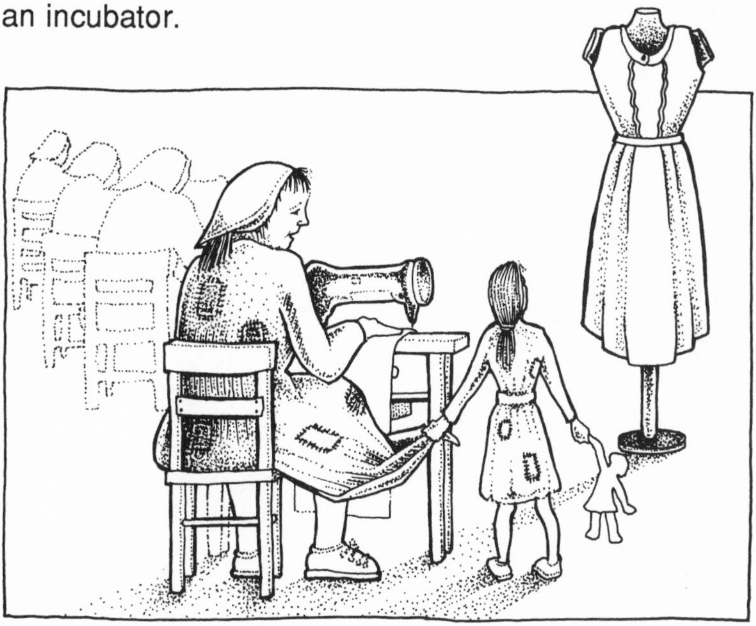

In this great land of ours, any man—or his children, or children's children—could become a captain of industry, or at least one of his assistants, or, short of that, a prominent investor. The present might involve back-breaking work at $5 a week, but there was dignity in it because the future glittered with promise.

The Colossus' peak of integration

By the end of the century Americans could point to industrial behemoths that dwarfed competitors everywhere in the world. Said one contemporary observer, U.S. Steel "receives and expends more money every year than any but the very greatest of the world's national governments; its debt is larger than that of many of the lesser nations of Europe; it absolutely controls the destinies of a population nearly as large as that of Maryland or Nebraska, and indirectly influences twice that number."[102] As with steel, so with oil, railroads, banking.

Many indicators point to 1900 as the socioeconomy's approximate peak of integration. Now Bantam Capitalists had virtually become cogs in the Colossus machine. Their children worked in the city, and they themselves were pillaged by the rate practices of robber barons who owned the great railroad lines.

From 1873 to 1900 "David" fought back. Farmers joined the Grangers and similar advocacy groups to help them fight bitter legal battles. Sometimes, as in *Munn vs Illinois*, they won. But increasingly they lost.

In the 1880s, led by the Knights of Columbus, labor attempted to dictate policy and failed. In 1890 the McKinley Tariff made a radical departure from the free-trade politics so dear to the Bantam Capitalist. (Along with states rights, low tariffs had helped to guard against any revival of that socioeconomy's favorite villain—the Big Business of the Mercantile Aristocrat.)

Despite David's efforts, Goliath was nearing its peak integration and the mindset was no longer sympathetic to the "little guy." In 1894, during a deep depression, Coxey's motley "Army" of the unemployed—including many ragged Civil War veterans—marched on Washington with a plea for help. Unmoved, and now in the pocket of Big Business, officialdom booted the Army out of town. As economic historian Howard R. Smith put it, "No better evidence could be had of the satisfaction of capitalism with itself in the last decade of the 19th century."[103] By 1900 the "war" was over.

Big Business was in firm command.

The third leading region

What region would best serve this new socioeconomy? Above all, it had to constitute a single national market. The thousands of separated local markets preferred by the Bantam Capitalist world would never do for the Colossus.

Tearing down the barriers of the small-scale socioeconomy would put companies in touch with millions of customers, giving life to giant corporations with a talent for mass production. Specialized machinery and labor would drive costs down so low that smaller competitors would be routed, leading to even greater size and even greater savings for the large corporations. Savings meant rapid accumulation of capital. Capital, invested and reinvested, would bring the endless industrial expansion so much prized by people of the Colossus. (Here was the model for post-World War II Japan.)

The third leading region is more difficult to determine than the second. In the earlier case, states of the Mississippi and Ohio valleys were found to peak around 1840. No longer confined to one geographic area as in the two preceding periods, migration was now directed to many discontiguous counties across the nation.

Counties in the third leading region met two criteria. They rose 1870–1890 and fell 1930–1950.[104] The first criterion eliminated counties belonging to the second region—they fell 1870–1890. The second criterion eliminated counties belonging to the fourth region—they rose 1930–1950.

Once again the evidence bears out the theoretical expectation. Following the rise and fall of the socioeconomy, we find a group of counties whose share of U.S. population began a steep ascent around 1840, reached a peak in 1900 with about *half* the U.S. population, then continuously declined until 1980. (See Figure 2.) The great cities of the Colossus peaked in the 1920s, while their hinterlands (a wide swath of rural counties across the nation) peaked in the 1880s. Averaging both cities and hinterlands results in a slower, gentler rise and fall in the overall curve of the third leading region's percentage of U.S. population. (See Figure 3.)

Figure 2
Third Leading Region and Third Socioeconomy
Percent of U.S. Population; Percent of Integration

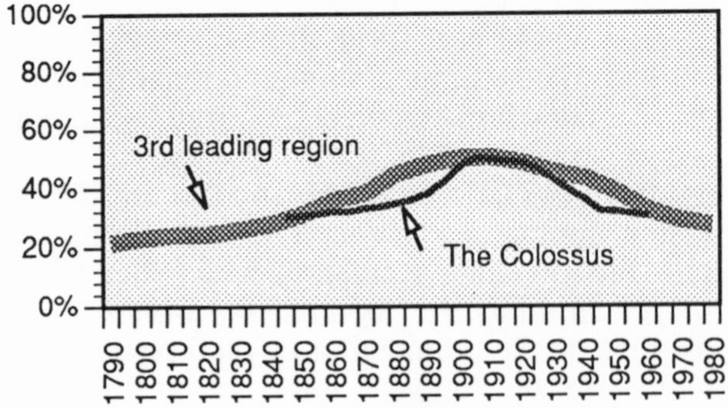

Figure 3
The Third Leading Region
Location of Counties

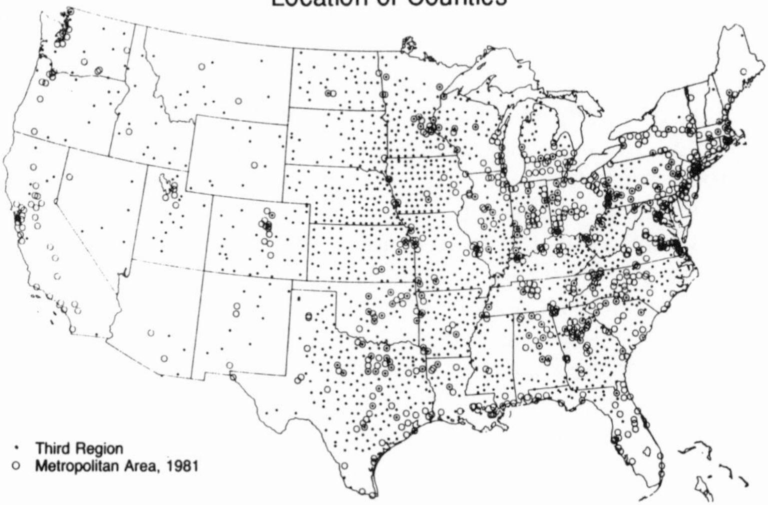

The former penchant for smallness was gone. On the prairies of the Midwest a new, highly mechanized farming industry grew and became an adjunct of the city. The city mass-produced plows, harrows, harvesters, processed the harvests, and offered its lusty appetite for food and raw materials as a ready market. Now the farmers were no longer independent, no longer small, no longer Bantam Capitalists.

Rural areas and big industrial cities were welded together by the railroads into a single well-regulated machine. The rise and fall of railroad construction—extending from the 1860s into the early 20th century—matched the rise and fall of the third leading region. (See Figure 4.)

Figure 4
Miles of U.S. Railroads (in thousands)
up to 1890, miles operated; after 1890, miles owned

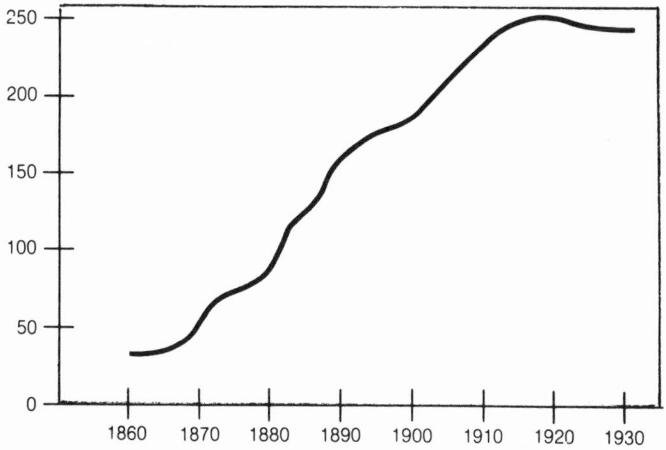

New York was ***not*** *a leading member of the third region*

Having grown early in the 19th century in the service of the Bantam Capitalist, New York was supposedly endowed with a superior capacity for further growth. That is the logic taught by conventional theory, even today. Where growth establishes an economic base, there further growth will be. Big cities will grow ever bigger. New York and other East Coast cities monopolized enormous markets. Accessibility to raw materials and industrial suppliers permitted the lowest possible production costs.

But New York, Boston, and Philadelphia did not leap into the new industrial age. They limped into it. From 1860 to 1890 (formative years of the 19th century industrial revolution) they barely kept pace with average increases in U.S.

population. At a time when small businesses were daily being swallowed by giant national corporations, cities catering to smallness couldn't compete. Constrained by obsolete real estate and the "small-is-beautiful" institutions of the Bantam Capitalist, these cities were unprepared for enormity. Manufacturers were often forced to operate in tiny, cramped quarters. Much of the existing retail trade was still conducted from lofts, stables, back rooms, basements, and one-room shops.

In contrast to the phlegmatic growth of the great Eastern coastal cities—and contradicting conventional theory—Chicago, a hick town in 1860, hurtled into the industrial age. It was both the archetypal city and hub of the third leading region. From a mere 50 residents in 1830, it grew to 29,963 by 1850, more than tripled by 1860 (to 109,206), and tripled again by 1870. It threw off every vestige of its ambience as a small river town. By 1900, 1,698,575 souls packed into that city of relentless and indefatigable growth. From muddy river village to world metropolis in half a century! (See Figure 5.)

Figure 5
Chicago Compared to East Coast Cities
Percent of U.S. Population

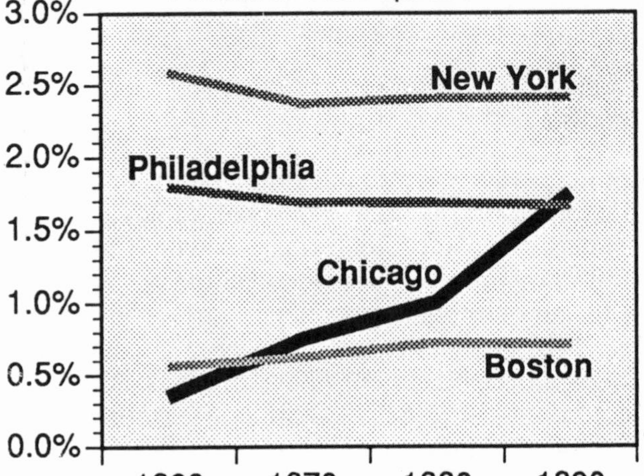

Why was Chicago "chosen" over other cities with a much more extensive economic base? There were, in fact, two reasons. One is well-known—Chicago's central location within the leading region and accessibility to main channels of transportation.

The second reason for Chicago's growth is not well-known, not acknowledged by economists—and in 1990 is the same reason that keeps the public from understanding the coming crash of suburbia and boom of penturbia. What Chicago had in the 19th century (and what penturbia has now) was *empty land by the mile.* 19th-century businessmen could play Prince Charming to a sleeping bonanza of flat, fertile and *vacant* prairie land.

Not having to make-do with quaint old Bantam Capitalist buildings and neighborhoods, Chicago could create its own kind of real estate—*geared to large-scale industry and dense living accommodations*—ideally suited to the emerging Colossus. (See Chapter 7.) Not only was Chicago built on new land, so was its hinterland of villages, towns and cities. The whole interdependent network of cities and rural areas enjoyed maximum freedom to shape the physical environment in accord with current preferences. Engineers planned centralized systems that could support armies of workers and machines able to move mountains of materials over half a continent.

The third season of depression 1873–1900

The economic seasons of the Colossus are choreographed in step with the rise and fall of the socioeconomy and the third leading region. (See Figure 6.)

After three prosperous decades (bracketing the Civil War) businessmen of 1873 were no less surprised than their counterparts at the end of the roaring 1920's—or, for that matter, the end of the high-spending 1980s—to see business activity suddenly suffer a free fall. The crash of 1873—allegedly triggered by the failure of financiers involved in the construction of the Northern Pacific railroad—sent convulsive tremors radiating across all economic and social boundaries.

Soon the nation became mired in the depression of 1873–1878. Half the steel industry shut down. The production of coal slowed to a dribble. Wages fell. Bread lines lengthened across the country.

Figure 6
Economic Seasons of the Colossus

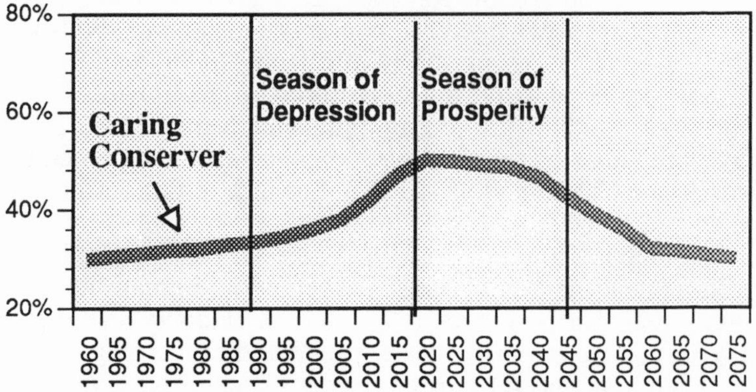

During the generally unstable period from 1873 to 1900, economic paralysis alternated with manic booms. After 1885 more than 40,000 miles of railroad track expanded the leading region. Railroads opened up the Great Plains—one of the most fertile agricultural empires of the world. The accompanying boom ended unhappily eight years later with a panic and the depression of 1893–1897.

Figure 7
Wholesale Price Index of All Commodities, 1875-1900

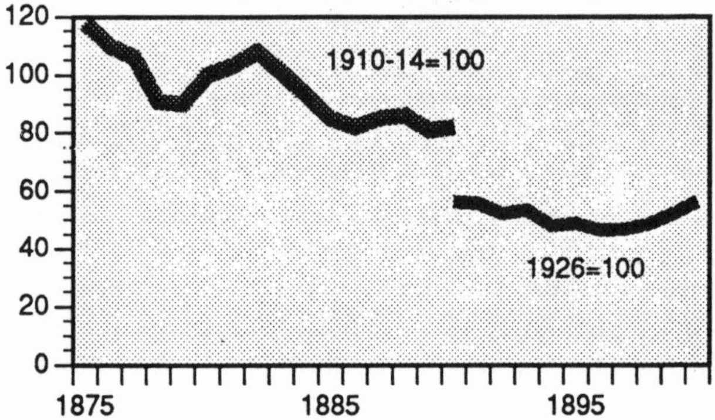

As in other periods of chronic instability, the booms and busts of 1873–1900 affected some areas more than others. In the region of obsolescence, depression sank real estate values to worrisome depths. In the leading region booms lifted them to unprecedented heights. The existence of a season of depression is once again supported by the record of declining prices. (See Figure 7.)

The third season of prosperity 1900–1929

For the third time we see that as a socioeconomy reaches its peak integration, a long season of prosperity begins. And again prosperity is interrupted by brief recessions no more frequent or severe than those encountered during our own post-World War II prosperity. *There is no depression in this season.*

That prosperity was the norm during this period is attested to by the upturn in the price level. (See Figure 8.)

Figure 8
Wholesale Price Index: All Commodities, 1900-1930[105]

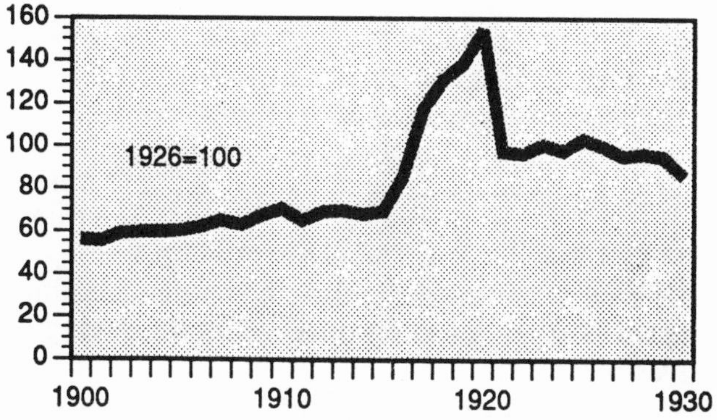

Again we see the paradox of prosperity and decline. Throughout the season of prosperity developing excesses lay the basis for an opposing socioeconomy and another leading region. After 1900, Chicago's growth began to slow. Where growth had once tripled in a decade, it less than doubled, and after 1930, fell *below* the national average. A new socioeconomy had appeared, but Chicago was unable to meet its requirements. Those cramped city lots were laid out before people changed their minds from saving all they could to spending all they could. Promoters of subdivisions with bucolic names like "Golden Meadows," "Sleepy Hollow Estates," and "Orchard Hills" were little tempted to invest capital in Chicago's gray and grimy neighborhoods. Unable to compete with suburban houses built on cheap, large, and sunny lots, aging industrial cities joined the region of obsolescence.

The third key problem: overproduction

As the Colossus was a trail-blazer in large-scale industrial production, its key problem was *over*production.

By 1920 supply was running far ahead of demand for steel, railroad lines, and industrial capacity. After 1920 railroad building came to a virtual halt. Cook and other favored counties reached their peak growth between 1900–1930. Migration slowed as Chicago and other industrial cities became congested, noisy, and expensive places in which to live. After 1930 the migration to industrial centers and their hinterlands no longer claimed an increasing percentage of U.S. population. The days of the Colossus were numbered.

The Colossus had reached its peak integration. But, as with every other mature socioeconomy, it could not slow the momentum of its excesses. It obstructed. It struggled. it multiplied its imbalances. The crisis now beckoning the next socioeconomy was a never-ending and self-defeating cycle: save and invest in order to produce still more saving and still more investment.

Save and invest for what? There was little demand for the socioeconomy's end-products. While its industrial plant had grown to colossal proportions, consumer demand had remained small and unpromising. Who was going to use the phenomenal capacity unleashed by the system? Unfortunately, the customers who might one day consume those good things pouring from the horn of plenty could not acquire the necessary purchasing power. Nor did they have the mindset predisposing them to consume rather than save. *The Colossus wasn't nurturing consumers.*

America's capacity to supply greatly outweighed its wizened powers of demand.

When supply is heavy
and demand is slack
The economy soon
goes out of whack

A world-wide disparity between the ability to produce and the ability to consume exacerbated that single and terrible problem. Everyone knew what to call it—overproduction. No one knew how to solve it.

Every socioeconomy attempts to cure its own key problem. Because it applies the same prescription that created the problem, its efforts remain dependably futile. For the Colossus, the futile effort was called Fascism and Naziism. Instead of opposing the excesses of the Colossus, they exaggerated them. What had begun as a benign corrective to the Bantam Capitalist became perverted into a Frankenstein.

In 1889 Andrew Carnegie had written, "We accept and

welcome ...great inequality..., the concentration of business... in the hands of a few, and the law of competition ...as being not only beneficial, but essential for the future progress of the race."[106] But by the 1920s, "future progress of the race" had moved disturbingly far from anything Carnegie envisioned. Italy, Germany and Japan attempted to wrest bigness at the expense of the rest of the world. Can't find markets? Take them away from other nations. Take their land. Take their colonies. *Force* them to buy our products.

Hitler solved the problem of overproduction by installing the State as ultimate consumer. At the same time, he overextended all the familiar themes of the Colossus. Served by iron will and discipline, the State would make the factories hum. Hum for what purpose? *For war.* And then a splendid future. After today's *sturm und drang* would come a golden tomorrow lasting a thousand years.

Around the turn of the century a more innovative solution to the problem of overproduction than Fascism was brewing deep in the recesses of the public mind. The curtain was being raised on *The Little King*.

Thirteen

Cycle 4—*The Little King;* Crowns for the masses

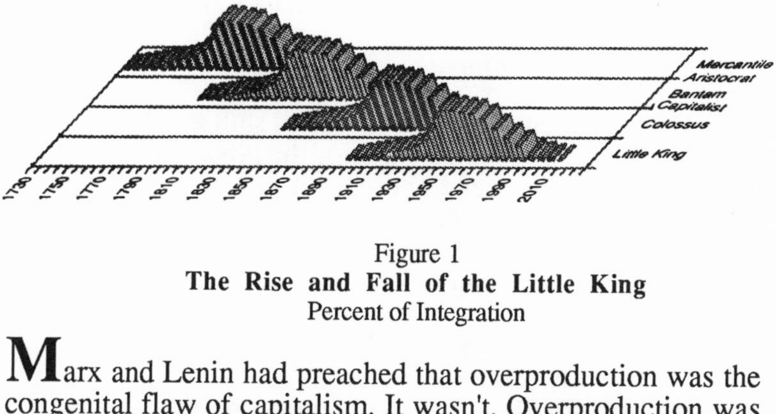

Figure 1
The Rise and Fall of the Little King
Percent of Integration

Marx and Lenin had preached that overproduction was the congenital flaw of capitalism. It wasn't. Overproduction was really the congenital flaw of only one perishable socioeconomy, the Colossus. In the next century capitalism cured itself—by turning from its emphasis on production to a new and unheard-of emphasis on consumption.

The new socioeconomy drilled away at its key problem like a dentist at a cavity. So comprehensive was its acceptance of the new mindset urging ever-greater consumption, and so complete the cure, that after almost a century, capitalism is suffering not from overproduction but from *overconsumption*—the diametric opposite of overproduction. Explain that if you can, Karl Marx.

Because the consumer is King, and because the Kings are many, I call this socioeconomy *The Little King*. Drawn from laborers earning little more than a dollar a day at the turn of the century, America's Little Kings soon boosted themselves into the great middle class.

On the way to peak integration

By what miracle did the Little Kings win their thrones? Was it an extraordinary propensity to save and invest? Was it the age-old capitalistic formula for inducing prosperity by driving down the cost of production? That was precisely what did *not* happen. Increased savings and investment would only have made things worse. What we did was far more appropriate. It was what we always do to overcome socioeconomic excesses. We change who we are and what we want.

Spend and consume

Thus commenced a little-celebrated shift in mindset: from concern for the future to concern for the present. To save and invest was *out*. To spend and consume was *in*. Americans were determined to "get it now."

We all learned to glorify consumption. "Don't hoard your capital as Grandpa used to do," became the sage advice of the Little King who now believed that Grandpa must have been a fool to bury himself so deep in the future. There *is* no future. Life is too short. *Get it now*.

It was difficult at first. Saving for productive purposes ran in the blood. How could a man of the Colossus, an earnest man, a man of integrity, a man of conscience, spend hard-earned capital on consumer goods? It would be unseemly, even wicked. Would he buy a house, a car, a motorcycle, a boat? Unthinkable. He didn't *need* them. That much money added to his savings would insure a solid future for his children and grandchildren. "Save and invest" had been the Eleventh Commandment.

With a smile bright as a silver dollar, the Little King

spoke, "Enjoy. Go on vacations—to the East Coast, the West Coast, Canada, Alaska, Europe, South America, Asia, Africa. And spend your capital. All of it. Spend more than your capital. Spend more than you earn, and that's okay too."

"How?"

"Haven't you heard about credit?"

Big Borrowers and Big Spenders became the new patriots who made the economy go 'round. And once again technology broke through all barriers to become the willing servant of rising new demands. Bankers took the technology of consumer credit to where it had never been before. They invented the "credit card." They became facile with consumption loans of every kind—for homes, cars, boats, vacations; and for every time period—from a few hours to 30 years, or an entire lifetime. The IRS taxed the savers and gave *incentives* to users of credit. And in our zeal to consume, we easily fell into a new American competition—to outspend the Joneses.

Equality: key strategy of the Little King

Congress gave its wholehearted assistance to the cause of equality. It levied progressive income taxes on the rich and distributed the proceeds in a dizzying array of welfare payments to the poor. Were we expressing an egalitarian passion to heal the wounds of the long-suffering poor? Perhaps. But bear this in mind: *The battle for equality was a perfectly logical strategy for a socioeconomy bent on conquering overproduction.*

The conquest of overproduction called for consumption, *voracious* consumption, requiring armadas of shipments to market. Let the earth be blanketed with consumers. But how? Most people were poor. And enabling the poor to buy seemed as impossible as getting the mute to speak.

The Little King's solution was simple. Take a dollar from a rich man—who will likely add it to savings because he doesn't *need* to spend it—and give it to a poor man, who *must* spend it or starve. Do it again and again, faster and faster, and in every kind of transaction. Eventually all incomes become more equal. Tremendous sums of money are put into circulation. Consumption spending rises up and up, soaring like an astronaut.

Implementing the mindset of the Little King

Theodore Roosevelt, symbolic man of the Colossus, spoke with a soft voice and carried a big stick, projecting nationalistic might. *But he was also America's first Little King.* As pioneer "trust buster" he aimed to reduce the weight of monopolies bearing down on average Americans. His trust-busting was a small but auspicious beginning to provide purchasing power to the poor.

By the 1930s—from Theodore to Franklin Roosevelt—the strategy of the Little King was completely clarified. The New Deal introduced a panoply of programs to moderate disparities in income—the progressive income tax, welfare programs, labor laws, public housing, social security, unemployment compensation, farm subsidies. And to further superintend the transfer of income from rich to poor we built the powerful welfare state, a collection of agencies, nearly every one of which was aimed at subsidies to the less fortunate—FHA, CCC, WPA, AAA, FCA, FSA, FWA, HOLC, NLRB, NYA, TVA and others.

In a slow, vacillating development up to 1930—and then rapidly thereafter—the political means to achieve a more equable distribution of wealth was incorporated into the character of the Little King.

After World War II, disturbed by a presentiment that the Great Depression had not yet run its course, we found additional ways to ensure sufficient spending. One of the most promising was the creation of what General Eisenhower later forebodingly called the *military-industrial complex.* With its insatiable hunger for big-ticket spending, it was an ideal institution of the Little King. It put money in worker's pockets while guaranteeing that, unlike productive investments, production for defense would not plague us by creating future unused inventories to depress the economy. All that was needed for expansion of the military-industrial complex was a likely villain. Had the Iron Curtain not appeared we might well have built it ourselves.

Peak integration of the Little King

Completing its integration in 1960, the Little King had decisively defeated the Colossus as a functioning system. Hitler and Mussolini—last European exemplars of the Colossus—had been routed in the 1940s. (See Chapter 12.) Ironically, America was the last fortress of that fading socioeconomy. Nourished by residual strains of the conservative Republicanism of Harding, Coolidge and Hoover and their insistence on business as the hierarchical center of American life, and repelled by the equalitarian trends of the Little King, the Colossus still had a breath of life. In America, a burst of nationalistic xenophobia touched off by Senator Joseph R. McCarthy sought to identify the equalitarian Little King with Communist extremism. The Senate eventually censured him in 1954. That blow to *McCarthyism* dealt the final coup de grace to the venerable socioeconomy. The relative equilibrium of peak integration lay just ahead.

After McCarthy, political strife was minimal. Democrats and Republicans were so much alike that, as a candidate for President, General Eisenhower could have represented either party. Once elected, the new administration was singularly somnolescent. Journalist Russell Baker brooded over the dullness of his job as White House correspondent. "It was a shock at day's end to discover that there hadn't been any work to speak of.... The main item of discussion among the White House reporters all day had been the president's forthcoming vacation."[107]

The Civil Rights movement of the late 1950s and early 1960s was not a disturbance to jar the Little King—it was living and breathing evidence of its peak integration. The Little King sought thoroughgoing equality. That was ingrained in its mindset. Most segments of white society had already cashed in their IOUs and been admitted to the great American middle class. The suburbs were filling up with formerly poor white families who now owned their own homes and shiny automobiles. As the poor grew prosperous, the economy leaped and surged in response—just as the Little King promised. How appropriate that, at the socioeconomy's peak, blacks too would at last be permitted to make their contribution to national prosperity.

Those were the palmy days before a stable consensus broke into a thousand troublesome issues: abortion, women's rights, gay rights, children's rights, animal rights, pollution, overspending, federal deficits, trade deficits, educational deficiencies, the dissolution of the Western Alliance, inflation and deflation. (After 1970, in an atmosphere of crisis, the movie industry spilled out a profusion of themes centered on nostalgic reminiscences of those earlier untroubled years.)

It was a time of stability, when women gave themselves to their families, when Rosalind Russell drew crowds of moviegoers to see the faithful wife awaiting organization-man husband with slippers in hand, when most of us hungered for a house in suburbia and knew we could buy it, when men wore standard haircuts and women wore skirts. We had a sense of everything being more or less right with the world.

Figure 2
Homicides[108]
Rate per 100,000

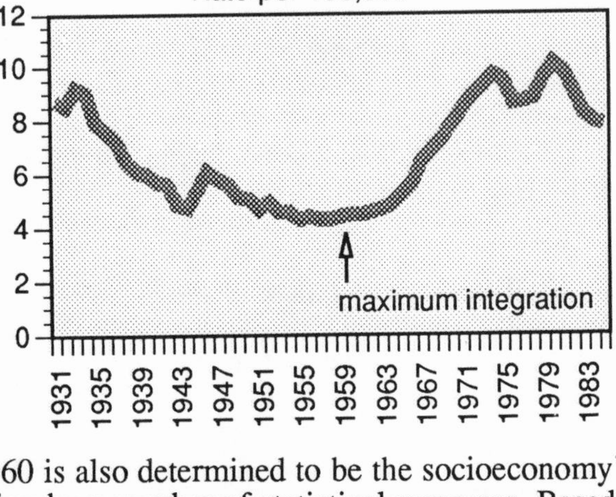

1960 is also determined to be the socioeconomy's peak integration by a number of statistical measures. Based on the homicide rate as one indicator, the record from 1931 to 1984 suggests 1958–1960 as a time of maximum social stability and integration. (See Figure 2.) Suicides and divorces, also at a minimum at this time, indicate the same conclusion. Finally, a stable economy suggests an environment conducive to raising families, and birthrates peaked around 1959.

The fourth leading region

One of the greatest obstacles to the creation of the new socioeconomy was the lack of a suitable place in which to consume. Within the tight circle of the old central cities land was expensive, lots necessarily tiny. There was no room for Little Kings and Queens to spread out, no feeling of spaciousness to inform the world of royal mastery, no space in which to accumulate wave after wave of automatic appliances and up-to-the-minute gadgetry.

Around the turn of the 20th century we embarked on a new migration—from dreary, tenement-filled neighborhoods to rustic meadowlands, from the raucus din of clattering subways and screaming factory whistles to the lowing of cows and the music of birdsong. Here, amidst peaceful green communities far beyond the city boundaries, was suburbia, *the promised land.*

As before, it took at least three decades before the new migration became visible—even to the experts. By 1940 most Americans dreamt of living in the suburbs. The dream, only mildly seductive at first, soon throbbed throughout the land. In the 1940s, despite the effort to win World War II, the suburbs grew by 2.4 times the national rate.

After the war suburbia became the New City, complete with industrial parks, condominiums, housing developments, shopping centers, and modern high-rises in smoky glass and concrete. Throughout the 1950s dream and reality converged in an explosion of suburban development. Census data show more than a 56 percent increase of suburban population in a single decade. In the decade of the 1950s the metropolitan population outside of the central cities grew from 35.1 to 54.9 million. After 1960, that pace could no longer be sustained.

The fourth leading region was estimated as the group of all counties growing faster than the national average 1950–1970, and slower than the national average 1970–1980.

Ideally, it should have included counties growing rapidly 1950–1970 that took longer to slow down.

The point map of county locations helps to confirm that the fourth leading region is really suburbia. Figure 3 shows that fourth migration counties are heavily represented in metropolitan areas.

Figure 3
Fourth Leading Region
Locations of Counties

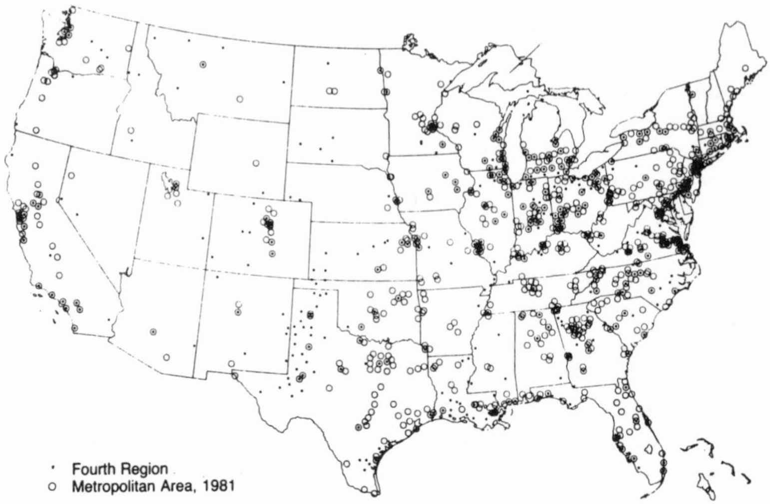

Once again we see the near-parallel development of a new socioeconomy and a new leading region. (See Figure 4.) The socioeconomy rises after 1900, peaks 1958–1960, and falls thereafter. The leading region also rises after 1900, reaches its peak rate of growth around 1960, and its peak share of U.S. population in the 1970s. At some future time, we may decide that suburbia's peak share occurred somewhat later, perhaps between 1970 and 1990.[109] As in previous leading regions, suburbia grows from small beginnings—about one fifth of U.S. population in 1900—to *one half* in 1970.

Figure 4
The Fourth Leading Region and The Fourth Socioeconomy
Percent of Population; Percent of Integration

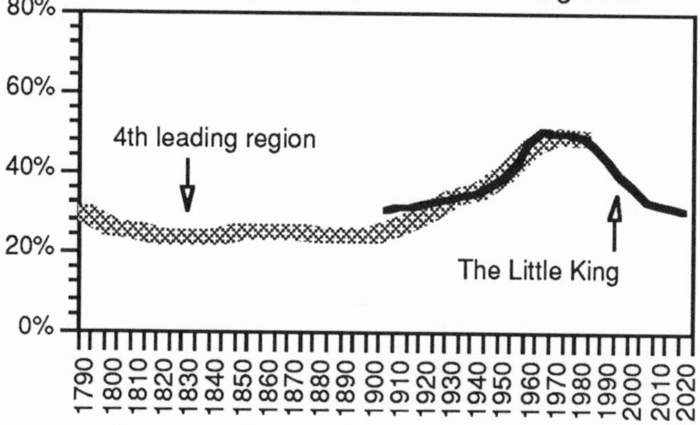

Los Angeles County, California shows the typical suburban growth pattern of counties in the fourth leading region. (See Figure 5.)

Figure 5
Los Angeles County, California
Percent of U.S. Population

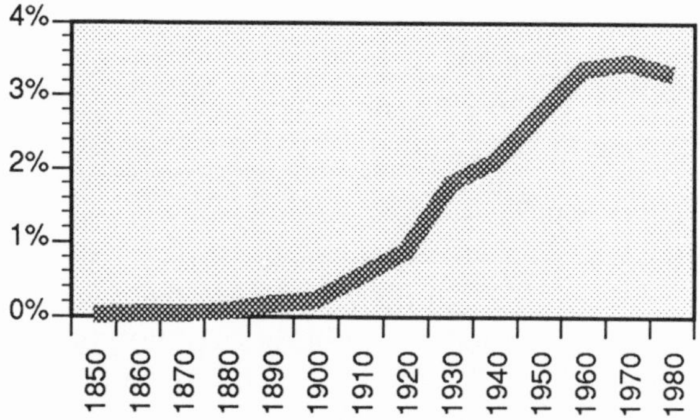

The egalitarian leading region

Every socioeconomy incorporates its mindset into all

aspects of its character. The very form of suburbia—its body language—shouted *egalitarian inspiration.* Made up of co-equal municipalities spreading at low densities over large metropolitan regions, suburbia brooks no dominant center. Though the word *sub*urbia literally refers to the dominance of an urb, the central cities were no longer dominant. With their skyscrapers and slums they didn't look like the homogeneous suburbs. But in function—as nodes in the urban archipelago—they were co-equals. Absorbing the central cities into the new pattern, suburbia was a confederation of equals—all subs and no urbs.

> Scattering the old downtown over an immense domain, the egalitarian Little King vastly expanded the urban land supply, brought down the price of real estate, made "dream" houses affordable and contributed to an unparalleled prosperity. (See Chapters 3–5.)

The flip side of equality—conformity

Lewis Mumford described the suburbs as "a multitude of uniform, unidentifiable houses, lined up inflexibly, at uniform distance, on uniform roads, in a treeless communal waste, inhabited by people of the same class, the same income, the same age group, witnessing the same television performances, eating the same tasteless pre-fabricated foods, from the same freezers, conforming in every outward and inward respect to a common mold."[110]

William J. Levitt's "ticky tacky boxes" of 1949 illustrated the conformist ideal then sweeping the country.[111] The microcosm Levitt created was suburbia's prototype. In his first assembly-line effort, Levitt built 17,500 identical houses. Bulldozers lined up and moved in formation like tanks across a battle line. On cue, a horde of street pavers arrived, followed by electricians, then by men with street signs. William Manchester describes the delivery trucks "tossing out prefabricated sidings at 8 A.M., toilets at 9:30, sinks and tubs at ten, sheetrock at 10:45, flooring at eleven." The mode of consumption was similarly circumscribed. "Everything was uniform. On Mondays wash was hung in 17,500 backyards; under no circumstances could it flap on Sundays." But the high order of standardization was no deterrent. The basic four-room house sold for $6,990, a fabulous bargain for the average young marrieds of the time. To them it was no "box" but a palace.[112]

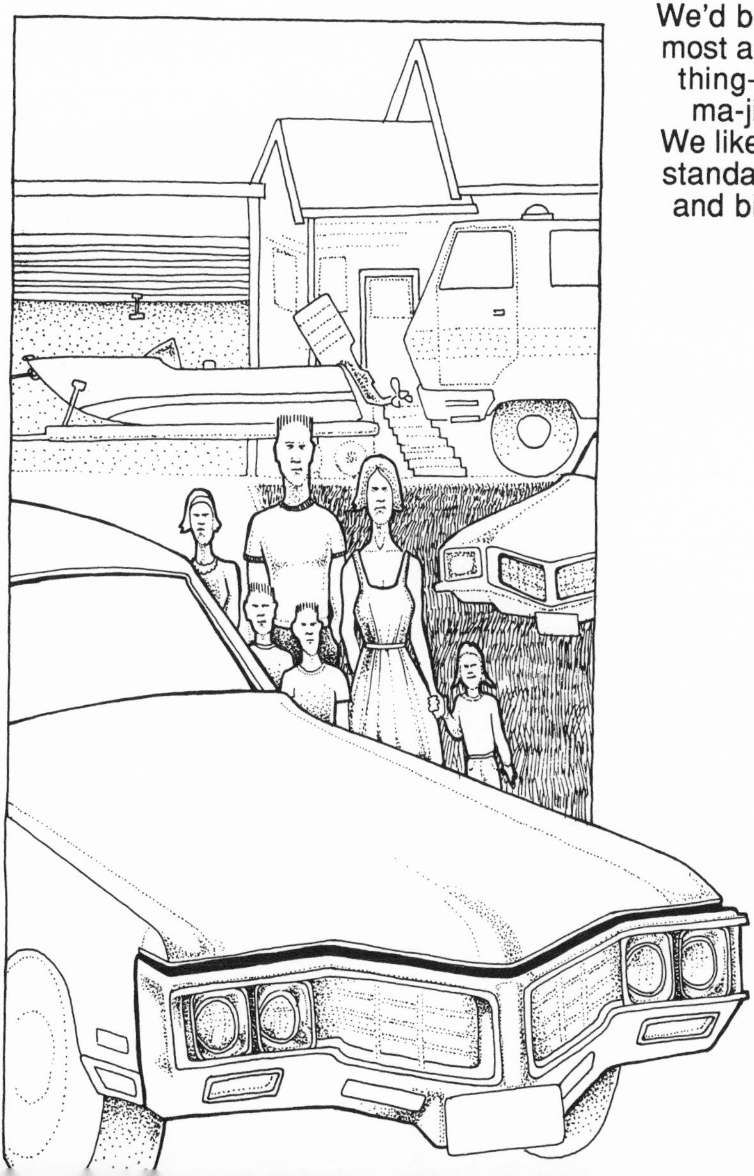

We'd buy
most any
thing-a-
ma-jig.
We like it
standard
and big.

The fourth season of depression 1929–1960

Figure 6 charts the theoretical seasons of prosperity and depression during the era of the Little King.

Figure 6
Economic Seasons of the Little King

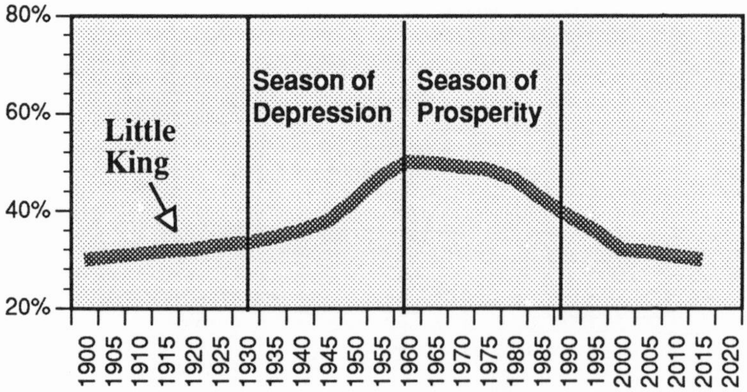

Many among us can recall the precipitous recession 1929–1931 that became the Great Depression of the 1930s—years of economic disaster right up to the attack on Pearl Harbor. By the middle of 1931, industrial production had dropped to less than half its maximum output in 1929. The average wage fell by 60 percent. Most dividends dropped to less than half of what they had been the year before. Unemployment rose to 15.9 percent in 1931, remained in the 20–25 percent range through 1935, and never dipped below 17 percent until after 1939. Season of depression: fourth

After 1939, World War II, the Marshall Plan, the Korean War and the Cold War staved off recurring symptoms of depression. However, the underlying season of depression continued until 1960. The high incidence of recessions and slower rise of GNP during this period of latent depression is documented in Figure 7 below.

Figure 7
US GNP 1929-1970
At Constant 1958 Prices

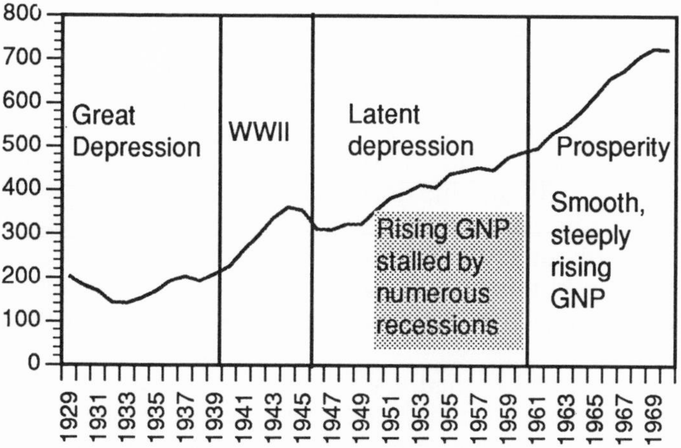

Prices declined after 1929 but not for long. After 1939 inflation was driven by the scarcities of war. Beginning with the New Deal, the Little King harbored a decided attachment to inflation. Rising prices drove consumers to buy sooner—and more abundantly. Inflation became one of the essential trends of the Little King. But in the 1930s inflationary policies *didn't* bring prosperity. What they did bring was inflation and more inflation—in bad as well as in good times.

Once again, as the season of depression ended, another leading region attained its peak growth—this time, suburbia, the fourth. Thereafter, though suburbia continued to grow faster than the national average, its rate of growth steadily declined.

Depression and migration; a personal note

For me, the fourth migration is a personal experience. In 1935, when the economy was still scraping along at the bottom of the Depression, my family joined the early fugitives from New York City. In that year, I turned thirteen, a bar-mitzvah boy. My proud parents were sufficiently prosperous to hold a splendid reception in my honor at what I recall as a middle-class, downtown night club. Among the guests were a number of pious old men, and I can still remember how my father enjoyed watching them steal guilty glances at the "*naketdeh maiden*"—scantily clad chorus girls who entertained us that evening.

Our good fortune we owed to my father, by profession a pharmacist and, by avocation, a speculator in real estate. A restless man, he loathed nothing more than waiting for customers to walk into his drugstore. To relieve his boredom he acquired the habit of perusing the classified ads, keeping a sharp lookout for good locations in which to build a new drugstore. In this he was successful. Every year or two, with awesome regularity, he would sell a store at a profit and build another.

It seemed he had a wizard's eye for good locations—until that fateful year of 1935. Soon after my bar-mitzvah in February, he met his nemesis. It was a store on Aldous Street in the Bronx that "done him in." Despite my father's earnest efforts, people could not be induced to come into that store. They were being lured away by the new cut-rate chains—the Tomashevskys and the Walgreens—now springing up all over the city.

These formidable competitors carried more varied merchandise. Their stores were larger, more modern, and lit up with as many lights as a theater on Broadway. But the severest blow of all was that they cut prices—not a little but deeply—and on just those items from which small neighborhood druggists like my father had to make a living.

In desperation, my father resorted to a tactic often used by his cutthroat competitors: loss leaders—merchandise sold below cost to attract customers into the store. After school one day, he asked me to help distribute circulars for a final effort, a do-or-die sale. His loss leader was Epsom salts, sold at a price far below cost. (Could it have been nine cents for five pounds?) Suddenly the store was packed. There wasn't enough room for all the customers. Everyone in New York, it seemed, was stocking up on a lifetime supply of Epsom salts. At dinner, after the second day of the sale, my father's voice was tinged with anxiety. He threw up his arms to the heavens and anguished. "Every package of Epsom salts I sell is pushing me into my grave."

Three days later he closed the store for good. He left for California—more specifically, for Rosemead, a tiny suburb of Los Angeles. (In a sense, all of Los Angeles was a suburb of New York, an increasingly popular alternative to Long Island.) Two weeks later, my mother, two sisters, and I received a fateful telegram. "Pack up immediately. Come to California. If we must starve at least it will be in the sunshine." And so it was that in 1935 we joined the pioneers of the fourth migration.

The fourth season of prosperity: 1960–1990

As the new mindset washed over the mind of America, the socioeconomy devoted to spending became a roaring reality. Average Americans migrated to suburbia by the millions to preside as Little Kings and Queens over their one-sixth-acre domains. Here, in sovereign splendor, plumbers, steelworkers, and pipe fitters lived in a lavishness of lifestyle exceeding the most impossible dream of their parents and grandparents. They filled their single-family palaces with freezers, furnaces, home laundries, vacuum cleaners, air-conditioners, stain-resistant nylon carpets, FM radios, television sets, electric blankets, electric floor polishers, electric pencil sharpeners, electric can openers. They filled their carports and garages with automobiles, boats, and recreational vehicles of every type and description. And to further bolster consumption, it all had to be *new*. "Planned obsolescence" accustomed us each year to discard 8 million automobiles. The throw-away society accustomed us to trashing 100 million tires, 40 million tons of paper, 48 million cans, and 26 million bottles each year.[113]

So faithfully did we follow the injunction to spend and consume, and so efficiently did the socioeconomy supply the desired consumables, that the *poverty* level of the 1970s probably exceeded the standard of living achieved by the *average*

American of 1900.

Inflation during the season of prosperity since 1960 is well known. No diagram of the price trend 1960-1990 is needed.

The fourth key problem: overconsumption

In the 1990s the sweet smell of rot pervades all institutions of the Little King. The socioeconomy had been a smashing success. Overproduction was conquered by the late 1950s and overconquered by the 1970s. The Little King had succeeded only too well in achieving prosperity through consumer spending. The new excess that increasingly summoned the next socioeconomy was overconsumption. To overcome that key problem, the socioeconomy of the Little King would eventually have to perish.

Overconsumption is dramatized by the plight of suburbia.

Because the suburbs have been growing so long, it's easy to imagine the unimaginable, that growth will continue for all time. That, at least, is the *feeling*. Maybe suburbia will stop growing...someday. By then the planet Earth will burn, freeze, or explode into cosmic debris...in billions of years. Nobody worries about it. In 1990, vacant land is still being surveyed, divided, and subdivided. Freeways are still filling with new migrants. And forecasters have not yet tired of predicting suburbia's future as a straight-line extrapolation of its past. "America's Suburbs Are Still Fine,"[114] they tell us, and, not to worry, 80 million suburbanites can't be wrong

By the 1970s, however, suburbia was no longer the solution but the problem. Suburbs springing out of farms in remote areas soon filled in the countryside, and then the corridors between suburbs and cities. Eventually, people who believed they had escaped the city found the city crowding in around them. Our former bucolic paradise was now being increasingly spoiled by congestion, pollution, and what some critics called "uglification."

A good strategy had been pursued too long. In the 1950s, alarmists warned of ill effects in the future. Ill effects?

We couldn't see any. Then the drumbeat of negative comment accelerated. Magazine articles told the story in titles. "Aging of the Suburbs,"[115] "Our Troubled Suburbs,"[116] the "Trek Back to the Cities,"[117] and, "Suburbia: End of the Golden Age."[118] Suburbs used to be a refuge, a place for big-city folk to escape pollution, crime, high taxes, exorbitant rents, and an unpleasant environment. But in recent years the suburbs themselves have fallen prey to those same afflictions. As one author put it, suburbanites resemble the people in Boccaccio's *Decameron*. They "ran away from the plague and took it with them."[119]

The battle against suburbia and its get-it-now attitudes is mounted by the forces of the next socioeconomy. I call it the Caring Conserver.

Fourteen

Cycle 5—The Little King is dying; Long live *The Caring Conserver*

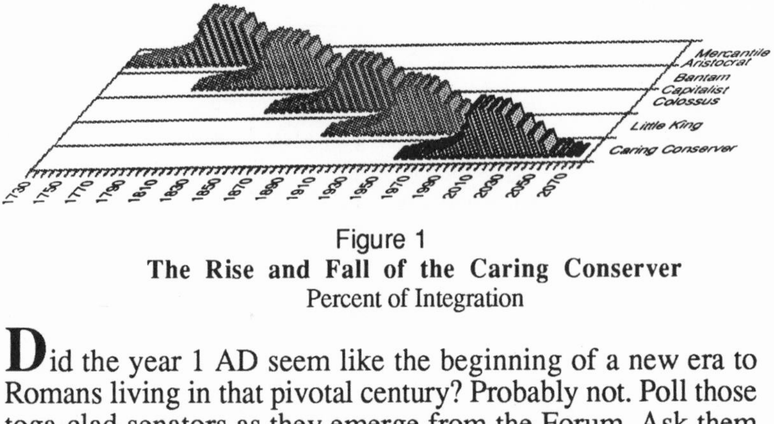

Figure 1
The Rise and Fall of the Caring Conserver
Percent of Integration

Did the year 1 AD seem like the beginning of a new era to Romans living in that pivotal century? Probably not. Poll those toga-clad senators as they emerge from the Forum. Ask them what the world will be like in a thousand years. They will tell you, "The gods, the forum, and Rome will prevail."

We needn't feel superior. The human propensity to project the immediate past into the indefinite future remains a constant. In the 1970s, the Little King seemed endless in its reach, though the Caring Conserver (its successor) had been alive and pulsing for more than a decade. Opposition to the wasteful Little King was mounting in America and the rest of the world—even the Communist world. In the 1980s, the Little King has been headed for extinction. The pollution-encouraging, fast-food swilling, cigarette-smoking, pop-and-beer-drinking devotee of get-it-now has become the very model of a dodo.

Cut the chatter about Earth-Day
To me it's only Dearth-Day

On the way to peak integration

As the Mercantile Aristocrat begat the Bantam Capitalist and the Bantam Capitalist begat the Colossus, and the Colossus begat the Little King, the Little King begat the

Caring Conserver.

The revolution against the mindset of the Little King dates from the 1960s (though dissent was noted in the 1950s). Led by a scattering of hotheads in places like California's Bay Area, a recognizable counterculture was coming on strong, challenging the establishment of the Little King in a guerrilla army of self-professed, bio-geo-religio-eco-anthro-socio-politico-cosmio-sexual revolutionaries. They were involved with natural foods stores, natural food restaurants, new age products of all kinds from organic growth to pyramids, to jewelry, to shoes. They were "into" growth experiences of all kinds—seminars and training and body work, like massage, polarity and rolfing. There were Hari Krishnas chanting mantras, Jews for Jesus, Schicsas for Jesus, Gay Vegetarians and Radical Lesbians. Every "body" was coming out of the closet at the same time as a new migration was beginning to reshape the American landscape.[120]

In the 1970s—though no one used the term *overconsumption*—a groundswell of feeling against it first appeared in force among masses of Americans. In 1976 a Louis Harris poll reported that a large majority of interviewees—almost three to one—agreed that it is "morally wrong" for Americans to consume 40 percent of the world's energy and raw materials when we constituted a mere 5.5 percent of the world's population.

Shortly afterward, a *Wall Street Journal* reporter asked, "Austerity ahead?"—and answered that "the idea wins surprising acceptance among Americans." Only a minority of those interviewed by all pollsters felt that traditional lifestyles could continue unchanged.[121] In a letter to the editor, one person complained that he couldn't buy bread in a plastic bag, eat a hamburger, wear knit pants, or flush a toilet without being guilty of abusing the environment or our own health. He had to cope with his individual guilt as a modern consumer, he said, "or run naked into the woods and starve."[122]

Those were the perceptions that brought the Caring Conserver to life. The socioeconomy is named for its unique mission: to rescue resources—natural and human—neglected by the Little King. In 1990 the mindset of this fledgling socioeconomy is still in flux. We cannot see it clearly. No textbooks exist to guide us beyond the frontiers of what is known.

Development cannot be quick. Like a quarterback attempting to run while being dragged down by tacklers, the new order will snatch progress however it can, despite controversy, accidents, miscalculations, feuds, misunderstandings, and false starts. Judging from the half century or more required by past socioeconomies to reach maturity, the ripening of the Caring Conserver will take us well into the twenty-first century. Only then, after the fact, when we can feel the new mindset deep in the solar plexus, when its dictates are accepted as "common sense," will we comprehend it with certainty.

Mission of the Caring Conserver

What, in 1990, do we know of the emerging socioeconomy? We know this much: that the Caring Conserver must solve the problem of overconsumption in all its guises. That is its mission. Until we are able to staunch the flow of our economic substance now bleeding away in excessive spending; until we are able to replenish our languishing capital stock with savings garnered from genuine increases in productivity, we will remain patients in intensive care, with ever diminishing prospects for a stable economic life.

What can be done to deal with our deficits, trade imbalances, high interest rates and other symptoms of overconsumption? Mainly we hear of impersonal policy solutions—tax consumption spending, get tough with the Japanese in new trade treaties, raise the interest rate. All helpful but secondary. The first and foremost task will be to make a radical change in our chosen direction—in *mindset.*

One mindset brought us into our present difficulties. Another will get us out of them. To solve the problem of overconsumption, the Caring Conserver must oppose every tenet of the consumption mindset. To conserve the huge capital sums routinely squandered by the Little King, the Caring Conserver must show an equally ardent determination to conserve.

It will happen because it must. But no one should expect the needed changes to come all at once. The pull of the past is strong. Change begins with a few Tom Haydens, Ralph

Naders, E.F. Schumachers and Steve Jobs—leaders revolted by the established ways of doing things—and even they are divided in their faith and conviction. The revolution spreads by fits and starts. And before its final triumph at the peak of integration there will be countless reversals, when the allure of the old socioeconomy, like the Pied Piper, carries off our young in renewed worship of obsolete idols.

Though the greatest rates of conversion are decades ahead, it is useful to chart the direction we're traveling. From what we can observe during the past quarter-century—and from what we know about past transformations—we can piece together a composite picture of the future Caring Conserver.

If the picture we construct seems too perfect, consider that it is only an ideal model, unblemished by the frailties inherent in real human beings.

This is what the emerging socioeconomy aims for. Conservation: to save and to safeguard—by law, by propaganda, by appeal to conscience. The will to conserve extends to capital: what we save and invest to support the new priorities; to all that nature gives freely: energy, pure air and water, an unmaimed environment; to culture: historic buildings, parks, folksongs and dances, all forms of art; and to people: the Caring Conserver encourages all people to realize their potential.

Whereas the Little King valued the poor for their *inability* to save (gladly shoveling billions into the maw of their limitless needs) the Caring Conserver values them for their potential as contributors to a capital-hungry economy. Treated as any other undeveloped resource, society's former rejects—women, minorities, senior citizens, high-school dropouts, drug addicts, the deaf, blind, homeless and hungry—are to be rescued, trained, and absorbed into the mainstream of economic life. Such is the faith of the Caring Conserver.

My theory suggests the shape of the new human type now emerging. To maximize the capacity to spend, Little Kings resolved to "give as little as possible and take all you can get." Shorter work days, higher pay, greater leisure and a sincere conviction that life is for living *now*, led to the permissive society. Many born-and-bred Little Kings slipped most naturally into careless work habits, white-collar crime, easy bankruptcies, and welfare frauds.

The Caring Conserver reverses the Little King's formula for living. Increasingly, eager volunteers apply for public service. The fast-growing hospice movement relies almost entirely on unpaid labor. Without a cent of compensation, rich and poor alike minister to orphans, the illiterate, the elderly, the sick, and the starving, providing care for the meaning it adds to their lives. In his 1988 campaign for president, candidate Bush knew what he was doing when he called for "a thousand points of light." (In 1991, did he know that, far from the Little King's lack of national feeling during the Viet Nam War, he could count on a new patriotism to support the Gulf War?) And corporations, so puritanical about the pursuit of profit in the past, now support the arts, public radio and television, numerous charities. Altruism, of course, is nothing new. The milestone is in the numbers. The numbers keep growing.

Advertising (the Little King socioeconomy's oldest profession), seduced us into a Dionysian intoxication with junk foods, cigarettes, and liquor. Nobody mentioned the death knells under each shiny wrapper. And nobody mentioned that from today's corruption of the palate and body would come tomorrow's costs in illness, doctors, and spiraling hospital fees. (Those Little Kings who lit up two packs of "coffin nails" a day, they didn't know? Not at all. They didn't *want* to know.)

Investments are "in." Congress debates new legislation to encourage higher savings. And savings extend to more than money. At the cost of a less indulgent present, the Caring Conserver directs us to choices that promise a more salubrious future. Here is one dimension of the new socioeconomy that is almost mature. We accept disciplines, make sacrifices for health and longevity. We jog, meditate, take vitamins, and show a preference for whole, natural foods.

The Caring Conserver trades present satisfactions for future benefits.

Farewell to slothful ease. Adieu to old age and disease.

The fifth leading region

For over a century the reigning assumption—that people would continue pouring out of rural locations into metropolitan areas—had remained unchanged. The trend was inexorable and the experts "proved" it. We could safely predict ever-increasing densities of urban populations. On the average, small cities would become medium-sized cities, medium-sized cities would become large cities, and the largest cities would become still larger.

Metropolis forever?

In 1975 the author of a well-known text on urban development asked, "Why then, do urban populations rise both relatively and absolutely, all over the globe?"[123] His answer came from the core of the profession: People *choose* large cities. They *always* do. They always *will*. Large cities permit greater specialization, which means low-cost production and distribution. The bigger the city the greater its capacity to produce what people want—houses, jobs, automobiles, appliances, schools, hospitals, theatres, bowling alleys, golf courses, political rallies, and gala celebrations.

But while urban economists were explaining that migration *had* to proceed from rural to urban areas, people were already reversing their direction. They were moving from *urban to rural* areas.

Early portents of a change

In 1975 Calvin Beale, an eminent demographer, was among the first formally to proclaim the change. He documented it in an obscure monograph published by the United States Department of Agriculture, entitled *The Revival of Population Growth in Non-metropolitan America*.[124] By 1977—long after the migration had actually begun—a spate of technical publications at last acknowledged the changing patterns.[125]

By 1978 news of the migration had filtered down to popular journals. However, by unduly emphasizing population changes *among* states, economists had overlooked a vital fact: populations were also shifting *within* states—from large population centers to smaller ones, from urban to rural. The narrow selection of facts gave the impression that the migration was from Frostbelt to Sunbelt. In fact, counties favored in the fifth migration are scattered throughout most of the fifty states. In 1981 a *Newsweek* cover story, "The Small Town Boom," presented a more accurate version of what was *really* happening.[126] It noted a shift in preference from the big-city lifestyle to the slower pace of the small-town environment.

The prospect of a new migration gains added perspective

and conviction when related to the launching of a new socioeconomy, and the full sweep of socioeconomic cycles beginning with the Mercantile Aristocrat.

Figure 2

The Fifth Leading region and The Fifth Socioeconomy

Percent of Population; Percent of Integration

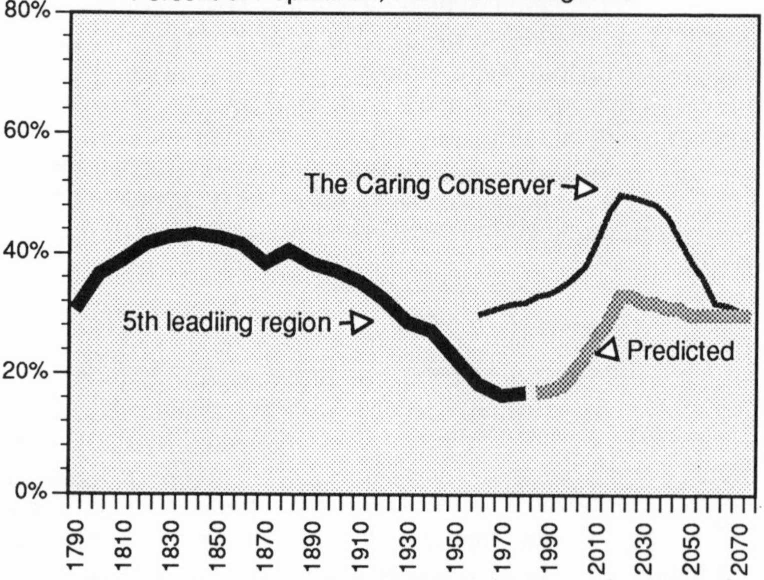

Once again we see the tandem initiation of a migration and a new socioeconomy. Both begin with the peaking of the Little King around 1960. A reversal of trends occurs in the 1970s. For the first time many suburban counties turn down as a percent of U.S. population. After decades of decline, many fifth-migration counties turn up. Figure 2 compares the present position of the fifth leading region with the theoretical curve of the Caring Conserver through 2070.

The three preceding regions of migration moved, respectively, from small percentages to peaks containing roughly half the total U.S. population. As a guide to policy (public and private) it will be useful to note some possible effects if penturbia (the fifth leading region) were to attain a comparable peak.

Judging from past experience, the year 2020 would be

the most likely year of penturbia's peak, with a population of no less than 100 million. (Estimate 308 million total U.S. population, of which 30 percent will be in penturbia—a conservative estimate compared to the 50 percent reached by the four preceding leading regions.) Penturbia's present population is already about 41 million. The estimate suggests a migration of at least 60 million distributed among 1708 counties, or, roughly, 35,000 people per county.

Critics of suburbia: yesterday and today

A quarter of a century ago—when early Caring Conservers denounced suburbia—we tuned out their vitriolic attacks. In addition to the usual complaints (boring conformity, "automobility," "ticky-tacky" houses, "sluburban" appearance) they claimed that there lay beneath that slick exterior a stone-cold heart. How unfair. With nary so much as a nod or a thank-you, they were railing against a socioeconomy that, after half a century had finally solved the desperate problem of the 19th century—overproduction. One can only hope that their criticisms—then and now—will be tempered by theory. Suburbia, like every leading region, served a uniqe socioeconomy. In its proper season it was constructive. *The Little King was constructive...then.*

Like every other leading region, suburbia grew rapidly while the Little King was rising. Now it obsolesces as the Little King declines. In our vast inventory of land, suburban real estate is the one type *least* suited to the emerging mindset. Not only has it become expensive as a result of a century of ever-increasing demand, but the very qualities that made it attractive to the Little King make it repugnant to the Caring Conserver. Suburbia—*wunderkind* of a yesteryear—will go down with the ship—along with the entire socioeconomy of the Little King.

If the symmetry of the past three cycles applies, the fourth region's 50-percent share of U.S. population in 1970 may dwindle to roughly 30 percent by the year 2020.

Obsolescence

As suburban real estate begins its long descent to the end of the line, an age-old process of decay returns. Let us not forget those sumptuous mansions lining Broadway near downtown Oakland, or downtown Manhattan, or a thousand other "Broadways" in cities still growing at the turn of the century. When the plutocrats migrated to suburbia, it was the poor who commandeered their elegant turrets and cupolas. Many of those palatial homes have been rehabilitated in recent years, but not before wasting away for decades in deepest slums.

Suburbia will show a similar deterioration. Not everywhere, and not all at once, but we will see miles of 2,500-square-foot behemoths, their wide windows broken and patched, their many rooms divided and subdivided into nondescript apartments, and betraying the indignities of poverty, the former proud front lawns will be littered with junk automobiles and broken furniture.

A conversation with HB, suburbanite

Author: That description of obsolescing suburbia is the down side. But the migration to penturbia has a bigger up side. It will help to solve the outstanding social and economic problems of our day.

HB: Are you suggesting that people are coming to these remote places because they want to solve the problem of overconsumption? An astounding idea.

Author: Let me ask what may seem to be a frivolous question. Why do people make love?

HB: Why ask? They enjoy it.

Author: Obviously. But why do they enjoy it? There's a stark reality behind that enjoyment—the necessity to assure continuity of the community and the species. Of course it is doubtful that any Don Juan ever seduced his lady love with anguished appeals to promote the general welfare, yet lovers do provide this community service. Without babies, society dies out. That is the exact, though abstract, truth. Nature found it expedient to make procreation attractive. Should the world become overpopulated, nature will revise its approach to accord with change. Even Don Juan will curb his instincts.

HB: But aren't you depriving the individual of her prerogatives and power?

Author: Behind all individual motivation there *is a higher imperative—the imperative of the group.* As individuals we are preoccupied with ourselves, with what we want and need. Without society we are quite powerless.

HB: Will the problem of overconsumption be addressed by some *higher imperative*?

Author: Solving that problem is as necessary to the perpetuation of our economic life as having children is to the perpetuation of the species. In the 1990s, overconsumption is our key problem. So long as it remains unsolved we are all aboard a foundering ship. If the ship goes down, everyone drowns. We all try to keep the ship afloat because somewhere in our consciousness we feel the *imperatives of the group.* We understand that each life can be saved only if *all* are saved.

HB: It's hard to believe that the ordinary individual will be much preoccupied with higher purposes of the group.

Author: We might not be conscious of those purposes, only that we're bored and repelled by the fast buck, fast foods and fast living—and that we're increasingly drawn to concern for the future, for ecology, and as philosopher, journalist and ex-U.S. ambassador Michael Novak points out, for home, family, church and the work ethic.

HB: You truly believe that average Americans will conquer overconsumption—that they'll vote for higher taxes to repair our roads, educate our children, and reduce our deficits? Will they curb their borrowing and save money to rehabilitate our ailing industries?

Author: Yes, I believe all of that. And I'll let you in on a little secret. In several decades, the Caring Conserver will create a very different problem: *too much* capital. We'll be drowning in it. Every new socioeconomy goes too far in solving its key problem. So it was with the Mercantile Aristocrat, the Bantam Capitalist, the Colossus and the Little King. And so it will be with the Caring Conserver. Eventually, it too will be be driven to its own form of excess and perish as a result of it. Meanwhile, you can look forward to a satisfying life in penturbia. There's only one hitch. A long period ahead of on-again-off-again depression, a *season of depression.*

HB: One hitch, eh? When will it begin?

Author: Soon. After the post-World-War II *season of prosperity.*

Fifteen

Prosperity and peak migration to suburbia

Economist: Having become the butt of stand-up comedians, we economists are very sensitive about prediction. Not that the jokes are unjustified. I admit that, on the average, the "inability of economists to forecast reliably remains a persistent criticism of the profession."[127] Could a socioeconomist do better?

Author: To answer your question I would first ask, Why do economists predict so badly? In my opinion, it's because they attempt to predict the short run—next quarter or next year. In our present state of knowledge it cannot be done. There are too many possibilities for small errors to accumulate into large ones. Failure is always waiting in ambush. Predicting GNP a year from now is as chancy as predicting the weather a week from now.

Economist: But if predicting the short run is practically impossible, surely predicting the long run is doubly so. Can you predict something in ten years that you cannot predict in one?

Author: Yes, so long as you're predicting *probabilities*. With unerring accuracy we can predict that the highest *probability* of cold weather will arrive in a precise number of days after December 21. We can also predict precisely when the highest *probability* of balmy weather will arrive.

Similarly, we can predict that the highest *probability* of prosperity will arrive at a socioeconomic peak. Like the long-run weather prediction, the socioeconomic prediction also relies on a single principle.

Economist: What is that principle?

Author: That a succession of socioeconomies rise and fall.

Economist: The rise and fall of socioeconomies and cycles of prosperity and depression are as sure as summer and winter?

The shape of the socioeconomic cycle

Author: I'll let you judge for yourself. Allow me to reproduce the diagram of the socioeconomic cycle from Chapter 9. (See Figure 1.) The height of the curve at any point represents the *degree of completeness with which the mindset is woven into the fabric of the socioeconomy*. The highest point represents the highest integration we can marshall, the lowest is the minium level at which the socioeconomy can function.

Figure 1
A Single Socioeconomic Cycle
Percent of Integration

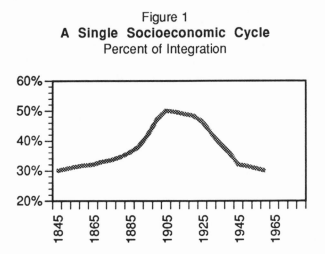

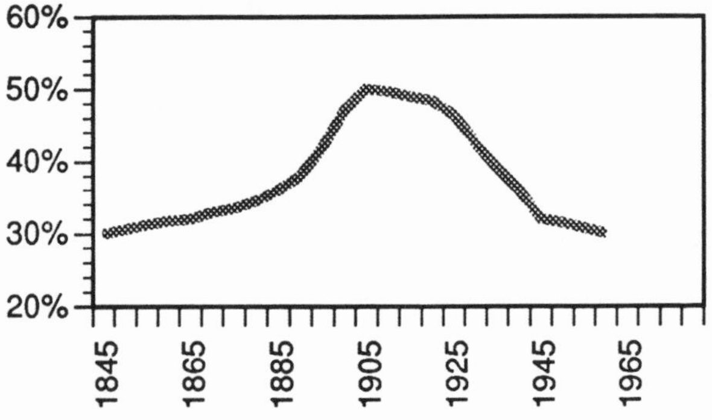

The initial plateau

Author: A socioeconomy's first two or three decades form a long plateau—the beginning of a learning curve. Masses of people must fix upon a common mindset and institutions must come into adjustment with that mindset.. Whether it is a new language, a new subject or a new socioeconomy that is being learned, difficulty in unifying diverse elements is always the reason for the initial plateau.

An additional reason for the plateau (one that is purely socioeconomic) is opposition from the reigning socioeconomy. From 1900–1930 the boisterous Little King was continually stymied by the Colossus. In 1919 the Colossus had sufficient clout to enact a constitutional amendment (Prohibition) squarely gauged to sober up the Little King. That was followed by three successive Republican administrations committed to policies effectively thwarting the Little King's efforts at promoting Big Labor. Such was the plateau 1900–1930.

Economist: And after the plateau?

Acceleration to the peak

Author: Change accelerates. Integration rises rapidly. Skeptics are transformed into believers. The emerging mindset takes hold. Stratagems to implement the mindset are quickly created, and in a surge of synergy, they prosper. You will remember that in the 1930s (under the influence of the Little King) a host of new institutions facilitated the transfer of income to poorer Americans. At the same time, accelerating migration to suburbia ensured the feasibility of the consuming lifestyle. Development accelerated towards a peak as the objectives of the Little King were increasingly realized.

Economist: And after the peak?

Decline: Slow, then rapid

Author: Development continues on a high but declining level, quickly fades, and eventually dies.

Economist: Gotcha. But I see no principle that explains prosperity.

Prosperity

Author: So far we've looked only at the shape of one socioeconomic cycle. To explain prosperity, you would have to consider no fewer than three successive cycles. The season of prosperity from 1960–1990, for example, involved the Colossus, the Little King and the Caring Conserver. (See Figure 2.)

Figure 2
Three Socioeconomic Cycles
The Colossus, Little King, Caring Conserver

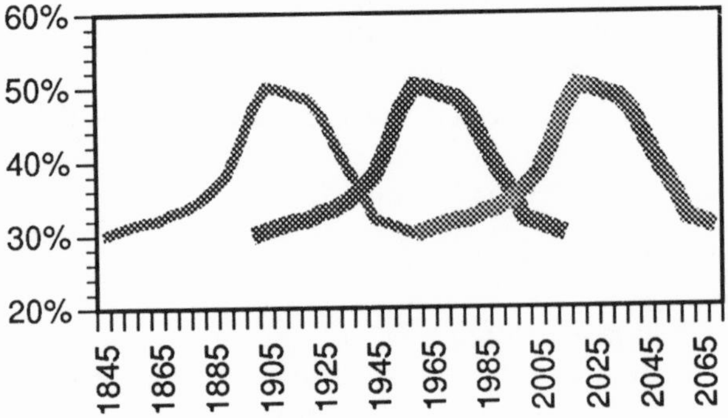

Economist: I see three peaks. Below the central peak, adjoining curves are at their lowest points.

Integration and the peak of the Little King

Author: Notice that the peak is a time of general agreement, an integration of many differing viewpoints. At the second peak, around 1960, the Little King reigns unopposed. The Colossus is ending, the Caring Conserver, beginning. (See Chapter 13.)

Economist: How does integration translate into prosperity?

Author: Integration brings certainty; certainty permits predictability; predictability minimizes risk and maximizes the pace of enterprise. Each peak carries with it the highest *probability* of prosperity and the start of a long *season of prosperity*.

Economist: You can show that?

Author: In the four preceding cycles I have found an invariable connection between prosperity and the integration achieved at the peak. (See Chapters 10-14.)

Economist: Would you say that prosperity at the peak is exclusively the result of integration?

Author: Yes, but integration has a number of facets. One not usually taken into account is the influence of a new leading region as a *stimulant* to prosperity.

The leading region as a "gift"

Let me put it this way: Suppose a mountain of precious metals came crashing out of the heavens into the great eastern desert of California. For only the cost of digging it up, we are suddenly enriched by a hoard worth hundreds of billions at present prices. But prices depend on supply and demand. Now, supply has suddenly increased and therefore prices must fall. First the precious metals. Then the capital equipment incorporating them, then the goods and services produced by that equipment. Cheaper goods and services stimulate demand. Purchasing power grows. The additional purchasing power measures the value of our heavenly gift.

Economist: But a leading region is no gift from the sky.

Author: True, the land under suburbia has been with us since the beginning of time. Call it a *sleeping* treasure. It was awakened by needs arising from a great social and economic transformation. But the effect was the same. A vast supply of land became available at little cost and a sluggish economy was quickened by it. Such an event is precipitated by the emergence of every new leading region.

Economist: Can other nations of the world enjoy the same gift?

Author: They can, providing they satisfy two difficult requirements at the same time. They must have available vacant land and a homogeneous population able and willing to migrate far from home territory. These are talents not readily found outside of America. Considering the diversity of cultures and languages, and the tenacity of old traditions, I think it will be very difficult for tomorrow's bold new Europe to garner much of that "sleeping treasure." Don't you agree?

Economist: Economics is silent on sleeping treasures.

Author: Economics does recognize other kinds of treasure which produce a similar effect. Take the Marshall Plan for Europe 1948-1952. With no strings attached, free of charge, we distributed nearly $3 billion a year to sixteen countries. To the starving and war-ravaged peoples of Europe this money from the United States seemed almost magical, rather like that precious metal raining down from the sky. It jump-started European prosperity—and greatly stimulated our own.

The gifts distributed via the Marshall Plan were even equivalent in size to the "sleeping treasure" supplied by suburbia. From 1950–1970 between one and two million houses a year were built at an average price of $15,000 per house. Assume that the savings due to using cheap farmland rather than expensive urban lots was as little as $3,000 per house. Suburbia's "gift" to the economy could have come to roughly $4.5 billion a year.

Economist: I don't know about $4.5 billion, but I'll have to agree that it was a lot more than nothing.

Author: A *lot* more. And don't forget, the Marshall Plan came to an end in four years. The gift of suburbia continued year after year.

Economist: The Marshall Plan may have been a gift to Europe. But it was a heavy cost to the United States.

Author: I agree. Suburbia, on the other hand, was *entirely* free, the result of a change in mindset—from the Colossus to the Little King.

Economist: That's where we part company. You say that suburbia's gift of "free" land was generated by a new socioeconomy. Most people would agree with me that suburbia was a gift of technology—the technology of the automobile. The automobile freed us from the need for public transportation and made those ubiquitous subdivisions possible. That's what created urban land. Not the Little King. I'd say it was the automobile.

Author: Automobiles are the superstars of a well-rehearsed balancing act. Twenty men with bulging muscles stretch a long rope; a smiling lady rides a bicycle across the rope; two men stand on each handlebar of the bicycle; two other ladies pose prettily as they balance on the shoulders of each man. In this perfect performance, everyone is dependent on everyone else. Should one performer sneeze or daydream, everyone topples and the performance is over.

The auto was a single component dependent on every other in the emerging socioeconomy—a big government, a strong president, a soak-the-rich welfare system and a range of specific aids—new freeways, new laws to regulate economic life, shopping centers, housing subdivisions, consumer credit... People of the Colossus would not have put themselves in debt to buy consumer goods like automobiles. Thrift and discipline had to yield to the spirit of *get-it-now*.

The demand for the automobile itself grew out of the same Little Kingdom. It was personal and instant transportation. Go anywhere. Go anytime. Door to door. In your own car *you* were the Little King. Furthermore, Little Kings behind the wheel developed a favorite game so essential to the consumption economy—beating the Joneses. The Joneses *had to have* the latest styles. And styles changed every year. My conclusion: it wasn't the automobile that made suburbia. It was mindset.

Economist: All right. For the sake of argument let me grant your conclusion—that "the sleeping treasure" is not a result of the automobile but simply another facet of socioeconomic integration. What other facets of the integration bring prosperity? Are there any other?

Author: Yes, two. First, the distinctive *form* of each new leading region is a stimulant to prosperity. Suburbia adopted a fragmented form which was exceptionally conducive to growth. (See Chapter 5.)

Second, integration creates new demands. By arousing a thousand appetites, the get-it-now mindset fueled an insatiable demand for consumer goods and an invincible thrust towards full employment. (See Chapters 4 and 13.)

Inflation

Economist: Do you suppose that insatiable demand for consumer goods had anything to do with the great post-World War II inflation?

Author: Without a doubt. Inflation just after the peak is traceable to a broad integration. Everyone wants the same goods. And suppliers are running out of capacity to respond to further increases in demand.

Demand for cars was never higher than after World War II. But by the 1950s the American automobile industry had settled into a mature equilibrium. Smaller companies had coalesced into The Big Three. They had learned how to make automobiles cheap, and, better yet, appealing. After 1950 there was little reason to expect price reductions due to new inventions, new plants, or new ways to organize the industry. (The Japanese challenge was an historical fluke.)

Suburbia figures hugely in that inflation. It was the conduit through which money was spent on consumption goods. A place in suburbia was what all Little Kings most wanted. But after the socioeconomy's peak in the late 1950s, and after half a century of population pressure, the supply of suburban land was increasingly exhausted. And under the gun of a fixated mindset, demand was never greater. Inflation was easily predictable.

Economist: Many economists believe that inflation will continue, though interrupted now and then by recessions. Inflation, it seems, has become fully acclimated to the world economy. To keep it within reasonable bounds is a priority for the Fed.

Author: But the Fed is not reckoning on socioeconomic cycles. Inflation is over. The season of prosperity is over. And suburbia as a dominant economic force in the nation, that too is over. Facing us in the 1990s is *deflation* and *the crash of suburbia.*

Sixteen

Depression, deflation and the crash of suburbia

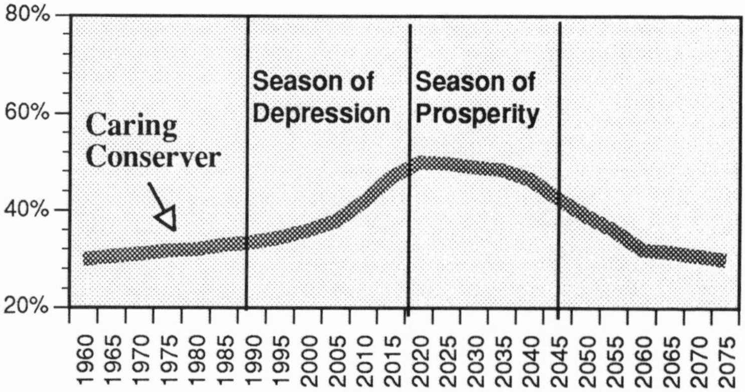

Figure 1
Prediction: 1990-2045

Economist: Let me be frank. I have trouble thinking of depression as periodic and predictable. We economists think it results from an accumulation of accidents—"external shocks" we call them. Early in the 1960s—when the U.S. government adopted John Maynard Keynes' advice on aggressive management of the economy—we believed our profession had made depression unnecessary. The word was all but stricken from the language. In the 1990s we seem to have lost our nerve. Now the "d" word is coming back, and it still means what it used to mean— millions thrown out of work, a calamity in the same class as wars, famines and epidemics, a black hole.

Author: Depression is no black hole. It's part of the regular and predictable pattern inherent in every socioeconomic cycle. The 1990s and 2000s will be decades of on-again-off-again depression—a *season of depression.*

Economist: Why *must* every socioeconomic cycle include a season of depression?

Author: Depression thrives on the awkward coexistence between two conflicting mindsets. You will find the perfect metaphor in human adolescence. A fifteen-year-old is pulled in two opposing directions—by the childhood she's leaving and the maturity she's entering. She wants both—the proud independence of an adult (to smoke and stay out late), and the cozy dependence of a child (parental love and the use of someone else's credit card).

Economist: What is the socioeconomic equivalent of adolescence?

The equinox

Author: I call it the *equinox*—when rising and declining curves intersect, and two conflicting socioeconomies are of equal strength, or equal weakness, however you choose to look at it. (See Figure 2.)

Economist: In adolescence the conflict is internal. Child and adult are the same person. In socioeconomies the conflict is between two separate entities.

Author: Socioeconomic conflict *is* internal. Think of Mr. Average. At the time of the equinox he is 50 percent persuaded by the Little King and 50 percent by the Caring Conserver. On the side of the Little King, he spends all his income and saves nothing. On the side of the Caring Conserver, he may jog for

Figure 2
The Equinox

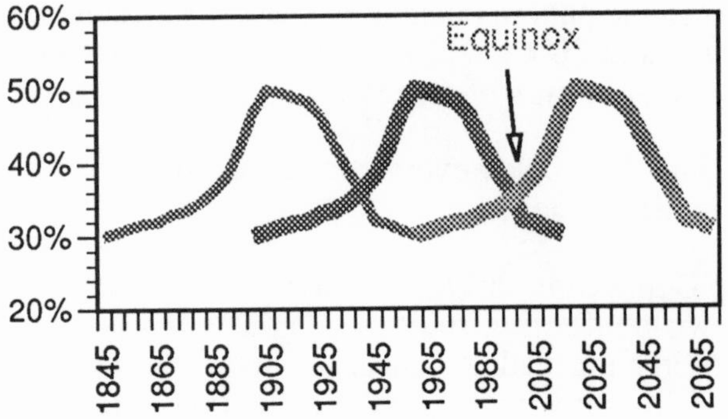

health and write letters of protest to Exxon over the oil spill. Any particular individual can be 80–20, 20–80 or any other combination.

In no period are contradictory values more vigorously espoused or more evenly matched than at the equinox. In the 1870s speeches by prominent leaders both glorified and vilified Big Business, encouraged and discouraged giant markets. In the 1980s politicians advocated more consumer spending ("Read my lips," said candidate Bush on taxes) and less consumer spending ("Unless we save more, America is in danger of becoming a second-rate power"). It's not that divisiveness is totally absent at other times, only that at the equinox the contradictions are greater, more passionately felt.

Economist: Have we come to the equinox of the Little King and the Caring Conserver?

Author: It is too early to fix a precise date, but I would put it somewhere around 1990. Before then, the Little King was far more powerful than the Caring Conserver. Now the Caring Conserver tops the national agenda for things to be done, whereas the Little King is increasingly viewed as something to be undone. It is the Caring Conserver in all of us who clamors to remove pollution from the skies, encourages a greater budget for education, proposes an across-the-board tax increase. Caring Conservers are showing their hand when we hear eminent economists commending greater savings. That translates into *reduced* consumption. To a Little King, attacking consumption is like attacking motherhood.

Economist: Without meaning to be overly agreeable I must report something I read in this morning's *New York Times* by Professor Nicolaus Mills. It is entitled "90's: The Payback Decade." The article begins by citing a new TV series called "Shannon's Deal" in which the hero is what *you* might call a recanting ex-Little King. Jack Shannon begins each program with a voiceover in which he says, "I thought I was big time—big money, big house, big car.... The whole thing was built on garbage. I started gambling big time, crazy stuff. I'm starting from scratch again." In his own words, Mills goes on to recite the excesses of the Little King—public and private deficits, banking irregularities, polluting the environment, shortage of capital etc.. And without using your terminology, the author speaks of the coming Caring Conserver—new human-scale architecture, new concern for ecology, new food habits and the recognition of "...what is most caring in us as a people."[128]

Author: That's a beautiful example. As of 1990 we are definitely past the equinox. From now on the Little King no longer rules. The Caring Conserver is fed up with our free-spending ways, our second-rate education, our permissive justice system, our depleted infrastructure, our inability to compete. And she is increasingly out-of-love with suburbia. But the transition will plunge us into a season of depression. There are four compelling reasons for it.

The first reason for depression: The insoluble key problem

After the equinox, every "old" socioeconomy becomes increasingly threatened by its key problem. For the Little King it is overconsumption, more specifically, the escalating *non-productive debt resulting from overconsumption.*

Mr. Goodtime is a devout Little King and a master builder of non-productive debt. Show him a new four-dimensional stereo and he'll probably buy it. Unfortunately, Goodtime yearns for more than he earns. Some years he spends as much as $50,000 over his annual income of $100,000. How does he do it? Until recently, by raising the mortgage on his house. But because he is already up to the limit, he continues his buying sprees with credit cards—at 19 percent interest. The roof on his house has started to leak and termites have invaded the basement, but Goodtime is reluctant to make repairs because he's planning a European vacation.. Will his house rot? Will it be foreclosed? Will he go bankrupt? Stay tuned.

A new 27-inch TV is nice to have, but it's non-productive. Charged to Goodtime's VISA card it will do nothing to reduce his mortgage. The same applies to public business. The Army's computerized tanks are also nice to have. But they won't reduce the deficit. A socioeconomy run by Little Kings is *predisposed* to non-productive debt. And the failure to make needed *productive* purchases results in the neglect of public assets—infrastructure, education, industrial prowess.

In time, the total debt—nonproductive spending plus neglected maintenance—becomes so large that it is impossible to find lenders able to fund it. Interest rates go up and there is a convulsive contraction in demand for goods and services.

Economist: And this, I suppose you would say, is the delayed price to be paid by the Little King for an extended binge.

Author: The real price is our dependence on other nations and the possibility—indeed, the probability—that they will abruptly jerk away the supports on which we depend. In the 1980s, whenever lack of cash presented a problem, foreigners, especially the Japanese, stepped in to lend us what we needed. During 1982–1988, foreigners provided a net capital inflow of $660 billion into the U.S.[129] But the time is approaching when they will abruptly deny us those funds.

Economist: Why do you say that?

Author: The Japanese will need their money. While the U.S. is reducing its rate of investment, Japan is accelerating its own internal investment—for R&D, for plants in East Asia and for expanding and modernizing factories in Japan. (See Figure 3.) Notice the sharp increase in their capital spending.

Figure 3
Total Capital Investments, U.S. and Japan*
Percent of Gross National Product

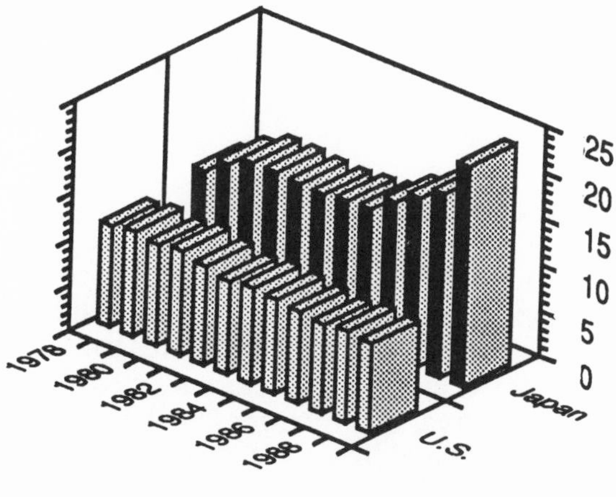

And there's another reason why we can't rely on them to fund our debt. The mindset of the Little King is crossing the ocean into Japan, inducing those hard workers and incurable savers to cut loose. Kazumasa Kuwahara is a 25-year-old stockbroker who says that he works from 9 a.m. to 10 p.m. He told a Wall Street Journal interviewer that, "...all of us, young and old, are more than just dissatisfied with this kind of workaholism. We're rethinking it." And from another young professional, "This isn't a fit country for a human being to live. It's only for work."[130] The title of an article in a Japanese newspaper says it all: "Japanese credit-card youth buy now, go bankrupt later." What do they buy? "Expensive luxury goods like cars and jewelry."[131]

The Little King's arrival in Japan is also revealed by the current passion for golf. Chiba Prefecture, a suburb to the northeast of Tokyo is blanketed by 104 golf courses, with another 16 under construction and 85 applications pending. "The surest sign of having really arrived is to belong to a golf club, and memberships can cost hundreds of thousands of dollars."[132] By the end of 1986, the propensity to spend for pleasure raised the consumer debt to about 16 trillion yen. Less than three years later, it had multiplied by four—to more than 65 trillion.[133] Now the Japanese are going into debt to finance their own consumption binges.

Economist: Without Japanese investment dollars the American debtor would be at the brink of a precipice. Interest rates might climb to high double digits, choking off normal business transactions. Because of our vast size, the effects would ricochet throughout the world.

Author: The Japanese aren't the only ones backing away from lending us the capital we need. Other lenders are about to join them. They're opting for higher returns from investments in Europe where whole industries need to be reorganized and rebuilt. Eastern Europe is an environmental disaster area. In the Romanian town of Copsa Mica, factory soot covers the landscape with a black layer of grime for about 15 miles around. Along the mountains that straddle the borders of Czechoslovakia, East Germany, and Poland, acid rain has reduced thousands of forested acres to a desert of shattered stumps: yet another spigot to pour out the world's capital.

Economist: I agree. And if our own capital reserves were greater than they are, we'd be less at the mercy of other nations who might at any time invest their capital elsewhere. But perhaps you have something even more serious up your sleeve. What's your second reason to expect depression?

The second reason for depression: Loss of social supports

Author: Anna Karenina, Tolstoy's tragic heroine, is a young and beautiful woman of noble birth. She violates a 19th century taboo by leaving her husband and running off with the dashing Count Vronsky. The two attempt to build a life together. But shunned by society, they can't. *There's* the tragedy. He loses his old regimental comrades, the opportunity to advance his career, and the stage on which to perform daring deeds. She loses her beloved child, her friends, and her position in society. After many bouts with despair, Anna Karenina throws herself under the wheels of an onrushing train.

An economy cannot survive without adequate support from society any more than Anna could. The prosperity of the Little King depends on a large range of *non-economic* supports—habits and institutions which grow out of a special mindset.

In the 20th century, one of the most crucial supports is our ability to incite the masses to demand consumer credit—including credit to buy houses. Equally vital are our institutions to supply massive amounts of consumer credit. The supply and demand of consumer credit on such a scale was unknown before the Little King. Both are essential to its continued survival. Both are under widespread attack.

I think fondly of one scene among my childhood memories. Uncle Jack was asking for a loan from my father, a stern man of the Colossus. It was in the 1930s during the depths of the depression. "Why do you want a loan?" My father was brusque. "Is your family starving? Are you being thrown out of the house for nonpayment of rent?" "Oh no," answered Uncle Jack. "We want to buy a complete set of new furniture for our apartment." Seeing the bewilderment in my father's face he added, "There's something you don't understand, Harry. Life is short. We only live once."

The loan was denied. But in that encounter I witnessed

the birth of one of the Little King's most valuable social supports—attitudes underlying the growth of consumer credit.

Around the turn of the century, average folks seldom borrowed for personal reasons. To go into debt to buy consumer goods was a *minor* sin—as irresponsible as going to a restaurant on a whim. But to undertake a consumer loan during a *depression*—with the ever-present risk of unemployment and starvation—that was a *major* sin, like turning your poor old father out into the street. And to make the request with all the moral conviction of a prophet on Mount Sinai—now *that* was different. Uncle Jack didn't feel the slightest guilt about asking for a loan. Buying furniture wasn't a *bad* thing. It was a *good* thing, and patriotic besides. It helped put people back to work.

In this encounter with my father, Uncle Jack was on the inside track. To accelerate demands for consumer goods he and his peers *had* to overcome the 19th century attitudes of people like my father. And a great new banking industry had to grow up during the century to finance the purchase of houses, autos, appliances, every kind of consumer durable. A nation teeming with "Uncle Jacks" and their suppliers would spend the nation into unprecedented prosperity.

In the 1990s—with the public revulsion attending the S&L scandals—we're seeing the beginning of a vast contraction of the housing-credit industry. Even profligate Little Kings are aware that a potential $500 billion loss is too high a price to be paid for the privilege of "getting-it-now." The momentum of public reaction will undoubtedly extend to all forms of consumer credit. Not only will our appetite for consumer credit be put on a diet but the industry supplying it must and will be disciplined. (See Chapter 8.)

In the 1990s true believers like Uncle Jack are long gone. Institutions they initiated are rapidly eroding—everything that multiplied, supplemented, provoked, aroused, incited, inspired, inflamed and coaxed big-time consumption. The Caring Conserver can't afford it and doesn't want it. Cut off from its supports, the Little King will be sent into extinction as surely as if it could be cast under the wheels of an onrushing Amtrak. As it loses crucial social supports, let us compose a requiem mass for the dying socioeconomy.

Economist: The Little King is dying. But why should we care? "Long live the Caring Conserver." The Caring Conserver will fill the breach. Let it support a very different kind of economy.

Author: Thank you. You have just introduced my third reason for expecting depression.

The third reason for depression: Immaturity of the emerging socioeconomy

Author: High above the ground two trapeze artists swing back and forth, back and forth in time to the music. Without breaking their rhythm, one hurls himself towards the other. But wait. A horrified gasp rises from the audience. The "catcher" is proving himself to be a rank beginner. It shows in his face, his body, his every movement. Will he miss? Everyone can see danger ahead.

At the time of the equinox we are faced with a similar predicament. In the 1990s—as the Little King increasingly loses our loyalties—responsibility for a stable economy passes into the keeping of the Caring Conserver. But the socioeconomy is so new, so immature, so poorly integrated that it cannot carry the load. *Time* is needed to develop a mature integration. Aerialists begin near the ground with simple movements. Through many trials and errors, they advance to more complicated maneuvers. Socioeconomies improve by trial and error too. New institutions are tried, found wanting, improved, expanded. Many fail. A few take hold. Decades pass before the needed bulwark of social support can be realized. Until then, the economy is exposed to awesome risks.

Economist: I'm willing to wait. But will the Caring Conserver *ever* be able to provide the basis of a stable and prosperous economy? You say that Caring Conservation means cutting down on consumption. Yet consumption is exactly what we must have to achieve full employment. Reduce consumption and you're cutting the heart out of *demand*, the very ground on which prosperity is built. You're not concerned about the anti-consumption bent of the new mindset?

Author: Not in the least. We can have full employment by developing industries that produce for conservation rather than for consumption. But it will take time. That's what will mire us in depression—the length of time to win the masses to the new mindset and gear up for the new socioeconomy. Here are some random examples of needed innovations which will take the Caring Conserver decades to accomplish:

• We can all agree about the need for a corps of inspired teachers. When teaching can attract our brightest youths, the Caring Conserver will have realized one of its priorities. But to improve the status of teachers, we will need to reward them with greater salaries. Not from $20,000 to $25,000, but to comparability with plumbers, doctors, perhaps even baseball players, whatever it takes to give them status in the community. How long will that take?

• There is a need to initiate effective programs of training and retraining to end our minority brain drain. Instead of spending $25,000 a year to maintain a youthful criminal in prison, we will learn how to direct latent energies to productive ends. But decades may pass before we do.

• We will eventually be able to rely on a first-rate work force. Many of today's high-school graduates are unable to read a bus schedule, figure a forty-percent reduction, or name the capital of China. Future graduates will be better trained at calculus and foreign languages, and their minds will be irrigated with art, literature and music. But we'll be lucky if that victory is won by 2020.

• We will live and work in the 1,708 counties of present and potential penturbia. But creating the conglomerate cities of the 21st century will take time. (See Chapter 23.)

• Maturity of the Caring Conserver will inevitably require curbing the advertising industry—*insofar as advertising incites consumer spending*. But the necessary revocation of rights and privileges is sure to be painful and time-consuming. Imagine the extended debates when some hapless senator proposes the stiffest tax possible on advertisers of non-productive goods—perfume, liquor, RVs, pleasure boats. The screams from

Madison Avenue will be heard from coast to coast. Million-dollar-a-year executives will hurl slogans like invectives. Advertising is the backbone of capitalism! First Amendment! Consumption keeps the economy healthy! In the end, after the smoke has lifted and the earth comes back to itself, the freedom so long enjoyed by the advertising industry will have been severely curtailed.

• How long will it take to apply the brakes to government as *instigator* of private spending—to say *no* to the chorus of appeals for tax reductions permitting consumers to spend more freely. Political lips long shaped to say "yes" will say "no" to economists who, confronted with a sluggish economy, prescribe increased consumption spending—the economic aspirin of the past half century. Like any addict denied a daily quota of crack, the nation will rave and writhe. Finally, government will give up its career as "pusher" of consumption spending.

Economist: In your view the Caring Conserver in its immaturity is like a partially built skyscraper. We don't see the completed building, only the steel trusses.

Author: It's earlier than that. We haven't finished drawing the blueprints. But even after the skeleton structure is complete, it will not be strong enough to prevent depression.

Economist: Aren't you forgetting about inflation? So long as prices keep going up, our burden of debt is continually eased, business more readily makes a profit, demands are stimulated, and the economy keeps growing.

Author: The progression you describe will not continue. *Inflation* will not continue. *Why* it will not is my fourth and final reason for depression.

The fourth reason for depression: Deflation

Author: In deflationary times, people behave quite predictably. It inclines them to postpone purchases, which weakens demand, which reduces prices, which shrinks profits, which discourages investment, which leads to unemployment, which further weakens demand and deepens deflation. The progression, you will observe, is the reverse of the one you gave for inflation.

Economist: But what we seem to be having at this time is nonstop *inflation*, not deflation.

Deflation in old industries

Author: The present inflation (since 1980) is like an unseasonably warm December. We should not be deceived into thinking that summer has arrived. To understand the *current economic season* we would do well to consider our *old* industries, because they tell us where we are in the socioeconomic cycle.

Economist: I assume you are referring to industries that developed in response to the old mindset. How do you connect them to deflation?

Author: My theory suggests that after the equinox, the old mindset increasingly loses its ability to influence tastes and preferences, which translates into a declining demand for the *old* goods and services. Television is an old industry. In 1990 Nielsen ratings showed for the first time a significant decline in TV viewing.[134] Auto manufacturing is an *old* industry. In 1990 young people are more often turned on by computers than by cars. To revive a sagging interest, the automobile industry has adopted an if-you-can't-beat-them-join-them approach. It computerizes its product every way it can. By adding microchips wherever possible, cars seem more wave-of-the-future, and, more to the point, *saleable*. But the old thrill is gone.

Economist: If the preference for cars is ebbing, why have the prices been going up rather than down?

Author: Automobile manufacturers—like many others—are able to *control* their prices. In 1990—despite sluggish sales, and a market glut that forced it to lay off workers—General

Motors *raised* the prices on a number of its options.

Economist: If you want a Cadillac, you can only get it from G.M. But raising prices reduces sales. And when many follow the example of G.M., the result is an unwholesome mix of stagnation and inflation—stagflation.

Author: There's no stagflation for producers of basic commodities like wheat, silver, soybeans, and iron ore. They exercise minimum control over price. People who market these commodities must cope with competition that is worldwide. Wheat of a certain grade—whether from Russia, China, or Australia—is the same as wheat of the same grade from Kansas, South Dakota, or Nebraska. A wheat farmer cannot get one cent more per bushel than the market price.

Figure 4
All-Commodities Price Index
USBLS; 1967=100; January

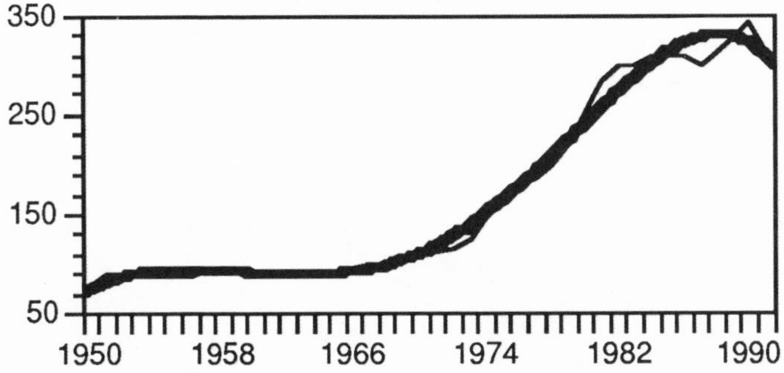

Economist: True enough. If people prefer less bread the price of wheat goes down—supply remaining the same. Commodity prices respond immediately to changes in supply and demand

Author: Let's go one step further. If world-wide demand for "old" goods is declining, wouldn't you expect the effect on prices to show up first in the commodity market? That's precisely what's happening. Adjusted for inflation, prices of *basic commodities peaked in the 1980s*. (See Figure 4.)

Economist: And "mindset" is the explanation?

Author: When the Little King flourished, so did a cluster of Little King industries. Oil and steel, for example, were mainstays of the automobile. Meat, grains, coffee and tobacco were the daily fare of Little Kings. In the 1990s all of these basic commodities are increasingly out of sync with the Caring Conserver's emphasis on health.

We eat less meat because we believe that cholesterol will clog our arteries. We use less grain because it is required to produce meat. We consume less coffee because we're avoiding caffeine. We smoke less tobacco because we're convinced it ruins our lungs. By government decrees requiring more miles per gallon, we cut down on oil because it pollutes the environment. We reduce our use of metals because metal makes cars heavy and heavy cars use too much oil.

Figure 5

Prices: Commodities and Existing Homes

Index of 21 Commodities (CRB; divided by $10)

Median Home Prices, in 1967 Dollars

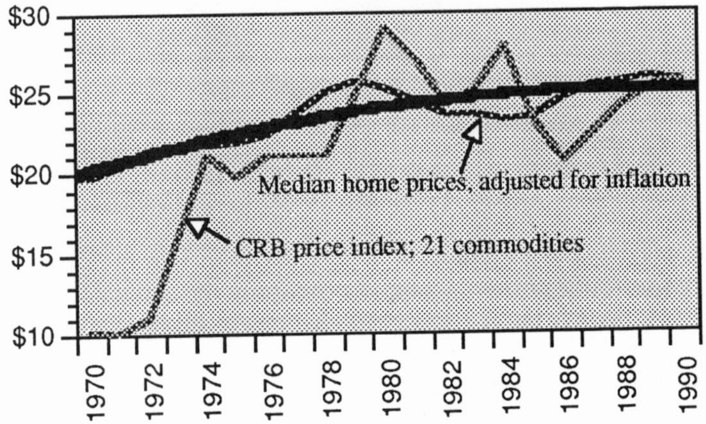

Economist: Do you apply the same reasoning to the housing market? I note that when adjusted for inflation, the trend of home prices during the 1970s and 1980s has been roughly similar to that of basic commodities. (See Figure 5.) Both peaked 1979–1980.

Author: Yes. The changing mindset is also reducing the growth of our metropolitan areas. And the effect on prices is immediate—just as in the commodity market. Individual home owners may hold out for a while. But they don't *control* the price. Those who *want* to sell—whether it's a house in suburbia or a truckload of corn— must sooner or later accept the verdict of the market. Look at the graph. When adjusted for inflation, home prices have been *falling* for a decade.

Deflation in new industries

Economist: But you are predicting a *general* deflation and I see no reason for it. As demand contracts in one sector of the economy it expands in another. If people buy fewer cars (an *old* industry), they buy more electronic equipment (a *new* industry).

Author: Sounds sensible, but it doesn't work that way. As those new industries expand, their prices go *down*. This is typical of new industries. In 1950 it took millions of dollars to buy 64K of computer memory. In 1990 you can get 4,000,000K for under $3,000. On the frontier of a new technology there is a bubbling up of related inventions which lowers costs. There are also economies of scale—due to producing a million units rather than a thousand. The new industries don't counter a deflationary trend, they *contribute* to it.

There's yet another reason for the deflationary trend. The required raw materials are still abundant. The microchip industry has plenty of silicon; penturbia has plenty of land. Both act as a powerful force for *deflation*. In the case of penturbia, supply far exceeds demand. I count 1,708 counties out of 3,096 in various stages of readiness for settlement. In the coming decade, penturban land will rise in value but that rise will not be as great as the fall in suburban land value. On the *average*, the trend of all urban land prices will be deflationary.

Economist: There's something we're forgetting. America is becoming part of a world market.

Deflation due to the coming crash of Japanese land values

Author: That brings me back to Japan. As we agreed earlier, we're increasingly dependent on the Japanese funding of our gargantuan debt ($11.06 trillion in 1987).[135] The Japanese are among our best sources to provide capital for every public and private purpose—real estate, Treasury bills, corporate bonds, stock equities, business start-ups, etc.

We think we know why Japan has all this money to invest— an inordinate propensity to save. But much of the collateral for those loanable funds derives from *the value of Japanese real estate.* A Japanese owner of a piece of land worth one billion yen can get a loan from the bank for some percentage of one billion. He pledges the land as collateral. Say he gets half a billion at a cost of five percent interest. The owner is now free to put his half a billion in U.S. bonds or other investments paying well over five percent interest. The difference is his profit.

In 1990, the value of all the land in Japan was estimated as *quadruple* that of the U.S.—an area one-twenty-fifth the size of ours.[136] In October 1987, a piece of prime Tokyo land the size of this page was worth $6,000![137] By 1990 it was worth still more and rising! Those trillions locked into the length and breadth of Tokyo are backing an increasing share of Japanese investments in U.S. assets.

Economist: That is a concern for those of us who ask ourselves what if.... What if those Japanese land values fell? What if they fell precipitously? What if they crashed?

Author: We'll find out soon enough. Those values *will* soon come tumbling down.

Economist: Why? Because Japanese land values are unreasonably high?

Author: The main reason is that once again *a new resource outcompetes an old one*. Over half the Japanese population is contained in a single "old" city. Call it Tokyo, but it's really a conglomerate of Tokyo-Nagoya-Osaka. That old city is now verging on obsolescence.

Economist: What's obsolescent about Tokyo?

Author: Nothing, if the emphasis is on production.

Economist: But in Japan the emphasis *is* on production.

Author: You mean it *has been*. Now the Japanese are becoming consumers. The world economy leaves them little choice. The U.S. can't continue to run so large a trade deficit with them. And no other country or combination of countries is willing and able to consume their goods on the required scale. If the Japanese cannot sell us what they produce, they will have to consume it themselves.

Economist: Why not? As people become richer I'd expect them to consume more.

Author: Our experience with the Little King teaches us that it isn't easy to build an effective consumer economy. To begin with, consumers need plenty of land for their spacious houses and grounds. For this, Tokyo is all wrong. Over half the country's population is crowded into tiny houses and apartments within that single, expensive, and super-crowded city—a singularly poor arrangement for a wealthy society interested in consumption.

Economist: Do you expect the Japanese to migrate to penturbia?

Author: Not necessarily. Penturbia is the next step only for those who are afflicted by excesses of the Little King. Though it increasingly interacts with the Western world, until 1854 Japan was still buried in its feudal cocoon. After 1900, while we learned to become consumers, Japan was catching up. Our voracious consumption was a perfect foil for their disciplined production. In 1990 Tokyo is still an industrial city (something like Chicago of 1900). Japan's next step is unclear. It may be the development of some version of suburbia or a hybrid suburbia-and-penturbia.

Economist: The country is too small. Its geography doesn't lend itself to anything but a compact city. There's no place for sprawl.

Author: If the Japanese cannot sprawl at home (including the largely unpopulated island of Hokaido) they may have to find the space elsewhere—perhaps by building economic colonies in Australia, North and South America, or on the Asian mainland. Many of the new Japanese plants established in the United States are even now permitting suburban or penturban lifestyles for company executives and workers.

Economist: Let me recap your argument. Competition is at the heart of the matter. *In 1930 Chicago could not compete with Los Angeles and the rest of suburbia. In the 1990s Tokyo will not be able to compete with a range of alternative locations around the world.*

Author: Tokyo land values will collapse because the city will no longer have what people want. The same thing has happened in every one of our U.S. migrations.The Tokyo crash, of course, will be much more spectacular than the Chicago crash. The drying up of the Japanese money supply will be felt on six continents.

Economist: Why hasn't it happened already?

Author: America's Little King refuses to be subdued. It keeps us importing Japanese goods, keeps reducing the pressure for adjustment. So long as the Japanese can export their surplus to us they are not *compelled* to change. And so long as we keep borrowing and consuming we can postpone our own development. Like Rasputin, the evil monk of pre-World War I Russia, the will to overconsume won't die until it is shot, drowned, poisoned and strangled.

Economist: So you expect today's inflation to turn into a deflationary rout, one more bullet killing off the Little King's prosperity. Do you see any common thread to your four reasons for depression?

Author: Depression is about transition. A whole civilization cannot be transformed into something better without slowing the pace of economic transactions. It is like the pause between acts of a play.

Economist: Do you have any evidence that in the 1990s we are approaching the "pause between acts of a play?"

Author: I do—compelling evidence. Angus Maddison, an economist of the OECD, has compared growth rates during two periods. By good fortune, the first of his periods, 1950–1973, is centered around the Little King's peak. The other follows immediately afterwards.

Table 1
Annual Average Rate of Economic Growth (in percent)[138]

	1950-1973	1973-1987
32 selected countries	5.1	3.4
16 OECD countries	4.9	2.4
United States	3.7	2.5
Japan	9.3	3.7
West Germany	5.9	1.8
9 Asian countries	5.4	5.9
U.S.S.R.	5.2	2.1
94 other countries	5.5	2.3

Growth is markedly lower in the second period—and not only in the U.S. but in nearly every nation of the world. In the

U.S., growth declines by a third, in West Germany, by two-thirds, in the sixteen OECD countries, by a half. (See Table 1.) The only increases occurred in a few late-developing Asian countries like South Korea, Taiwan and Thailand.

Economist: That's a slowdown that cuts across both socio–economies, doesn't it, the new and the old?

Author: That's right. It involves the whole society and economy.

Economist: But I thought you said that the pause occured during the season of depression. The world slowdown revealed by Maddison's data has been going on during the entire post-World-War II season of prosperity.

Author: The slowdown begins as soon as the new socioeconomy emerges. At first the change in pace is imperceptible, then it gradually increases. After the equinox "slowdown" advances to "pause."

Economist: Aren't you overlooking a very important factor in the equation? I'm talking about the recent fall of Communism and the new opportunities for economic growth offered by the consolidation of Europe into a single market.

Author: Europe is outside of our present scope. But I see the New Europe you speak of as just another feature of the emerging Caring Conserver. Even casual observation suggests that a remarkable effort will be required to perfect a *reversal* of the old socioeconomy. (How far has the USSR's perestroika come in five years of Gorbachev's revolution?) It will take time. A lot of time.

Economist: Ah. I see your point. According to your theory it will take time to move the props around, adjust the lights, prepare the actors for their next scene.

Author: And that's only part of the problem. Economic actors don't have a prepared plot, script, lights, props. The play goes on but not without confusion, anguish and bitterness, *depression and deflation.*

Economist: What's the track record of the theory? Could it have predicted past depressions and past deflations?

Author: *Every major depression of the last two centuries occurred during a season of depression—between an equinox and the subsequent socioeconomic peak.* (See Chapters 10–14.)

Economist: Deflation and inflation appear to follow the economic seasons. But the occurrence of depressions is decidedly irregular.

Author: As expected. Seasons of depression are periods of heightened *probabilities* of depression, not *actual* depressions. The irregularities are usually due to random events—an unexpected disclosure of corruption in an S&L, a sudden outbreak of war in the Middle East, a failed industry in Texas. Such events are truly unpredictable.

Economist: Suppose it's all true, that prices will be dropping and a season of depression is in the offing. What can we do to prevent it?

Author: Nothing. I see depression as a necessary and recurring feature of human existence. It is no more possible to prevent depression than to prevent winter. But, as we prepare for winter, we can prepare for depression. We protect ourselves against icy blasts with suitable clothing—warm coats, woolen sweaters, scarves, hats, and gloves. The seasons of depression are equally predictable; strategies to mitigate their effects equally feasible. But perhaps we shouldn't go too far in softening the bite of depression.

Economist: Would you recommend that we provide coats but no gloves?

Author: I only mean to suggest that depression can be a useful whip to hasten needed adjustments. Hardship in massive doses whacks at our lethargy and quickens our passage from the present to the future. Perhaps you will recall how quickly we moved from the passivity of the 1920s to the urgency of the 1930s.

In describing the reception to Roosevelt's first inaugural speech, William Manchester wrote: "...in the three-decker tenements with radios the hungry children looked up; in county courthouses the embattled farmers looked up; housewives patching threadbare clothes looked up; there was a kind of magic in the air...."[139] In times of depression, people hunger for action.

Don't underestimate the benefits of depression. It is the ideal time for rejecting the old mindset and sharpening our appreciation for the new one. Depression is the mother that necessitates invention. Philosopher-comedian Will Rogers commented on the popular support behind *whatever* Roosevelt proposed: "If he burned down the Capitol, we would cheer and say, 'Well, we at least got a fire started somehow.'"[140]

Part three

3,096 county predictions

Part II presented a theory of socioeconomic cycles. Part III projects the theory into the 1990s and beyond. Counties are classified based on the observation that 1970 was a peak year for suburbia and a trough year for penturbia—as well as by a wealth of historical information confirming the preceding decade as a turning point for the two socioeconomies.

Over three thousand counties in the contiguous United States are assigned to seven major classes. Each class is a prediction representing a distinct probability of growth or decline in the 1990s.

Probabilities however are not certainties. Not every Class I county will grow rapidly in the 1990s. Nor will every Class VII county grow slowly.

In *Regions of Opportunity* (Lessinger, 1986) a county's assignment to one of the seven classes is based on data available up to 1980. The present book is updated to reflect data available up to 1988, extrapolated to 1990. To take into account growth trends of the 1980s, the original seven classifications are here expanded to seven pairs. (See Chapter 21.)

We begin with Class VII, primarily older suburbs now declining.

Seventeen

Counties of decline in the 1990s

Class VII: Primarily older suburbs

***H**ow to recognize a Class VII county:*
• *1950–1970 The county's percentage of U.S. population increased.*
• *1970–1980 The county's percentage of U.S. population decreased.*

Class VII counties include those furiously growing suburbs of midcentury which began to decline in 1970. Some contain older central cities (Oakland, Seattle, Denver) established during the third migration before the turn of the century. These cities typically weight the county statistics in a downward direction.

As part of the fourth leading region, Class VII counties are primarily located within the nation's metropolitan areas. (See Figure 1.)

Although Class VII counties are identified by statistics pertaining to only thirty years, 1950–1980, a common long-run pattern also sweeps through the preceding 160 years. In the early 19th century, a number of Class VII counties were lagging members of the second migration. Others were settled much later. In either case, they soared to a peak in the 1960s or

1970s. (See Figure 2.)

Figure 1
Class VII
Locations of Counties

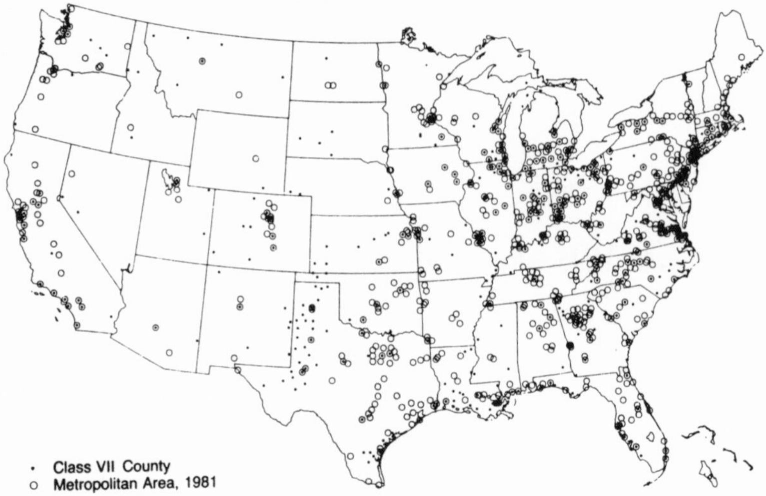

Figure 2
Class VII
Percent of U.S. Population

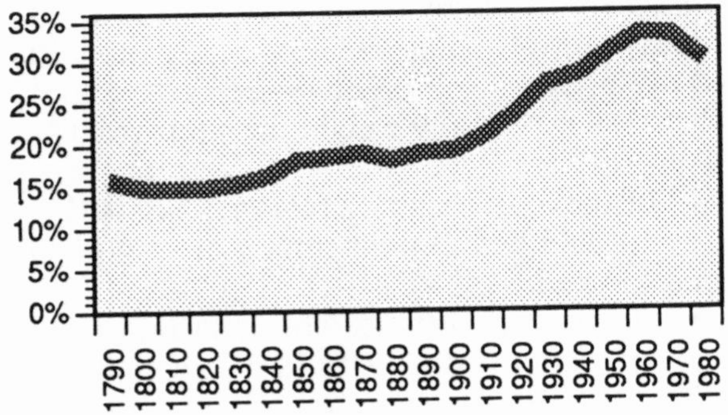

The growth trends of Class VII counties can be discerned

in the patterns of individual counties.(See Figures 3 and 4.)

Figure 3
Alameda County, California: Class VII
Percent of U.S. Population

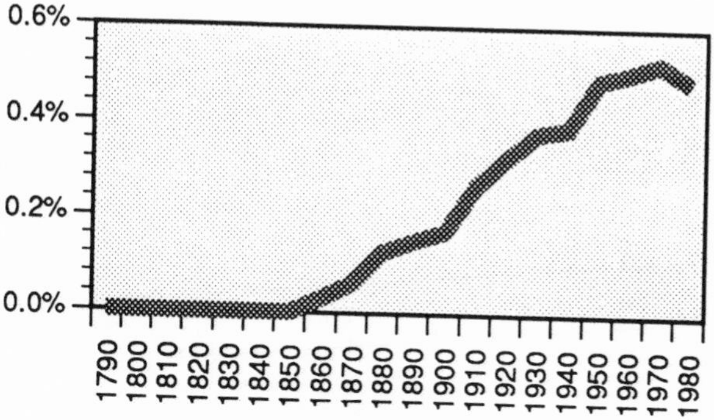

Figure 4
Westchester County, NY: Class VII
Percent of U.S. Population

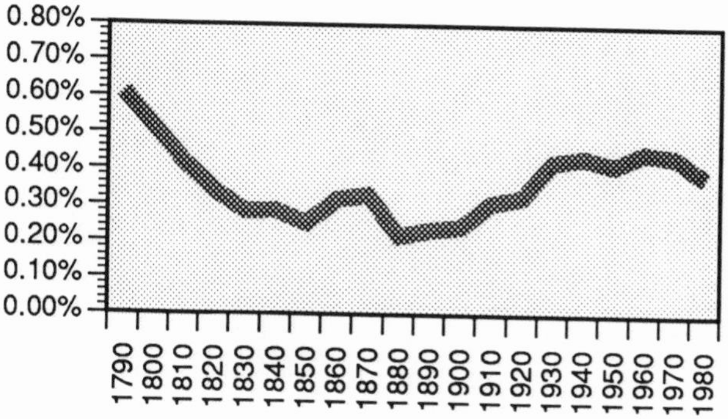

Logic suggests a bleak outlook for most Class VII counties. Favored by the fourth migration and the socioeconomy of the Little King, these counties supported a social and economic structure that will be increasingly out of favor in the 1990s.

As a result of special factors, some Class VII counties may

escape the fate of the group. King County, Washington, for example, may be accorded an economic transfusion by the rise of trade with Pacific Rim countries, particularly with China. Selected counties of Class VII could therefore prove highly susceptible to growth, especially in the short run. In general, however, the future is likely to be grim for this class.

Eighteen

Counties peaking in the 1990s

Class VI: Suburbs younger than Class VII

***H**ow to recognize a Class VI county:*

- *1950–1970 The county's percentage of U.S. population increased.*
- *1970–1980 The county's percentage of U.S. population increased.*
- *The increase 1970–1980 was less than half the increase 1950–1970.*

Suburbs mushrooming across the San Gabriel Mountains northeast of the city of Los Angeles are typical of Class VI. In 1988 several communities joined to form the city of Santa Clarita. Two years later, in 1990, Santa Clarita houses more than 150,000 residents. Such rapid growth is typical of fringe suburbs and brings the typical retinue of suburban problems: gridlock, inflated real estate prices, inadequate sewers, lack of parks. The new residents often continue in their old jobs, simply extending their commute. Santa Clarita "has been invaded by middleclass homebuyers fleeing the increasingly expensive and crowded San Fernando Valley to the south."[141]

Almost as much as Class VII, Class VI counties tend to be located close to or within metropolitan areas. (See Figure 1.)

Figure 1
Class VI Counties
Locations of Counties

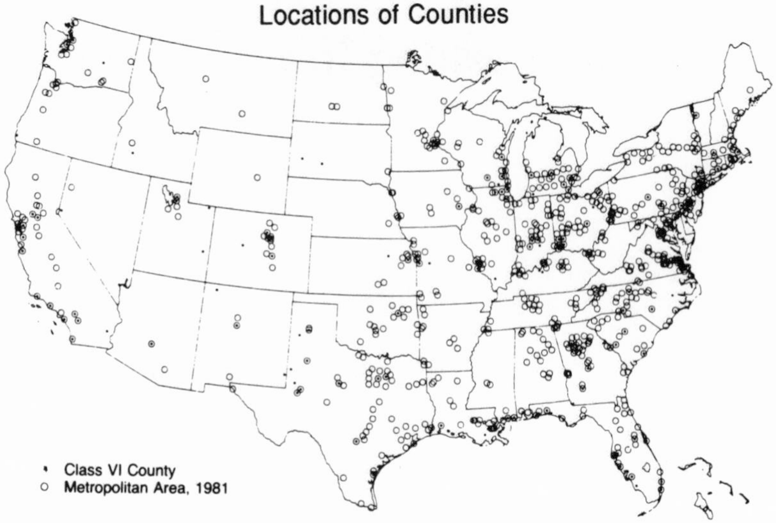

Figure 2
Class VI Counties
Percent of U.S. Population

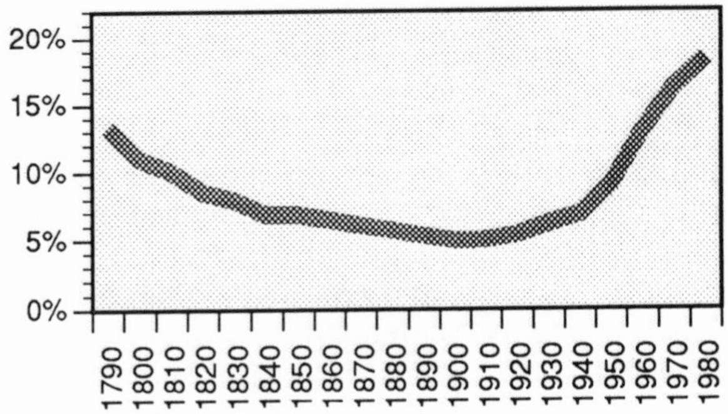

Although Class VI counties are identified by only three decades of population data (1950–1980), like Class VIIs, they too follow a distinctive pattern of growth over the preceding 160 years. Counties of this class that were settled early—those in the East—declined throughout the 19th century. Growth accelerated after 1900, with the greatest gains in the 1960s, and slowing in the 1970s. (See Figure 2.)

Santa Clara County, home of Silicon Valley, and Orange County, both in California, are two Class VI counties which noticeably decelerated in the 1970s. (See Figures 3 and 4.)

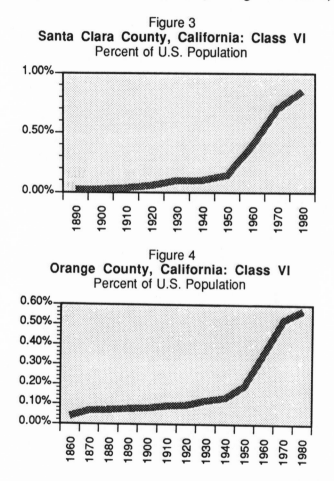

Figure 3
Santa Clara County, California: Class VI
Percent of U.S. Population

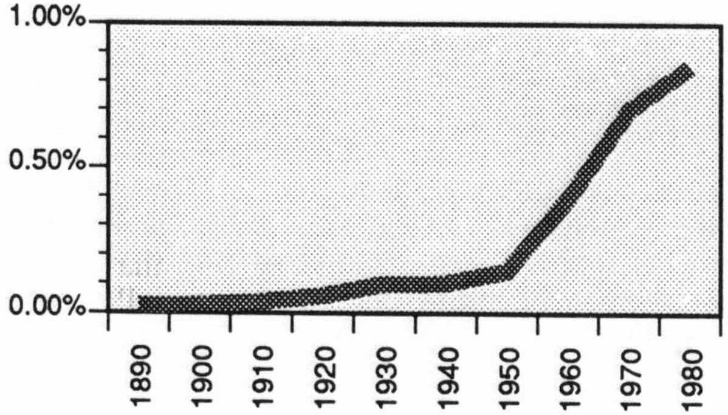

Figure 4
Orange County, California: Class VI
Percent of U.S. Population

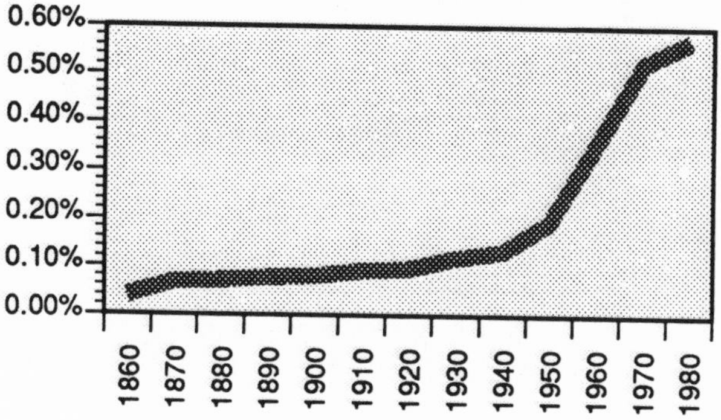

Class V: Youngest suburbs (borderline penturbia)

How to recognize a Class V county:
• *1950–1970 The county's percentage of U.S. population increased.*
• *1970–1980 The county's percentage of U.S. population increased*
• *The increase from 1970–1980 was at least twice the increase 1950–1970.*

Class V counties showed strong growth in the 1970s. While the VIs slowed down in the 1970s, the Vs continued as rapidly as before. It is interesting to note that the VIs grew more rapidly earlier in the 1950s and especially in the 1960s. (See Figure 5.)

Figure 5
Class V Counties
Percent of U.S. Population

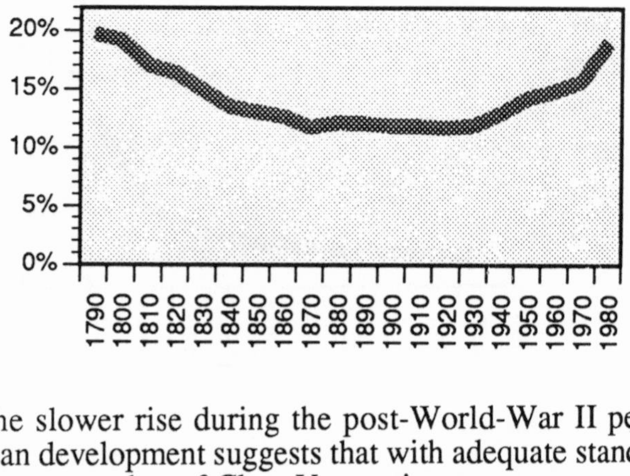

The slower rise during the post-World-War II period of suburban development suggests that with adequate standards of planning, a number of Class V counties may escape suburban status and eventually evolve as part of penturbia. This outcome depends on their residents, whether, if given the opportunity they will vote for superior environments. Counties growing rapidly from 1950 to 1970 (Class VI) are more likely to be set in their ways.

A *leaning* towards penturbia is also suggested by the location of Class V counties—many are less dependent on metropolitan areas than is typical of Classes VI and VII. (See Figure 6.)

Figure 6
Class V Counties
Locations of Counties

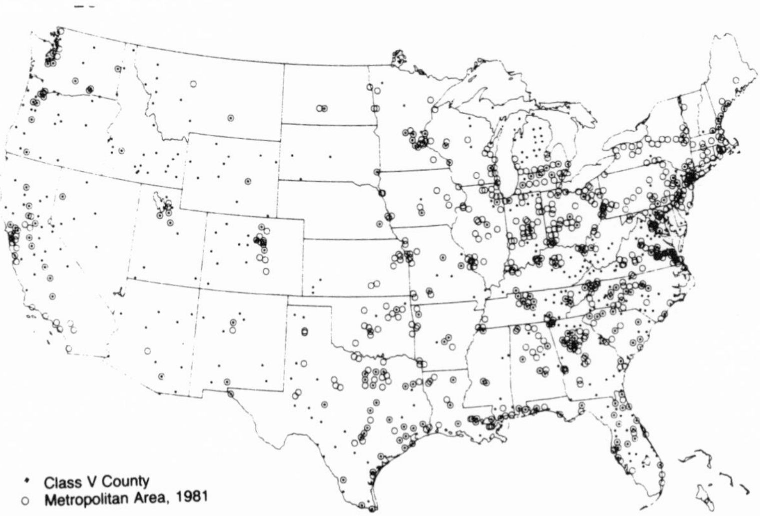

Whether they evolve towards obsolescence or fifth-migration growth, Class V counties present an important disadvantage for investment purposes. Decades of population pressure have raised land values far above those in counties where growth has either lagged or fallen during the same period.

Class V counties present a serious challenge to planners. In some counties, there is still time to pre-empt suburbanization. Comprehensive planning programs, while likely to be expensive due to high land values, can ensure healthy continuing growth.

Camas, in Clark County, Washington (a typical Class V

county) is the site of a new RCA-Sharp electronics plant. Camas is a timber town in Southwest Washington, a short drive from the Portland metropolitan area. Because of that accessibility the county grew faster than the national average during the suburban era 1950–1970. By 1970, however, much of the county was still lightly populated. Depending on voter activism or apathy, Camas could develop as either penturbia or suburbia.

Counties in Classes VII, VI and V make up suburbia, ranging from most to least mature. Class I is "prime" penturbia, the area developing rapidly in the 1970s after declining during the era of suburbanization. To contrast suburbia with penturbia, we now consider Class I.

Nineteen

Counties of growth in the 1990s

Class I: Prime penturbia

***H**ow to recognize a Class I county:*

- *1950–1970 The county's percentage of U.S. population decreased.*
- *1970–1980 The county's percentage of U.S. population increased.*
- *1970–1980 The increase was large enough to place this county among the fastest-growing 16 percent of all U.S. counties.*

On the average, the percentage of population in Class I counties rises to a long plateau beginning in 1830 (encompassing both the second and third migrations) and falls steeply after the turn of the century. One shouldn't be surprised that the percentage rose steeply after 1970. That was the way the class was defined. (See Figure 1.)

The shift after 1970—from slow growth or actual loss to rapid growth—is no accident.

• Until 1970 hundreds of Class I counties had been declining for up to a century or more. Something extraordinary had to happen to induce such an unlikely shift at the same time.

• The down-up shift of Class I came approximately at the same time as the up-down shift of Class VII.

Figure 1
Class I
Percent of U.S. Population

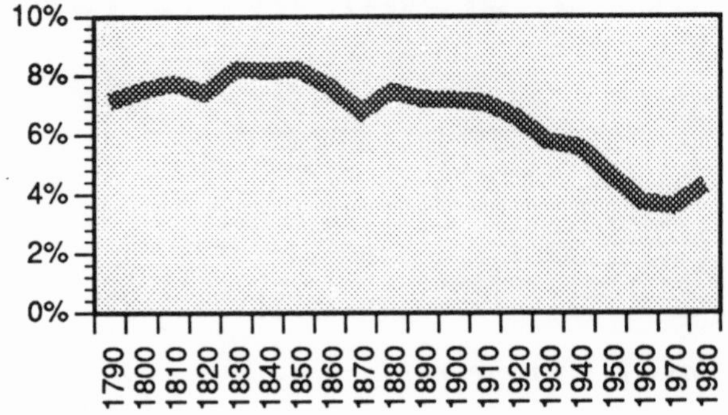

• The decline of the Little King in the 1970s can explain both reversals—down-up of Class I and the up-down of Class VII. By the 1970s, the Caring Conserver had impressed these declining counties into a new role.

From 1950 to 1970, when suburbs were the target of the biggest land rush in American history, Class I counties were "out in the boonies." Today, that former isolation is their greatest resource.

Because Class I counties did not participate in the growth of the Little King, they are not shackled to an obsolete suburban structure, the curving superblocks, manicured lawns, and homogeneous dormitories of the swinger generation. They are free of dated regional shopping centers and vast gray parking lots, from miles of freeway congestion and air pollution, and they are only slightly vulnerable to municipal deficits and drug traffic. Remoteness also insulates them from wage demands often imposed by labor unions. Finally, they are unburdened by the Little King himself, that prisoner of belief in the merit of get-it-now-and-pay-later.

What these rural and semirural communities lost during the fourth migration they are now able to reclaim in the fifth. They should not be considered as simple extensions of suburbia.

Here is a clean slate on which to write lessons for the future. Class I counties are least committed to patterns of suburban development, least albatrossed by a spent history. The map of Class I counties shows their rejection of metropolitan locations. (See Figure 2.)

Figure 2
Class I Counties
Locations of Counties

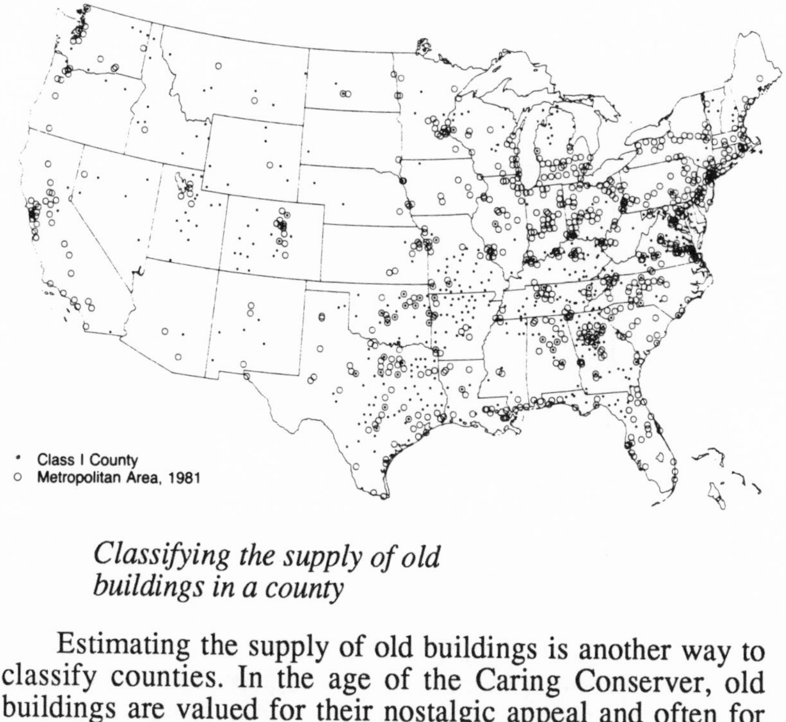

Classifying the supply of old buildings in a county

Estimating the supply of old buildings is another way to classify counties. In the age of the Caring Conserver, old buildings are valued for their nostalgic appeal and often for lower construction costs. I refer to counties with a large inventory of old real estate as "A" counties, those with a smaller inventory as "B" counties. Because data is unavailable for this purpose, the inventory of old buildings is estimated on the basis of population. In any year, the combined inventory of private and commercial structures should correspond roughly to the size of population. In 1930 or before, Class IA counties had larger populations than in 1970, Class IB had smaller populations than in 1970. A and B classifications for Classes I and II are provided in Appendix D.

Due to increasing demands for raw materials from its forests and fields, Stevens County, Washington grew from 10,543 in 1900 to 25,297 in 1910. Then, as with many other third-migration counties, Stevens fell behind in the era of the Little King. It declined to 17,405 in 1970—below its former peak of 25,297—and is therefore classified as IA. Its growth profile is typical of the group. (See Figure 3.)

Figure 3
Stevens County, WA: IA
Percent of U.S. Population

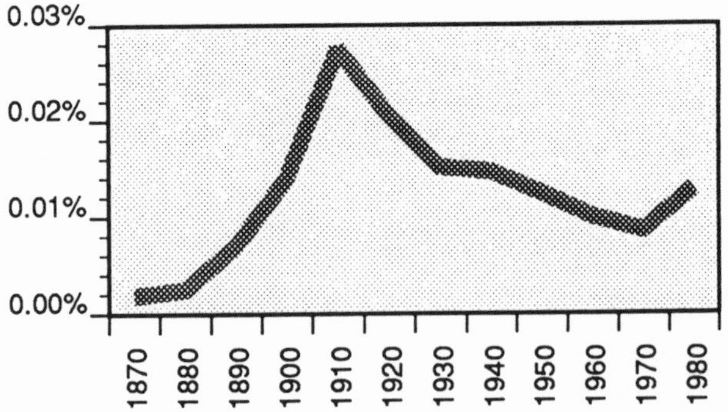

A Class I designation does not guarantee a sound investment potential. Within each county, special factors should be taken into account. For example, a county may be judged Class I based on the criteria outlined in this chapter but yet prove unsuitable for investment purposes because growth in the 1970s reflected a heavy influx of unemployed migrants.

Counties classified as IB are indistinguishable from those in IA except for their smaller inventory of old buildings. Klickitat County Washington, and White County, Arkansas, for example, follow the typical profile of the class. (See Figure 4 and 5.)

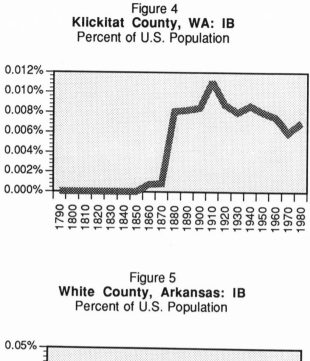

Figure 4
Klickitat County, WA: IB
Percent of U.S. Population

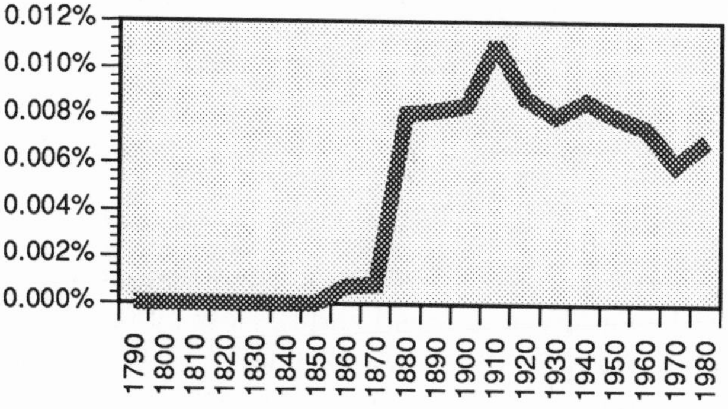

Figure 5
White County, Arkansas: IB
Percent of U.S. Population

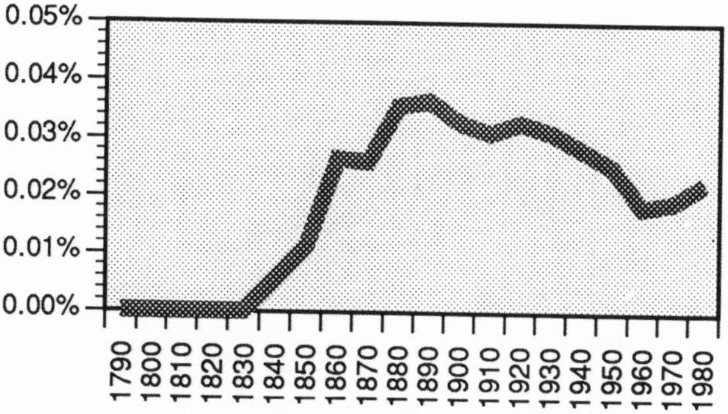

Class II: Secondary penturbia

How to recognize a Class II county:
• *1950–1970 The county's percentage of U.S. population decreased.*
• *1970–980 The county's percentage of U.S. population increased.*
• *1970–1980 The increase was less than the increase for Class I counties.*

During the peak years of suburban migration, from 1950 to 1970 counties in classes I and II grew more slowly than the national average. After 1970, prompted by the rise of the new socioeconomy, both sped up their growth, but II less than I.

The growth of Class II counties suggests an overwhelming presence of counties formerly in the second leading region. Typical of the second region, Class II counties peaked in the 1840s and then began a long decline until 1970. (See Figure 6.)

Figure 6
Class II
Percent of U.S. Population

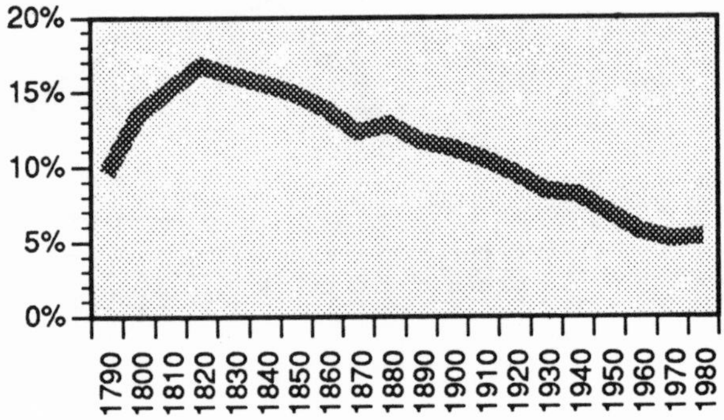

Class II counties are heavily represented in the Mississippi Valley, location of the second leading region. (See Figure 7.)

Figure 7
Class II
Locations of Counties

Figure 62:
LOCATIONS OF CLASS II COUNTIES

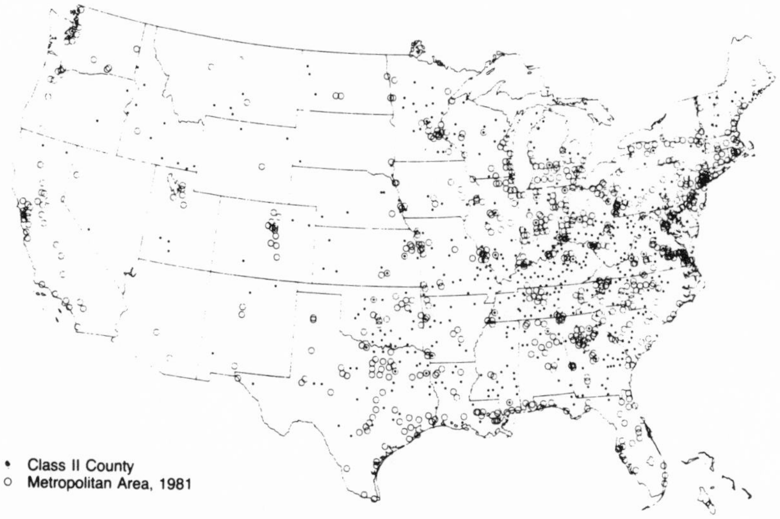

Individual Class II counties follow the typical pattern. As before, the A and B designations identify the different inventories of old buildings, with A greater than B. The accompanying graphs show the percentages of U.S. population for sample counties in Classes IIA and IIB. (See Figures 9 and 10.)

Figure 8
Hancock County, Maine: Class IIA
Percent of U.S. Population

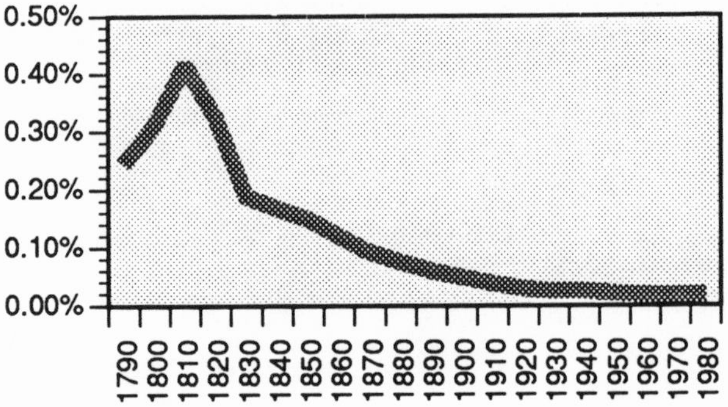

Figure 9
Coffee County, Georgia: Class IIB
Percent of U.S. Population

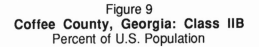

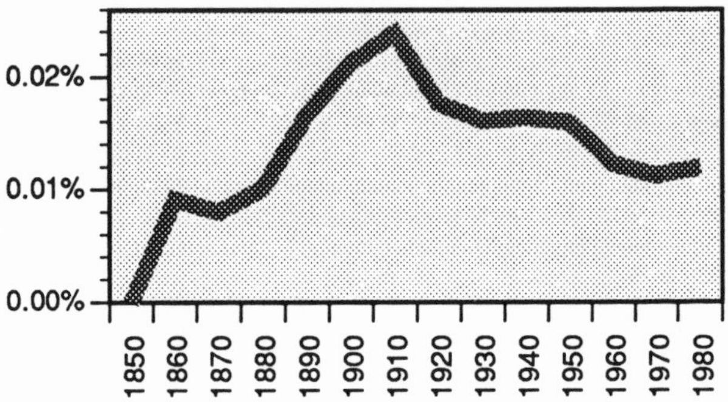

Twenty

Counties less likely to grow in the 1990s

Class III: Latent penturbia

***H**ow to recognize a Class III county:*

- *1950–1970 The county's percentage of U.S. population decreased.*
- *1970–1980 The county's percentage of U.S. population decreased.*
- *1970–1980 The decrease in the county's percentage of U.S. population was* less *than half the decrease from 1950 to 1970.*

From 1950 to 1970, Class III counties were indistinguishable from Classes I and II. All three grew at rates below the national average. Differences among them, however, became visible only after 1970. Though Class III counties continued to lag, after the 1970 turning point, they lagged less.

Figure 1
Class III
Percent of U.S. Population

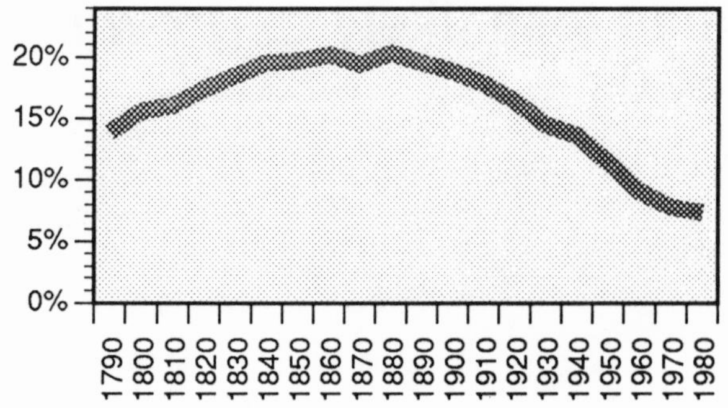

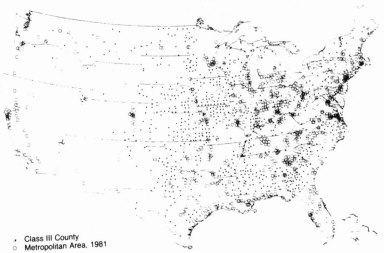

Class III counties are located throughout the nation, with a smaller concentration in the West. (See Figure 2.)

Figure 2
Class III
Locations of Counties

Figure 3
McDowell County, West Virginia: Class IIIA
Percent of U.S. Population

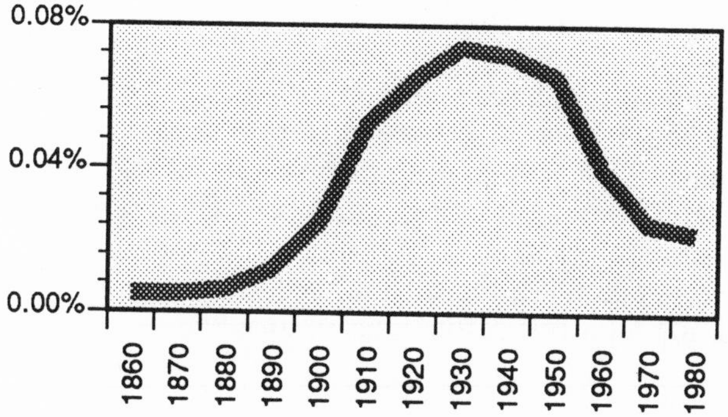

Figure 4
Caswell County, North Carolina: Class IIIB
Percent of U.S. Population

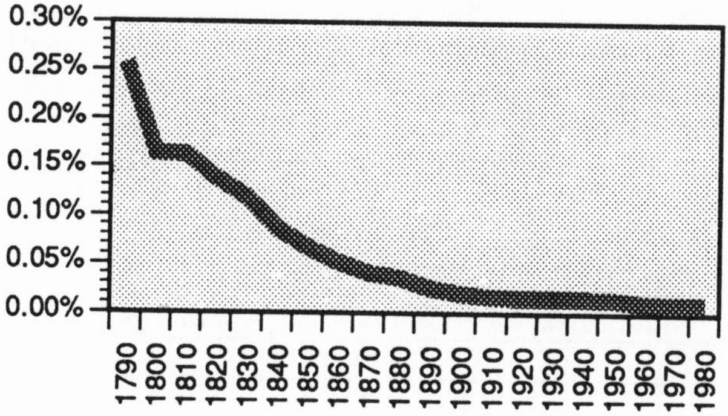

Can the disparities in growth rates of Classes I, II, and III be expected to continue?

The three classes have been identified by their different trends during the 1970s. Are they differentiated by other, deeper differences? We need more information. Accordingly, the three have been compared using a number of economic, social and demographic measures. Though their averages are often narrowly separated, the differences are logically consistent in explaining their respective rates of growth.

Lifestyle

Of the three classes, Class I is most immediately adaptable to the lifestyle of the Caring Conserver. (See Chapter 12.) Penturbia is neither rural nor urban. It is urban-rural, a rural location settled by urban-minded people. Residents of Class I (prime penturbia) show a preference for a rural lifestyle but earn their living mainly in non-agricultural pursuits. Consider the following comparisons based on the 1980 census.

Farm population as a percent of total population

Class I	7.4 percent
Class II	9.6 percent
Class III	14.4 percent

Average value of farm land per acre

Class I	$688
Class II	$716
Class III	$746

Urban population as a percent of total population

Class I	22.6 percent
Class II	24.9 percent
Class III	26.3 percent

Percent of individuals commuting to work outside county

Class I	30.8 percent
Class II	26.9 percent
Class III	21.6 percent

Number of in-county jobs per hundred population

Class I	5.7
Class II	6.1
Class III	6.7

Income

Residents of Class I counties are richer on the average than those in Class II—who are richer than residents of Class III counties.

Percent of families at the poverty level

Class I	13.3 percent
Class II	13.8 percent
Class III	14.4 percent

Percent of households earning less than $10,000 annually

Class I	37.8 percent
Class II	39.0 percent
Class III	40.3 percent

Percent of households earning $20,000–$29,999 annually

Class I	18.6 percent
Class II	18.1 percent
Class III	17.3 percent

Percent of households earning $30,000–$49,999 annually

Class I	9.2 percent
Class II	8.5 percent
Class III	8.1 percent

Average value of owner-occupied houses

Class I	$34,844
Class II	$30,822
Class III	$27,579

Average monthly rent (residential)

Class I	$188
Class II	$173
Class III	$164

Age

Class I counties have the smallest percentage of population over 65, Due to the exit of younger age groups from rural resource occupations, Class III counties have the highest.

Percent of population over 65

Class I	13.1 percent
Class II	13.7 percent
Class III	15.8 percent

Despite evident disparities in growth and socioeconomic characteristics among the three classes, no one should assume that *every* Class II or Class III county is less sound as a candidate for investment than any in Class I. As a class, I shows more potential than II, II more than III. But some properties in Class II may prove to have far sounder investment potential than some in Class I. And some counties in Class III may be authentic "sleepers."

Class IV: Long-standing decline in population—rural and urban counties

How to recognize a Class IV county:
• *1950–1970 The county's percentage of U.S. population decreased.*
• *1970–1980 The county's percentage of U.S. population decreased.*
• *1970–1980 Decrease in the county's percentage of U.S. population was more than half the decrease that occurred between 1950 and 1970.*

The chart of Class IV percentages of U.S. population most resembles that of Class III except that the two differ in the 1970s. Although both continue to decline in the 1970s, Class IV dives more steeply. (See Figure 5.)

Figure 5
Class IV
Percent of U.S. Population

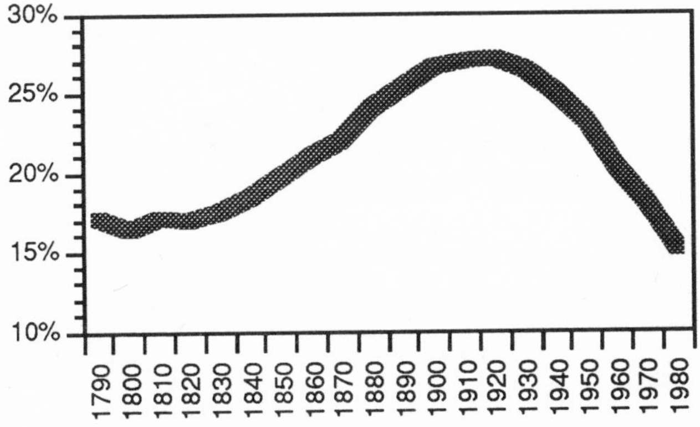

Class IV counties—many of them in the third leading region, like penturban coutnies—are unlikely to turn around any time soon. However, some will prove to be rare "sleepers." Recent "gentrification" and/or redevelopment programs have typically been unable to reverse the long-term trend. While many Class IV counties are primarily agricultural—with few amenities prized by urban residents—others are in obsolescing industrial areas where low-income migrants have already partly filled the vacuum left by the departing middle class.

Class IV also contains a group of "rich" counties containing hub cities like San Francisco or Manhattan. These counties are losing populations but gaining in another way. Inextricably linked to their surrounding suburbs, they have become valuable as commercial sites—for shops and offices. As the suburbs decline in population, the Class IV hubs will inevitably suffer an economic decline.

Class IV counties likely to grow the most in coming decades will be those containing small urban hubs with less than 200,000 population—including industrial mill towns, state capitals or university towns.

Figure 6
Class IV-Counties
Locations of Counties

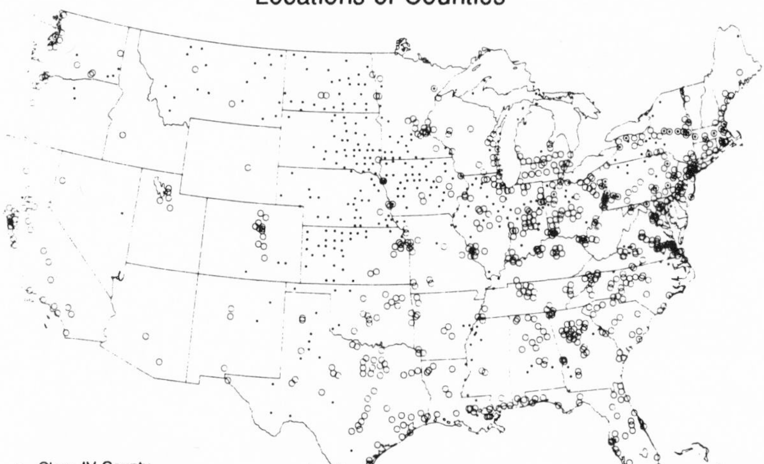

Individual members of Class IV show the typical downward trend after the 1920s. (See Figure 7.)

Figure 7
Colusa County, California: Class IV
Percent of U.S. Population

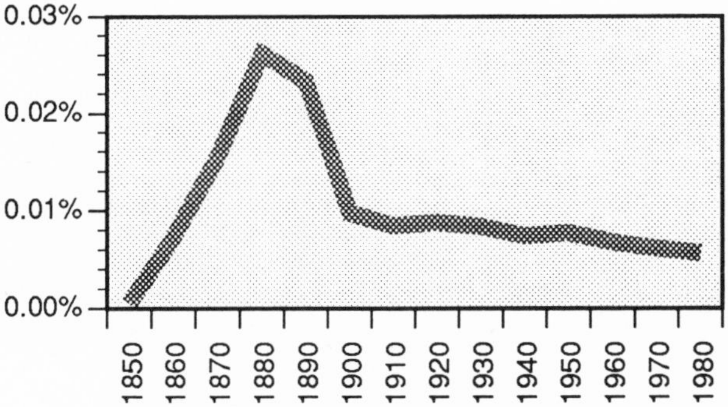

Twenty-one

Ten years later: How good were the predictions?

County predictions for the 1980s and beyond made in *Regions of Opportunity* (Lessinger, 1986) were based on census statistics from 1790 to 1980. Those predictions are now tested by rates of growth registered in the 1980s based on preliminary counts of the 1990 Census.

• Class I (prime penturbia) was expected to grow substantially faster than the national average. It did. Based on the prelimary 1990 Census counts, fom 1980 to 1990 it grew *over sixty* percent faster than the average rate. (For the counties surveyed, average growth was 8.6 percent; prime penturbia grew by 13.8 percent.)

While any Class I county was given a high probability of growth during the 1980s, it is in the very nature of probabilities that some counties would grow little, later, or not at all. (Similarly, perhaps half the companies in a prosperous industry may be expected to fare worse than those more successful.) Half of the total Class I population lived in counties where growth had fallen from 28.7 percent in the 1970s to a mere 1.6 percent in the 1980s. However, in the 1980s, the other half of the Class I population—declining for many decades up to 1970—grew by an astonishing 30 percent, or over three times the national average.

Why did Class I split into two such disparate groups? The best explanation in most cases is that the declining counties were in the path of the commodity depression of the 1980s—agriculture, mining, oil and timber. (See Chapter 16.) In a smaller number of cases it is also possible that the early pioneers of the migration were disappointed with what they found. A third explanation is that these counties were never qualified to be included as Class I. The essential criterion—that a surge of migration begins in the 1970s—may have been due to some anomaly, such as the discovery of oil, or the unexpected influx of migrant workers.

• *Classes II and III* (secondary and latent penturbia) were predicted to grow, but at rates ranging from negligible to less than Class I. In fact, these counties were hit hard by the basic commodities depression of the 1980s. In-migration was often overwhelmed by a massive exodus of bankrupt farmers, loggers, miners, oil workers and dependent services. It is surprising that any net growth could have occurred at all. Yet the growth rate of counties containing 13.6 percent of the Class II population was 73 percent greater than the average rate—14.9 percent.

• *Class IV* (a region of decline and old urban core cities) was expected to continue in its loss of population. It did. While the national average grew by 10.7 percent, Class IV declined by 3.4 percent.

• *Class V* (youngest suburbs) may develop as penturbs—with suitable planning. For example, most of the counties of California's Central Valley, its agricultural empire responsible for much of the nation's fruits and vegetables, are Class V. Kaplan McLaughlin Diaz, a leading planning firm has proposed a comprehensive plan for the entire region. In many such areas, growth is limited by legislative action pending more active planning. During the decade, approximately a quarter of the Cass grew by an astounding 37.7 percent. Three-quarters dropped from 33.5 percent in the preceding decade to 13.9 percent between 1980 and 1990.

• *Class VI* (newer suburbs typically on the fringes of the metropolitan area), behaved much like Class V. Between 1980 and 1990, counties containing nearly 40 percent of the class population grew by an astonishing 34.3 percent. The rest dropped in their rate of growth from 26.4 percent in the preceding decade to 12.9 percent. The heavy growth of the class as a whole testifies to a popular thrust out of the metropolitan area. Class VI is often a temporary stopping place on the way towards penturbia.

• *Class VII* (mature suburbs) was expected to decline during the 1980s and for decades to come. These counties, which in the 1950s and 1960s had exceeded the national average, now grew by only 3.4 percent—about one-third the national average. Growth might well have been even lower except for large infusions of foreigners and migrants from the inner cities. (See Chapter 2.)

Using the test results to improve the classification

The information provided by the additional decade of growth permits a major strengthening of the original classification scheme. The seven classes are now divided into two groups on the basis of growth during the 1980s. The result is an updated and, I believe, more powerful set of predictions for the 1990s.

Each of the seven classes is divided into a *plus* and *minus* pair. *Plus* counties grew faster during the 1980s than minus counties. But how this difference is defined varies with each class, as follows:

Class I

How to recognize a Class I-plus county
Start with a Class I county
1980–1990: The county's percentage of U.S. population increased.

How to recognize a Class I-minus county
Start with a Class I county

1980–1990: The county's percentage of U.S. population did not increase.

Class II

How to recognize a Class II-plus county
Start with a Class II-county
1980–1990: The county's percentage of U.S. population increased.

How to recognize a Class II-minus county
Start with a Class II county
1980–1990: The county's percentage of U.S. population did not increase.

Class III

How to recognize a Class III-plus county
Start with a Class III county
1980–1990: The decrease in the county's percentage of U.S. population was smaller than the decrease during the 1970s.

How to recognize a Class III-minus county
Start with a Class III county
1980–1990: The decrease in the county's percentage of U.S. population was at least as great as the decrease during the 1970s.

Class IV

How to recognize a Class IV-plus county
1980 Start with a Class IV county
1980–1990: The county's percentage of U.S. population increased.

How to recognize a Class IV-minus county
1980 Start with a Class IV county
1980–1990: The county's percentage of U.S. population did not increase.

Class V

How to recognize a Class V-plus county	
	1980 Start with a Class V county
	1980–1990: The increase in the county's percentage of U.S. population was greater than its increase in the 1970s.
How to recognize a Class V-minus county	
	1980 Start with a Class V county
	1980–1990: The rise in the county's percentage of U.S. population did not exceed its rise in the 1970s.

Class VI

How to recognize a Class VI-plus county	
	Start with a Class VI county
	1980–1990: The county's percentage of U.S. population exceeded its increase in the seventies.
How to recognize a Class VI-minus county	
	Start with a Class VI county
	1980–1990: The county's percentage of U.S. population did not exceed its increase in the seventies.

Class VII

How to recognize a Class VII-plus	
	Start with a Class VII county.
	1980–1990: The county's percentage of U.S. population increased.
How to recognize a Class VII-minus	
	Start with a Class VII county.
	1980–1990: The county's percentage of U.S. population did not increase.

Twenty-two

Las Animas, Colorado— a Class III-minus county

Early in 1990 I was intrigued by a story in *The Wall Street Journal* about Trinidad, the principal—but tiny—city of Las Animas County.

Written by Dennis Farney, a reporter for the *Journal,* the story provides independent evidence on a critical question: Can counties that are still losing population—like those in Class III minus—be considered viable candidates for sustained growth in the long-run future?

Because he appears to be unfamiliar with my concept of penturbia, Farney's report offers a revealing counterpoint to the statistics of Part III. His story is reproduced below in its entirety.*

Trinidad, Colorado—Tom Mix, the Hollywood cowboy, stayed at the grand old Columbian Hotel here. His room was 214. His horse's room was 212.

Miners stood up to John D. Rockefeller Jr. here—and died when he and other Eastern coal barons struck back. Men, women and children were mowed down indiscriminately when the Colorado militia crushed their bitter 1914 strike with machine guns and Springfield rifles. That was the Ludlow Massacre. People here talk about it as if it happened last week.

The Santa Fe Trail once ran right through the center of town. Bat Masterson was a Trinidad sheriff. In its coal-mining heyday, the area boasted an astonishing 32 different nationalities—Montenegrins, Italians, Lebanese, Welsh, Hispanics—babbling in 27 different tongues.

---

* **By Dennis Farney. Reprinted by permission of *The Wall Street Journal*, ©Dow Jones & Company, Inc. 1990. All Rights Reserved Worldwide. Originally entitled "A Struggle for Survival: a small Colorado town that has lost population for decades seeks to find a new rationale for existence." *The Wall Street Journal*, March 3, 1990. Emphasis added. Photos by Dave Neligh.**

Clearly, Trinidad has a history. The question is, Does Trinidad have a future?

Numbers that hurt

Few places await the 1990 census results with more trepidation and hope than this gritty, gutsy little town in the pinon pine foothills of southern Colorado. For the grim fact is that surrounding Las Animas County has lost population in every census since 1920. And lost big, to an estimated 14,500 today from 39,000 then. Trinidad city, meanwhile, has slipped to an estimated 9,200 from some 11,700 in 1930.

The unrelenting decline, crippling the local economy, has scarred the collective psychology as well.

Grimaces economic director Frank Granberg: "We still have people who tell visitors, 'Boy, if I could get out of here tomorrow, I would.'" A 1972 history—co-written, incidentally, by presidential candidate George McGovern—described a town that seemed "to have retreated into private contemplation of its unadvertised past." Even the current walking-tour guidebook talks of life "among the tarnished splendor built by former wealth."

But now there's something new in the air. Something is happening here that parallels broad trends in the Midwestern industrial belt and, indeed, the nation as a whole. Trinidad is embarked upon a perilous journey, from the Industrial to the Post-Industrial era.

It's a tortuous process—partly the product of a conscious strategy, partly the piecemeal response to national economic forces beyond Trinidad's control. There's no guarantee that this town, like so many others, won't go right on dying by degrees. But for the first time in a long time, there is guarded optimism.

The town has a splendidly intact collection of Victorian commercial buildings, some of them empty, whose original brick and stonework is gradually re-emerging as 1950-era aluminum false fronts come down.

Of necessity, Trinidad is trying to move to a service-based economy from one based upon natural resources and cattle. Once known as "the Pittsburgh of Colorado," it hasn't entirely given up on its abundant coal. But the inescapable fact is that the coal mines now employ only several hundred workers, not the 10,000 or more needed at the population peak. Trinidad's vital signs, mixed though they are, suggest a town in transition.

High-school graduates continue to leave for lack of jobs, but retirees have begun filtering in. Some demographers predict continued population decline, yet building permits are up. Mr. Granberg counts some 30 new business concerns, but most employ only a handful of workers. Trinidad is on an interstate highway, a crucial advantage many struggling towns lack, and has built a handsome new Welcome Center to lure tourists down off it. The town counted some 116,000 "turnoffs" last year. But in a state that glitters with places like Aspen and Vail, Trinidad must fight to overcome its stereotype as a scruffy industrial town.

"To the rest of Colorado, we're downstate, downtrodden and downgraded," protests Beatrice Davis Klodzinski, a live-wire entrepreneur, business consultant and relative newcomer who arrived a year and a half ago. "*It's not true*. If people could only see what we have here."

Saw-Toothed Peaks

What Trinidad has are old-fashioned brick streets, winding like the arroyos they originally followed, and the scent of pinon smoke in the air. To the west the saw-toothed peaks of the Sangre de Cristo Mountains gleam white with snow. To the east, there are the limitless plains, ghostly beneath a rising moon. The town has a splendidly intact collection of Victorian commercial buildings, some of them empty, whose original brick and stonework is gradually re-emerging as 1950-era aluminum false fronts come down. Trinidad remains a decidedly Western place. A sign in the courthouse plaintively requests: "Please do not spit tobacco in cooler."

What Trinidad doesn't have—not yet, anyway—are many jobs that come close to replacing the high-paying mining jobs lost decades ago. That's why the town is arm-wrestling others to land a state prison for its industrial park. Prisons aren't glamorous. But they do provide steady work at good pay for blue-collar workers. Small towns, which once would have shunned them, now see them as economic salvation.

But there are limits to how far this town will go. Although isolated and politically vulnerable, it is fiercely resisting a proposed nuclear waste storage facility nearby. "Nuclear waste is just not in sync with what we see as the future of this city," insists Mayor Robert Fabec.

Trinidad today remains a better place to live than to make a living. Travel agent Louise Abeyta, 44, was born here and has moved back from Denver. "I think this is the best town in Colorado!" she says. Still, she doubts that a college-age daughter will return—"not the way things are now." As an airline employee in Denver, Mrs. Abeyta explains, she made about $15 an hour. Here "it's a little over minimum wage."

Past and future hopes and fears mingle in the Park Street School's fourth-grade classroom of teacher Kathy Humphrey. History is alive here, as real as a weight on your shoulder. (The saloon of Ms. Humphrey's own grandfather was destroyed by the militia in 1914.) So is a sense of ambivalence about the future.

Asked what Trinidad will look like in 20 years, nine-year-old Kirk Borden predicts: "A ghost town."

But not if Leroy Mestas can help it. He's one of the few class members who intends to stick around. His father remains a coal miner, and he wants to be a miner, too. Other pupils, while uncertain where their adult lives will take them, describe the kind of childhoods that urban kids can only dream about.

Climbing Simpson's Rest

Shandell Mangino, a diminutive blonde with curly hair, talks of regularly seeing deer and eagles in the wild, and of climbing the towering butte called Simpson's Rest to look upon the town and its distant wall of mountains. And Cori White, who firmly intends to live in Paris someday, likes Trinidad "because you can ride your bike anywhere."

Things like that—intangible things—are worth preserving. And so Trinidad struggles. It struggles, ultimately, to give itself a new rationale for existence.

"We're trying to reorient ourselves," says Mayor Fabec, "not just to tourism but to retirees. Retirees are a pretty affluent group. You don't have to build new schools for them, and they don't make many demands on police services." But they do need quality medical services, and so Trinidad must try to upgrade hospital facilities that are becoming outdated.

Mr. Fabec, 43, is another embodiment of a town in transition. To many residents, he represents a break with old-style politics, more preoccupied with turf battles than with the city as a whole, that long dominated the town. He and his wife, Sally, a doctor, also are among the small but growing group of natives who've returned—not because they had to but because they wanted to. *Finally, his economic vision of the city is anchored in the Post-Industrial era.*

Ultimately, the mayor would like a town with "the flavor of Santa Fe, without the problems."

'Racing the Rooster'

That's shooting high, and may be unattainable. This is a town, after all, that in frontier days was known for its bordellos and the stomach-churning sport of "Racing the Rooster." According to Gerald H. Stokes, author of a lively town walking-tour guidebook, roosters were buried up to their necks in sand on Main Street. Then Hispanic horsemen would try to grab the neck as they galloped by. It was one of those things that tended to repulse Anglos. Even today, Trinidad's two dominant ethnic groups, Hispanics and Italians, have a tenuous working relationship. There are two separate chambers of commerce. The town has no commercial airport, but it has persuaded U.S. West to upgrade its ancient telephone-switching equipment.

Still, there is a Santa Fe-quality art gallery, Southwest Legacy, on Main Street that wasn't there three years ago. It's a gamble, but it's already attracted other galleries and a handful of artists. Owners are potter Trish Keck and her husband,

Jerry, himself another native come home.

"We came to stay, not to make excuses," he says. And speaking of the town, he adds: "Everybody was sitting here waiting for a break, waiting for something to happen. Now we're getting enough momentum to make things happen."

Part four

Socially responsible and profitable investing in penturbia

Profit smiles on goodness when the good is profitable.

Rabindranath Tagore (1928)

It must be a good thing to be good or ivrybody wudden't be pretendin' he was.

Finley Peter Dunne (1902)

Waste no more time arguing what a good man should be. Be one.

Marcus Aurelius (2nd century)

Twenty-three

Creating penturbia

In its first two or three decades, every leading region remains indistinct from its predecessor. Thirty years after inauspicious beginnings around 1900, suburbia was only a word flaunted by a few intellectuals. By 1930 what did it amount to anyway but a few houses built beyond the last trolley stop? Nothing to suggest the new kind of settlement about to dominate the nation's heartland. The inventors of our postwar shopping centers and mass subdivisions were still cooing and crawling in their diapers.

In 1990, thirty years after the first exodus from suburbia penturbia is still indistinct. What will it look like by 2010? Nobody knows precisely. Could Rodin describe in advance the final form of his "Thinker?" Even Mozart's great Requiem Mass may have begun in the composer's mind as a vague repetition of rhythms. Development is a delicate process, leaping and twisting, but in the end, slow, often painful, always the cumulated effect of one effort building on another. Any turn along the way could change everything.

All we can see clearly is bits and pieces of a brilliant composition. We see the *direction* of change. But we do not deceive ourselves. The ingredients will be combined and recombined in surprising ways before the mature penturbia finally appears, when people will know it as profoundly as the taste of apple in the mouth.

To plan for penturbia will take time—to crystallize the

requisite mindset, to experiment and to apply lessons learned. Fortunately, time is available. While counties of Class I are already growing far more rapidly than the national average, most of penturbia still slumbers. Judging from previous cycles it may be another thirty years before we see growth peaking in the new leading region. As the socioeconomy becomes more disposed to regional planning, penturbia will assume its distinctive form.

County classes and planning for open space

The classifications in Part III can help identify counties lying in the path of future demand and also serve as a guide to purchasing land for open space. The table of counties in Appendix A and the maps of Appendixes B and C classify potential for growth or decline in 3,096 counties of the contiguous United States.

The longest lead time for buying land inexpensively will be in Classes II and III. Their slower development will permit surer protections for fragile ecosystems and better regional and economic planning. For this reason they may ultimately enjoy an even greater prosperity than Class I. The rush of demand, already driving up prices in some Class I counties, may prove to be more curse than blessing. At this early stage, voters are not always ready for penturbia. Commitment to controlling the environment does not always or easily overcome the Little King's commitment to short-run economic growth.

Setting aside land for open space is not an impossible dream. In 1990 many privately owned, non-profit institutions are buying large parcels of land and putting them into local land trusts. These are people-to-people organizations dedicated to preserving open space.

It's happening in Dutchess County, New York, two hours north by commuter train from New York City.[142] In 1985 a couple of large farms came on the market. Eager developers leaped to attention. Think of it, only two hours from the Big Apple. Were those prize plums seized by some alert subdivider? Not this time. The farms were bought and paid for by a local land trust. From 1985 to 1989 the Dutchess County Land

Trust bought 3,500 acres. Their plan: to restrict the land with permanent conservation easements, then sell it back to farmers and other users who will keep it in open space.

Isn't Dutchess County and its 3,500 acres of protected land a drop in the U.S. bucket? Yes, but the Dutchess County Land Trust is not alone. Aided by a central agency, the Land Trust Exchange, land trusts are growing at a spectacular rate. In 45 states, 640,000 Americans now belong to local land trusts. Figure 1 shows the recent acceleration of investments in land-trusts.

Figure 1
Investments in Land Trusts since 1950[143]
in Millions of Dollars

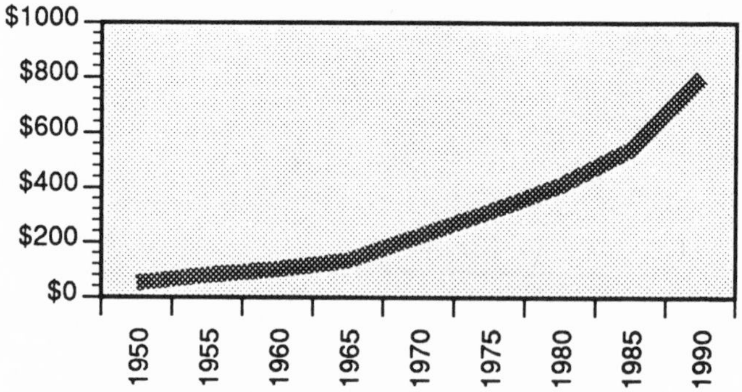

Want to buy a five-to-twenty-acre farm in penturbia?

Setting aside millions of acres for open space collides head-on with another trend—the purchase of hobby farms, five-to-twenty-acres each.

Until higher prices can apply a brake to that trend, it poses a real danger. If *both* open space and small farms are to be accommodated, penturbia's growth will be severely limited—as surely as if the borders had been closed. Whereas limiting growth is a noble objective for many, it has a less appealing side effect. The smaller population reduces the number of taxpaying families essential for cost-efficient settlements. In spite of its generous land supply in 1708 counties, penturbia could become an exclusive enclave for a tiny elite.

Conclusion: Hobby farms do not compute. They will have to go. Their space is needed for clusters of penturban development.

Does eliminating hobby farms mean that people will be packed together in a repeat performance of the worst of suburbia—only this time surrounded by countryside?

2010 AD: Your life in Penturbia

You live in a small cluster of houses and take pride in your community, and your 2,345 "neighbors," including little Sasha Kositsky and Benjamin Luria born last week. Yours is a single-family house on a half-acre lot. Half your windows face out towards rolling hills framed by blue-gray mountains. From your desk upstairs you see a trail winding along a tree-lined stream. You tell relatives in New York that it's your Sanity Trail. Here, amidst the pungent splendors of ponderosa pine, douglas fir and Oregon grape, you regain your equilibrium. You and a few of your close friends enjoy a hike on that trail after wrestling with the day's computer tasks.

Like many of your neighbors, you don't leave the house for work. No need. You are *electronically* employed. You exchange fax messages with associates around the world and confer by modem. On occasion, you arrange a "meeting" by teleconference. Your workday generally begins with reading overnight fax communications. By the time you finish scanning your electronic copy of the *New York Times*, you're enjoying your second cup of decaffeinated espresso.

You are a member of a new breed, cosmopolitan yet proudly provincial. Your outside world is wide, but here it is deep—here among the ten towns scattered throughout your valley. All of them, as well as the green and mystic open spaces that separate them, are yours. This is *your region*. You identify with every part of it—every mountain , forest, barber shop, and fire hydrant.

There is much to love here. Celebrating the vital community that rose and prospered here a century ago, a number of its buildings have been magnificently restored. Almost at the center of a great open space are two organic farms that supply produce to the local restaurants. In the same general area there is a ballet school, a music conservatory, some funky shops. Three monumental sculptures in brass, steel, and stone adorn the parking lot of the mag-lev train station. At 185 miles per hour you can be whisked away to the opera in New York or a computer fair in Chicago. (And you and your wife venture to the big city several times a year.) A new regional airport—almost completely hidden from nearby roads by clever landscaping—is a ten-minute subway ride away. But there isn't much need for the big cities. The other day you were chatting with some friends about the region's "best restaurants." Gourmet sandwiches and freshly squeezed carrot juice in one town, warm bread right out of the oven in another, best wines in the world in still another. Between all of them you aren't badly off. Not at all. Everyone agrees.

P.L.A.N.

The first organization you joined after arriving here seven years ago in 2003 was the local chapter of a new national organization called ***PLAN*, acronym for Penturbia League of Active Neighbors**.

One of P.L.A.N.'s many notices on the big wall in Harry's cafe caught your eye. "MAY 12, 2003—BIG DOINGS AT TILDEN MEADOW—POTLUCK DINNER FOR YOUNG AND OLD"

Your whole family went—you, Maia, her three children and your two. Everybody's kids took off in a flash to watch the volunteer jugglers, clowns, musicians and story-tellers. Pretty soon the action settled down to organizing the food and consuming it. Then came the meeting. People sat on a motley assortment of chairs, couches, and stools or cross-legged on cushions.

Chris Barker, a housing expert, who lives three houses south of you, was the featured speaker. His subject was Softbelts—A Revolutionary Approach to the Purchase and Use of Public Land. This is how you remembered it.

Softbelts

Go to any settled urban area. Measure the acreage owned by the public for purely public functions—streets, roads, freeways, rapid transit, parks, playgrounds, dams, disposal sites, schools, city halls. Don't even include land for open space. You'll find that the public owns roughly half of all the developed land.

It's also a fact that the public almost always buys its land in response to private developments. A farmer sells ten acres of land with frontage on a county road. Other people add some houses and a gasoline station. Soon there are more houses and maybe a shop or two. Within a few years, the roads are congested and the old country school is inadequate to serve the growing community. When the County Council gets daily phone calls from irate citizens, plans are made to buy land for new roads and schools. But it's very late in the process. The prices are high.

Along comes the Softbelt idea, and it's so simple it makes you smile. Don't *re-act*. Act. Buy all the public land now, enough for the next fifty years. Buy the full half the county will eventually own anyway. Buy pasture and meadow land *now* for five percent of its future worth.

You raised your hand. "If you buy land so far in advance," you asked, "how will you know how much and what kind of land to buy?"

"That's where the Softbelts come in," Barker said. The county acts like a retailer who invests in a stock of computers, knowing that sooner or later customers will appear. The county buys a stock of acres appropriate for a variety of uses and holds it until it's needed. The stock has to be flexible, not rigidly earmarked, because future uses are unpredictable.

This is the meaning of Softbelts. It's a county's inventory of *flexible* public land bought in advance of need. Flexibility also extends to county land already in use. Suppose a certain area has been designated for a park, but the park isn't being used. Perhaps that land would be far more useful as a vocational school or a civic center. It can be traded for another piece of land that is owned by the county. All county property would be tradeable: a school for a park, a park for a firehouse, a firehouse for a senior citizen center. Trades may even be made between public and private users. What must always be kept in mind is whether or not the trade is *beneficial to the region as a whole.*

The Parable of the Painting

Seeing the questions in our eyes, Barker responded with a story, the Parable of the Painting.

Imagine a painting executed by a Master Painter. It is a huge oil painting of a certain valley, not as it is now, but as it will be thirty years from now. It shows towns interlaced with farms, forests, a broad river, and surrounded by white-peaked mountains. The critics love it. But when the people who live in the valley see it they are extremely angry. What angers them about it is the evident lack of democracy. "We want a picture of *our* valley, not *yours*. You never consulted us. Live in it yourself if you want to. We want to paint ourselves into our own environment."

Now imagine a second attempt. A thousand citizens are invited to help paint the picture. The Master is allotted as many brush strokes as all the thousand painters put together, but his colors are limited to black and white. The thousand can paint in all the other colors—red, yellow, blue, and in any combination or intensity. The painting begins with each of the thousand dabbing a single colorful stroke on the canvas. Then comes the Master with his thousand strokes in black and white. The procedure is repeated again and again.

The painting quickly inclines towards incoherence. Blobs of color and form appear here and there. Some are interesting or beautiful in themselves, but there is no single conception pulling the pieces together. A number of the artists attempt to draw attention to their own efforts by using fluorescent colors and vulgar forms. The result begins to look like the work of a madman—disconnected and jarring. As time goes on, the picture becomes increasingly outrageous, crowded and muddled. Nobody likes it. The Master tries to introduce some semblance of beauty and organization into the picture. But because the other painters always take the lead, he continually fails.

A third attempt is made. *This time, the Master takes the lead.* He begins by laying out a few intriguing black and white outlines. But not without consultation. Still smarting from the criticisms of his first, "undemocratic" effort, he discusses his intentions and invites comments from the group. Then, in round after round, he acts first. All the other painters apply their colors in cunning and interesting patterns as an accompaniment. There are still some who violate the picture's integrity with wanton and raucus details. But by and large, *compelled by the logic of the Master's conception*, most willingly fit their contributions into the general scheme. Indeed, the citizen-painters point out to each other how much the Master's overall plan enhances their individual efforts. They see that their work is wasted when they do not pay attention to the overall plan and that they get the most gratifying results when they do.

Barker stressed a single point. How does the Master planner achieve his ability to lead penturbia's development? Not by buying private land, but by acquiring the public land it would have to buy eventually—*before* development occurs.

Many questions were raised. Wouldn't Softbelts assign too much power to government? Would Softbelts be constitutional? Where will rural counties get the money to finance the purchase of Softbelts?

Later...

It is now 2018. The questions asked have long since been answered by the flow of events. Looking back you see things in clearer perspective. To protect the environment and provide for a higher quality of life, local governments have assumed far more power than ever before. The Federal Government has long since conceded their priority. In a sweeping, historic decision, the Supreme Court voted 6 to 3 in favor of the widest application of the Softbelt concept. Senator Harold Tacker won a great legislative victory when he persuaded his colleagues in the U.S. Senate to vote for Federal loans and grants to finance Softbelt purchases.

Softbelts have become the central institution of penturbia, defining its shape and character. They have helped to preserve open spaces, historic structures, clean air and water. Several counties have merged into regional conglomerates. Having comprehensive control over their softbelts, it has been possible to maintain easy accessibility over a large region and to integrate many rural and urban functions. Indeed, Softbelts have become the favorite metaphor for the Caring Conserver's interweaving of public and private interests.

The next two chapters focus on private interests—*when as well as where to invest.*

Twenty-four

Invest: The season of depression is coming

The following fictional examination of an investment strategy is a composite of numerous actual conversations.

Investment Club: Our strategy for real estate investment is based on common sense. Buy when prices are rising; sell when they are falling. Be active on the market when the potential for profit is high, stay out when it vanishes. An ideal strategy, wouldn't you say?

Author: For the short-run, perhaps—if the objective is to take advantage of trends lasting for weeks, months or a few years. As the cycle veers towards the season of depression, your formula is a recipe for disaster. It's too risky to jump in and out of the real estate market.

Long-run real estate investments

Investment Club: Then you're interested only in long-run investments?

Author: If well chosen, long-run investments make the most sense. But they require patience. For the long-run my plan is the reverse of yours: Conduct your real estate investments during the season of depression. Buy during a deep depression. Sell during the subsequent boom. I can show you why this strategy is safest and most profitable.

Investment Club: Safest? You're advising us to go against the tide? To buy during a depression? I believe the word for that is *chutzpah.*

Author: Precisely. It's part of my three-fold strategy.

Investment Club: And that is. . . ?

Author: First, the best time to buy is during a low spot when the season of depression is well under way.That's a buyer's paradise: few competing buyers and many sellers.

Second, the best time to sell is during a subsequent boom within the same season, when prices are rising. That's a seller's paradise: few competing sellers and many buyers.

Third, the best places to invest will be carefully selected locations within penturbia. The worst places to invest are in suburbia, the region of obsolescence.

Investing in Chicago during the season of depression

Those who invested their savings in Chicago's real estate at the end of the devastating depression (1873–1878) earned remarkable profits. Even if they had chosen properties by throwing darts at a map—*blindfolded*—and even if they had sold during any at any time during the boom years 1880–1894 they would have earned, on the average, a gross return of *15 percent*![144] By contrast, stock yields ranged around 4.5 percent. And think of the possibilities for those who took off the blindfolds and chose locations carefully. During the period 1877–1894, twentyfold increases in land value were not at all uncommon within Chicago's commercial loop.[145]

Wayne County, Nebraska, 1873-1900

In 1990, Wayne County, Nebraska is a Class IV, rural

county. From 1873 to 1900, during the migration to the leading regions of the Colossus, this county enjoyed a brief moment as part of the nation's growing edge. It has been declining now for almost a century.

As before, the period from the preceding equinox (when the Colossus had barely overtaken the Bantam Capitalist) to the peak (of the Colossus) was a season of depression. (See Chapter 16.) Two serious depressions, 1873-1878 and 1893-1897, accompanied a general deflationary trend.

Nevertheless, land values in Wayne County climbed steadily.[146] Annual appreciation varied, in the main, between 7 and 11 percent. This made for exceptional returns during that unstable period. By comparison, stock yields fell from 7.02 percent in 1876 to less than 4.5 percent after 1885.

Instabilities during any season of depression create the volatility essential to profitable real estate investments. Just as pessimism during depression unduly depresses prices, optimism during the ensuing boom unduly inflates them. A suitable time to buy property in Wayne County was during the last years of the severe depression of 1873–1878. A suitable time to sell was during the subsequent boom of the late 1880s. That strategy would have returned an annual rate of at least 11 percent—high for those unstable years.

Wise and hardy souls who understood the inevitability of Wayne County's growth could easily have earned a 15-percent annual return on their investment. They could have bought almost any random property in 1880 or 1881 and sold any time during the subsequent boom. They would have profited by more than three times the return received by common stockholders. Carefully chosen locations—those having unusual fertility, accessibility to railroad marshalling yards, or proximity to towns and villages—could have yielded much greater returns.

Twenty-five

Parting words

In the 1940s invincible competition from the Thrifty Drug chain in Los Angeles closed two of my father's stores, depleted his capital, punctured his self-confidence, and made him a Thrifty employee. Until he retired, my father filled their prescriptions, sold their toys and nylon stockings and gave thanks for the medical insurance that came with the job. No longer did he scour the classified ads for great real estate buys. Instead, he spent hours with his old crony, Shomstein, reminiscing about bygone adventures in real estate—their past triumphs and near-misses.

When he drove through Hollywood in his 1937 Chevy he would occasionally slow down near the corner of Gower and Sunset Boulevard: "See that drug store? It's the main hang-out of Western bit players. Could have bought it for $7,500 down. Today..." He would lift his shoulders in a gesture that mixed past glories and present defeats. It was the same with an old mansion near the intersection of Wilshire and Western. A thousand dollars down would have captured that prize. "So what can I do? Those days are gone forever."

Yes, those days *are* gone forever, but the era of rising prices lasted far longer than he could have imagined. He died in 1952. Had he lived into the 1960s he would have been amazed at the heights to which prices had climbed in Los Angeles.

In the 1990s the new leading region is as burgeoning with promise as Los Angeles was in the 1940s. To help the investor recognize opportunities and avoid pitfalls, I offer some final words of caution and advice.

Do not count on inflation for capital gains in real estate

In the late 1970s inflation was predictable and bankable. From 1975 to 1980 the general price level flew up anywhere from 5.8 to 13.5 percent a year. Real estate was never far behind and often ahead.

Inflation was the explosive force wired into every investment strategy. "Mavens" urged, "Get your money into real estate as quickly as possible." Leaving money in the bank was to see it wither away. And the faster people spent their money on real estate—and everything else that caught their fancy—the more rapidly inflation progressed. In Los Angeles it was not unusual in 1979 to overhear any neighbor at the next table in any restaurant along Wilshire Boulevard say, something like: "It was a steal at $98,500. By the time I finish putting a coat of paint on it, it'll sell for $125,000."

But as we made a transition to the economy of the Caring Conserver, conditions changed. (See Chapter 12.) The inflationary spiral created by the preceding socioeconomy had at last become intolerable. The American public was ready for strong action. At the time of this writing, the Fed has put the fight against inflation above every other policy objective.

Do not base real estate investments on metropolitan growth

Seeing adjoining metropolitan areas grow and more growth filling the corridors between them, we easily visualize massive urban consolidations. Because metropolitan growth is being increasingly arrested by the migration to penturbia, investments in metropolitan areas should be considered high risk. On the other hand, an area likely to be designated as metropolitan should not necessarily be ruled out. Howard County, between Washington, D.C. and Baltimore—rated V—may yet develop into an authentic penturb.

Determine the reasons for a county's growth in the 1970s

The major reason for growth should be an abundance of resources attractive to the emerging socioeconomy. Be wary of a county whose growth depends upon a very few large companies or government agencies.

Although growth patterns provide the basis for initial screening, it is essential to broaden the inquiry. Make first-hand explorations. When you come to an area to interview for a job or to start a business, take time to talk to recent migrants. Find out what drew them to this area rather than to any other. Do those original attractions still hold? Does the county still seem beautiful, peaceful, friendly, unpolluted, safe? How does this area compare with others in which they have lived? To what extent are they pleased to have made the move? Has the new area improved or deteriorated in its ability to meet their needs?

On military bases

Plans to construct a military base provide an illustration of a *wrong* reason to invest. Say the army announces that it is going to locate a new base for satellite research in County X. Immediately—like prospectors thronging into the gold fields on news of a strike—investors rush to buy. The lucky ones buy cheaply and realize some short-term gains, but they must beat the *insiders* who were first to get wind of the plan. They must also contend with long-time resident-owners now convinced of an unrealistically bountiful future.

Another factor adds to the risk: What the army gives, it can also take away. The billion dollar program funding the base in Xanadu County is part of one president's strategy for the defense of the country, but an opponent in the next election may vow to dismantle the program. If the opponent is elected, and if the base is in fact dismantled, property values will fall as quickly as they rose.

Start investigations with the county unit

After you isolate a favorable county, divide it into smaller areas. Counties are never uniform throughout their domain. If a county is classified as "obsolete," that condition is likely to prevail throughout much of it. But there may also be portions which are not representative of the county as a whole.

The potential of an individual census tract (compared to that of the county as a whole), can be roughly estimated by rates of growth from 1960 to 1980. Promising tracts—those that show unusual growth after 1970—should be examined further. Seek interviews with local real estate agents, businessmen and residents, and based on the analyses of Part III, make tentative classifications. Does the accumulated evidence show this part of the county as typical of the class of the county as a whole? In which direction does it differ? Does it show the characteristics of a promising Class I or II county? Or does it suggest maximum risk, as in a Class VI county?

Investigate attitudes towards planning

To confirm a county's suitability for your purposes, inquire into the record of past and present planning programs. Interview analysts in the county's planning department and, if possible, planning commissioners. Request copies of the latest master plan, building and zoning codes. Examine minutes covering recent meetings of the planning commission. Find articles in the local newspapers dealing with current land-use issues.

Does this county demonstrate a willingness to support a high level of planning activity? For without that support, a county's standing may be seriously compromised.

Do not confuse industrial recruitment with comprehensive planning

Restoration of old industrial cities—like Youngstown,

Fort Wayne, or Detroit—cannot be guaranteed by even the most spirited efforts to attract new industries. A complex of adverse factors inherited from the past cannot be dismissed at the will of a local Chamber of Commerce. My theory dictates that many decades are likely to intervene before an obsolete or obsolescing area will prove useful to an emerging socioeconomy. Though exceptions do exist, extreme caution is recommended.

Avoid inflexible planning

Avoid states and counties where "planning" attempts to lock in obsolete patterns. Consider Oregon. In 1973 this verdant state enacted Senate Bill 100 to protect its forests and farm land from urban encroachment—a helter-skelter and capricious growth reminiscent of Los Angeles and other large metropolitan areas. "Keep the barbarian developers at bay," argued the bill's proponents, "we want both cities and countryside. But we don't want a chaotic mongrelization of the two. Let them be equal but separate."

Motivated by rising sentiment against unplanned growth, Oregon legislators created a kind of fortress wall around its cities. Urban migrants to Oregon were enjoined to locate on land *inside* the wall. Those aspiring to locate *outside* the wall had better be prepared to farm, mine, or grow forests. But those boundaries, hardened by legislation, were created by now-defunct socioeconomies. They are no longer relevant. Today we need to develop a very different type of regional city, the penturban interlacing of small settlements and open spaces that balances growth and high-quality environments.

Coordinate investment and career decisions.

Investments, like careers, should develop and grow increasingly profitable over many years. Ideally, investment decisions should be made at the same time as career decision.

Say you are offered two positions. One is in Boise, Idaho and the other in Oakland, California. In Boise you are within commuting distance of Ada, Canyon, Boise, Elmore and Gem counties. In Oakland, you are within commuting distance of Contra Costa, San Francisco, Solano and San Mateo Counties. Appendix A reveals that the Boise location offers superior advantages for long-run investments.

Choose improved real estate for current income

Real-estate improvements such as stores and houses bring income which can offset current costs and also offer a degree of tax shelter. A strategic purchase made near the end of a depression (see Chapter 24) needs to be buttressed by current income. That income will help insure against the risk of foreclosure due to the involuntary loss of a job or business. The plan is to weather all storms until the next boom.

And finally...

Prepare for an era of turbulent adjustment. You are about to witness the surrender of one socioeconomy and the victory of another. You'll discover increasing numbers of migrants leaving metropolitan areas to create a new kind of life in the fifth leading region. You'll encounter an economic winter generated by immense upheavals. But do not be deceived by the negative aura surrounding depression. It will be a time of challenge—and perhaps of pilgrimage.

Reader: I sense that we're coming to the end of your book. What is the essence of your advice for practical decision-making.

Author: Remember two themes for the 1990s that run through the whole book: social responsibility and private interest.

As the fifth socioeconomy emerges we see these two themes in a new light. For over two centuries we have been taught to tend our own self-interest, to let Adam Smith's *invisible hand* translate private incentives into public well-being. That attitude is obsolete and must be set aside. Contemplate the public interest. Tend the public interest. In the coming decades, you will be most successful culti-

vating your private and public gardens with equal vigor. Make the invisible hand visible by your conscious efforts to improve your community, your nation, your economy, your world.

Reader: I'm curious about one more thing. What do you see as the most enduring contribution of your book?

Author: The basic principle of socioeconomics—that at any time, conflicting trends belonging to *the* society and *the* economy can be separated into two overlapping and opposing socioeconomies, one rising, the other falling. Both are ever-present. Both are ever-changing.

Epilogue

Socioeconomics versus economics

Every exit is an entry somewhere else.

Tom Stoppard (1967)

Cycles in history*

Author: You and I both started out in economics over forty years ago. We studied at the same school, read the same books, heard the same lectures, were caught up in the same intellectual winds. Then we parted ways. I'm curious to know your reaction to my book.

Economist: I simply cannot reconcile your ideas with the teachings of economics, or social science, or history, or even common sense.

Author: I suppose it's my socioeconomies that you find so troublesome—the Little King, the Caring Conserver, and the others.

Continuous vs discontinuous history

Economist: Ah. The Little King, the Caring Conserver. You tell us that your socioeconomies are cycles, that each begins, develops, peaks and declines, after which it is finished, done with, kaput.

---

* In portions of this debate I quote anthropologist A.R. Radcliffe-Browne, historian Richard Jenkyns, economist Leonard Silk, and at the 1989 annual meeting of the American Economic Association, Nobel prize-winning economists Herbert Simon and Kenneth Arrow. For readability each is identified by reference note rather than in the text.

Author: Socioeconomic cycles are at the heart of my theory.

Economist: I see that quite clearly. What I do not see is the cordoning off of history into chunks that are nearly free-standing. In my view, all "periods are artificial concepts. They are used as a convenience in teaching or exposition...."[147] To speak of epochs and eras is nothing new, but it is understood that their timing is not absolute. One historian approximates an epoch from 1820 to 1860, another from 1840 to 1900.

Author: You will concede, will you not, that the United States of today is a very different kettle of fish from the United States of one hundred years ago.

Economist: Certainly. But that misses the point. Call the U.S. of 100 years ago "A" and the U.S. of today, "B." The change from A to B is gradual, evolving as it always has—by adding, subtracting, changing with every tick of the clock. At which month or year does the change come? "I would say it does not come precisely anywhere. Where you draw the line is more or less arbitrary. You are facing the same problem always in all history of social development."[148] *Evolution is continuous.* Economists, social scientists and historians are in full agreement on this.

Author: I do not join that agreement. Socioeconomic cycles begin and end at precise times. In my view *continuous evolution is an illusion*, a magician's sleight of hand.

Economist: I would have sworn it was the other way around, that socioeconomic cycles were the illusion.

Author: What appears to you as a seamless progression is actually the *overlapping of two socio-economies*. You look for the consistency and uniformity that tells us we're in a distinctive period, and you don't find it. Why not? Because you're always seeing two socioeconomies at the same time. There is no moment that is not a combination of

both, one rising, the other falling.

An illustration of overlap

The Colossus	1846__________1958		
The Little King		1900___________2020?	
The Caring Conserver			1958__________2070?

Two socioeconomies overlap, never three. When the Colossus died, the Caring Conserver was born. One day the Little King will die, and a new socioeconomy will be born, one that is completely unknown at this time. Without understanding the nature of overlap there is no hope of understanding my theory. *Two contrary movements camouflage each other—one rising the other falling.*

Perishability

Economist: I can understand the perishing of individuals, corporations, even institutions. But a socioeconomy? I see people working, cities standing, industries producing, Congress meeting. With so much that is living and lasting, what's perishing?

The rules perish

Author: What's perishing is a set of rules, like the rules of a game. Imagine we have a deck of cards on the table and we invite friends to play poker or bridge. Each game will have its own rules. Suppose we play poker first, then bridge. Physically, the cards are the same. But when we go from poker to bridge, the *meaning* of every card is transformed. A ten of diamonds means one thing in bridge and another in poker. One game perishes and another begins.

Economist: And you see a parallel between a socioeconomy and a poker game.

Like a poker game

Author: The "cards" are the people, industries and cities which you said were "still standing." When the rules change, those structural elements do not disappear but come to have an entirely different meaning. Structures created by one socioeconomy are junk to another. When that happens, they either disappear or find new uses. A warehouse no longer serviceable to the Colossus may succeed as a restaurant or an art gallery of the Little King. A suburban rambler built by the Little King may become low-income apartments of the Caring Conserver.

Economist: Now show me how the rules of poker are like the rules of a socioeconomy.

Author: In poker, the rules regulate how we compete, how we value each card, and how those values determine a winning hand. In a socioeconomy too, there are rules regulating how we compete for goods and services, how we determine their values, and how we calculate winning positions.

Examples.

Unique rules regulating competition for goods and services:
Accelerated by F.D.R's New Deal, the Little King rewrote the rules governing competition between Big Business and Big Labor. The effect was to deal labor a better hand.

Unique values of a socioeconomy's goods and services:
The Colossus gave high value to the city and low value to the suburbs. The Little King reversed that priority.

Unique ways to calculate winning positions:
During the Colossus you won admiration for your hard work and thrift. As a Little King, you won it for your leisure and an ability to spend.

However divergent, all of these rules arise from one and only one source.

Economist: And that source?

Mindset

Author: Mindset is the body of assumptions and convictions—heavily freighted with emotion—that we adopt in common. It is the shared mental climate that converts us to members of a specific socioeconomy. (See Chapters 4 and 9.) Every socioeconomy is governed by a unique mindset.

Economist: But you say there are two socioeconomies, two sets of rules, two mindsets. Do you not find this confusing? How can you tell them apart?

Author: By their opposition. The Little King extols the *short run*. That is the mindset urging us to get-it-now-and-forget-the-future. The Caring Conserver promotes responsibility for the *long run*, exhorting us to save capital, the environment, infrastructure, our fellow humans—to *plan* for the future.

Economist: Strange, isn't it, that the two are so conveniently opposed to one another?

Natural opposition

Author: Not strange at all. Nothing could be more natural. The two are problem and solution. Each socioeconomy develops to excess (that's the problem). The next socioeconomy is the corrective (that's the solution). (See Chapter 9.) The Colossus, intent on production, eventually overproduced. (See Chapter 12.) The Little King, intent on consumption, was the corrective. (See Chapter 13.) Each emerging socioeconomy becomes the special vehicle to overcome the excesses of its predecessor. That's why there must always be two.

Economist: And the "solution," I suppose, corresponds to the rise of a new socioeconomy.

The mandate

Author: Precisely. The new socioeconomy appears as a mandate to correct the excesses of the preceding socioeconomy.

Economist: All right. Now let me show you where you're wrong. This mandate you speak of, at what point does it occur? I expect it does not come in any one month or year.

Author: But it does. The mandate to end excesses of the preceding socioeconomy is like an embryo. At one precise moment, the moment of conception, the embryo possesses *100 percent of all the genetic individuality it will ever have.* That individuality is inscribed in its DNA and governs every inherited characteristic of the developing individual. Subsequent development will not be haphazard but the creative unfolding of potentials inherent at the moment of conception.

Economist: What is that moment of conception for a socioeconomy?

Author: When the new mindset is formed under the compulsion of accumulating excesses. It all comes down to mindset. The DNA of the socioeconomy is a unique mindset.

Economist: Ah. I see that mindset is the centerpiece of your theory. It identifies unique socioeconomies and determines their economic consequences. The term socioeconomics derives from the central role of socioeconomies.

Author: Hallelujah, I am completely understood.

Understanding is not enough

Economist: I understand you, but you may not find the economics profession ready to graft mindset onto the tree of economic theory.

Author: Why not?

Economist: You might say that mindset is beyond the pale of economics. We leave such things to sociologists, anthropologists and historians. They are directly concerned with society, we are not—except insofar as society is the sum of rational individuals looking out for Number One.[149] Our province has always been the rational behavior of individuals—unmind-setted if you will.

Author: Without mindset, socioeconomies do not exist.

Economist: And without mindset history is once again the continuous evolution that economists assume.

Author: At least we've narrowed our disagreement. The issue is mindset. Without it, evolution is continuous; with it, evolution is *dis*-continuous, a succession of overlapping socio-economies.

Winds of reform

Economist: Please don't imagine that economists seal themselves off from change, even in the fundamentals. Nor are we indifferent to the shortcomings of economic theory. At the 1989 meetings of the American Economic Association one outstanding member discussed experiments made by cognitive psychologists who "...had found systematic kinds of bias...strongly contradicting the economists' assumption of rational behavior."[150] I suppose you think mindset could illuminate that "systematic bias."

Author: I do. In the real world, whether recognized or not, economic decisions depend on rationality *and* mindset. That pair is as inextricably linked as hydrogen and oxygen in molecules of water. To exclude mindset is to waste an immense bank of organized information seeping into the decisions of millions of separate, rational individuals.

A scientific theory must be testable

Economist: I'd be more inclined to accept mindset if it were subject to thorough scientific testing. Inadequate testing of theory is the cardinal sin of science. At the 1989 meetings the profession itself was indicted for that sin. "When theories and facts are in conflict," said one of the Association's luminaries, "the theories must yield. Economics has strayed from that simple principle, and it must return to it."[151] So I ask, can your theory be tested by the facts?

Author: The theory makes innumerable inferences to social and economic facts which can be checked. Here are just a few:

- Rising and falling socioeconomies must follow an exact and invariable sequence.
- Development of each socioeconomy must be traceable to a single mindset.
- Every socioeconomy develops step-by-step to its peak integration at which time the preceding socioeconomic cycle comes to an end and another begins.
- Two overlapping mindsets must be in opposition.
- The opposition of mindsets is always an attempt to solve an insoluble problem, one that is traceable to excesses of the previous socioeconomy.
- A major migration and a season of depression begins during the rise of a new socioeconomy.
- The target of migration—a new leading region—is selected by virtue of its serviceability to the emerging mindset.

Economist: And the tests you've made, you're satisfied with them?

Author: There can never be enough testing, and I wholeheartedly welcome others to join me. But I have studied five cycles since the 1730s and have found considerable supporting evidence. To record the progressive unfolding of each socioeconomy, I've made decade-by-decade analyses of demographic as well as historical facts. I've also tracked decade-by-decade shifts in mindset as revealed in speeches, laws, literature, art and music. What convinces me is the gradual rise of one socioeconomy in each successive decade, and the accompanying fall of another. That progression is entirely visible and can be verified.

Public policy

Economist: The ultimate meaning of any theory lies in what it portends for public policy. How would socioeconomics differ from economics in its use of taxing and spending policies?

Author: In their taxing and spending policies, economists too often act like Little Kings. In this respect they are part of the problem rather than the solution. In the 1980s politicians collaborated with economists to postpone recession. But they did it by outrageous deficit spending. They reduced taxes and increased spending at the same time. Recession was further postponed by granting a combination of tax advantages and generous credit terms that encouraged corporations and individuals to assume enormous debts. The great Keynes himself would have blanched at that much red ink.

Economist: Don't you think it was important to postpone recession? Think of the millions all over the world who were benefitted. Their incomes would have been lower, many would have lost their jobs.

Author: We postponed recession by encouraging the Little King to linger a little longer, and that was detrimental to our future. The cost was far too high. It is Little Kings who waste our capital. It is Little Kings who lose our technological edge. It is Little Kings who give our children mediocre educations. It is Little Kings who abuse our environment. And it is Little Kings who would spoil penturbia. I say cut the bonds. The longer we wait, the greater the damage. Make the transition to the Caring Conserver as quickly as possible.

Economist: Your theories and policies are a radical departure from traditional economics. Socioeconomics will have to slug it out in the marketplace of ideas.

Author: It will indeed.

Addendum

Notes

1. Grateful acknowledgment is made to *The New York Times*, for permission to quote from William Safire's article of September 25, 1989.
2. Ibid.
3. Called "regions of opportunity" in *Regions of Opportunity*.
4. Unless otherwise indicated, the U.S. Bureau of the Census is the source for all population data, 1790–1980; data on 1790–1960 were assembled from historical tables in the 1900 and 1930 census volumes as well as from *Population Abstract of the United States*, ed. John L. Androit (McLean, VA: Androit Associates, 1980). County populations on July 1, 1988 were obtained from *County Population Estimates: July 1, 1986, 1987, and 1988 and Series* P-26, No. 88-A (Washington, D.C.: USDC, Bureau of the Census, August 1989).

   Unless otherwise indicated, all diagrams and tables not pertaining to county and city populations were derived from *Historical Statistics of the United States: Colonial Times to 1970*, Bicentennial Edition, Parts 1 and 2 (Washington, DC: USDC, Bureau of the Census, 1975) (*H.S.*) and updates in later *Statistical Abstracts of the United States* (Washington, DC: USDC, Bureau of the Census) *(S.A.)*.
5. "The Determination of Land Use in Rural-Urban Transition Areas: A Case Study in Northern Santa Clara Valley," Ph.D. diss., University of California, 1956.
6. [To avoid cyclical implications, Simon Kuznets named the periodic international migrations he discovered, Long Swings, rather than Long Cycles.]
7. Jack Beatty, "Brigadoon, USA," *World Monitor*, September, 1989, p. 103.
8. September 23, 1989, p. 69.
9. Ibid.

10. "Many Caught in Housing Crunch," *Seattle Times*, August 1, 1989.
11. Scott Armstrong, "Study Finds More Poor in Los Angeles," *The Christian Science Monitor*, June 21, 1989.
12. [In 1980, blacks and hispanics alone accounted for 48.75% of the L.A. County population.]
13. Ibid.
14. Dirk Johnson, "As Inner-Ccity Areas Decay, Blacks Flee to Small Towns," *The New York Times*, December 4, 1989.
15. Ibid.
16. Ibid.
17. *S.A.*
18. Total households in 1986: 88,458,000, (*S.A.*)
    Total 1986 population: 241,078,000, (*S.A.*)
    Population per household: 2.7.
    Per capita money income in 1986: 11,670, (*S.A.*)
    Income per household: 11,670 * 2.7= 31,509.
    Total households in 1950: 43,554,000, (*H.S*)
    Total 1950 population: 150,697,361. (*H.S.*)
    Population per household: 150,697,361/43,554,000= 3.46
    Income per household: 1491 * 3.46= $5158.
19. [Median values of new homes-- 7,400 in 1950 (*S.A.*) and 80,300 in 1986 (*S.A.*) Part of the increase is due to larger, better construction.]
20. *County and City Data Book*, 1988. [Benton County is Class V, borderline penturban.]
21. James B. Treece, "Here Comes GM's Saturn: More Than a Car, It Is GM's Hope for Reinventing Itself," *Business Week*, April 9, 1990, p. 57.
22. Ibid, p. 62.
23. Marilyn Hoffman, "Home Is Where the Office Is," *The Christian Science Monitor*, June 20, 1989.
24. Paul Edwards, *Working From Home* (Jeremy P. Tarcher Inc., Los Angeles, 1987). Cited by John Edwards, *MacWeek*, November, 22, 1988.
25. Cynthia Furlong Reynolds, "Goodbye City, Hello Country Life," *The Christian Science Monitor,* January 1, 1989.
26. [Broken Bow is in Custer County, Class IIIA, potential

penturbia.]
27. Sue Shellenbarger, "Country Soil Fertile for Small Business," *The Wall Street Journal*, September 8, 1989.
28. Susan Benner, *Inc*, September, 1982.
29. *Seattle Times*, July 3, 1983.
30. David DeVoss, “Penturbia: The New Great Migration,” *Los Angeles Times*, October 25, 1987, Part VI.
31. Larry Bensky, "Little Big One," *The Nation*, November 13, 1989, p. 553.
32. Robert C. Wood, *1400 Government* (1961; New York: Anchor, 1964) p. 1
33. Cited by Neal Peirce and Curtis W. Johnson in the "The Peirce Report," *Seattle Times*, 1989.
34. Frederick Lewis Allen, *Only Yesterday* (New York: Harper & Row, 1959) p. 135.
35. Ivan Illich, cited in *Utne Reader*, Nov-Dec. 1989, p. 90.
36. Peter T. Kilborn, *The New York Times*, July 20, 1989.
37. Howard Gleckman et al., "The Quiet Crusader," *Business Week,* September 18, 1989, p. 81.
38. Ibid.
39. Joan C. Scabo, "Our Crumbling Infrastructure," *Nation's Business*, August, 1989m, p. 16.
40. "Economic Scene; the Changes Forced by Deficits," *The New York Times*, October 27, 1989.
41. Brad Kessler, "Down and Out in Suburbia," *The Nation*, September 15, 1989, p.312.
42. Linda Keene, "Region's Future Linked to the Hero in All of Us," *Seattle Times*, June 13, 1989.
43. Richard L. Berke, "Oratory of Eenvironmentalism Becomes the Sound of Politics," *New York Times*, April 17, 1990.
44. *The Christian Science Monitor*, October 23, 1989.
45. [“Conglomerate municipalities” suggested by Natalie Lessinger.]
46. Daniel Yankelovich, “New Rules in American Life: Searching for Self-fulfillment in a World Turned Upside Down,” *Psychology Today*, April 1981.
47. *Seattle Times*, July 3, 1983.
48. [Some studies have shown that even excluding farmers and others working at home, work trips in nonmetro coun-

ties are 40 percent shorter on the average.]
49. Interview with Gail Appel, Catskill, N.Y., April, 1988.
50. Herb Robinson, "A Dissent from Part of Peirce Report," *Seattle Times / Seattle Post Intelligencer*, October 8, 1989.
51. [Estimate based on 357 acres required for 6.9 miles of I-90 in Seattle (51.7 acres/mile)].
52. Scott Armstrong, "US Watches California's Smog Plan," *The Christian Science Monitor*, June 16, 1989.
53. Neal Peirce and Curtis W. Johnson, "The Peirce Report; 4. No One's in Charge," *Seattle Times*, October 4, 1989.
54. John Kenneth Galbraith, "The Ultimate Scandal," *The New York Review of Books*, January 18, 1990, p. 15.
55. National Association of Realtors, Washington, DC, *Existing Home Sales.*
56. Cited by Eric Schmitt.
57. N. Gregory Mankiw and David N. Weil, *Regional Science and Urban Economics*, May 1989.
58. [The study by Mankiw and Weil took other factors into account, but by means of regression analysis, a methodology which, in my view, makes questionable assumptions.]
59. [Purchasing power of the dollar, *S.A.*, 1988. Population numbers 25-34 , *S.A.* and *H.S.*. Home Prices, *S.A.*, 1960 and 1988.]
60. Nancy Miller, "Housing Starts at Lowest Level since 1982," *USA Today*, May 17, 1990.
61. Source: Federal Deposit Insurance Corp. Cited by Roger Lowenstein in "Real Estate Loans May Loom as the Next Threat to the Banks," *Wall Street Journal*, December 13, 1989.
62. John Meehan, "Suddenly, All this Terra Doesn't Feel so Firma," *Business Week*, October 23, 1989, p. 64.
63. [The names are fictional.]
64. William Celis, III, op.cit.
65. Richard W. Stevenson, "Where Savings Crisis Hits Hard," *The New York Times,* January 16, 1990.
66. Roger Lowenstein, "Leveraged Optimism, a Key to the '80s, Is Giving Way to Conservative Investing," *The Wall Street Journal*, December 29, 1989.

67. John Steinbeck, *The Red Pony* (New York: Viking, 1945) p. 130.
68. [The recommended method for future determinations would involve testing every decade as a potential peak.]
69. [Later refinements may include definitions of economic spring and autumn.]
70. Letter to Thomas Cooper, September 10, 1814; reprinted in Martin A. Larson, *Jefferson, Magnificent Populist* (Greenwich, CT: Devin-Adair, 1984) p. 46.
71. Roy Porter, *English Society in the Eighteenth Century* (New York: Penguin, 1982) pp. 222–224.
72. Letter to William Short, January 8, 1825, Larson, op. cit., p. 116.
73. Debates of the Federal Convention, June 18, 1787.
74. Letter to Colonel Arthur Campbell, September 1, 1797, Larson, op. cit. p. 119.
75. [*Regions of Opportunity* based the first region primarily on North and South Carolina. Review of the data suggested that, while population changes in the other colonies were not entirely synchronous with those of the Carolinas, their rise and fall was controlled by the same socioeconomic cycle.]
76. [Since county population data were not available in the period before 1790, the first region of migration is roughly approximated by data on all of North and South Carolina.]
77. Otto C. Lightner, *The History of Business Depressions* (1922; New York: Burt Franklin, 1970) p. 48.
78. Ibid.
79. Ibid.
80. Ibid., p. 91.

* While 1790 was the approximate beginning of the season of prosperity and the birth of the new socioeconomy, 1789 seems more appropriate— not only because it was the year of the French Revolution but also because it was the inaugural year of the American republic.

81. Adam Smith, *The Wealth of Nations* (1776: New York: Modern Library, 1937).
82. Ibid., p. 364.
83. Letter to Colonel Arthur Campbell, September 1, 1797, Larson, op. cit., p. 119.

84. Letter to Colonel Arthur Campbell, op. cit., p. 119.
85. Talbot Hamlin, *Greek-Revival Architecture in America* (New York: Oxford, 1944).
86. Allan Nevins, ed. *American Social History as Recorded by British Travellers* (New York: Henry Holt, 1923) pp. 5–6.
87. William Cobbett, in Nevins, ibid., p. 91.
88. Charles M. Wiltse, *The New Nation* (New York: Hill and Wang, 1961) p. 143.
89. Charles Augustus Murray, *Travels in North America* (London: 1839) pp. 155-6.
90. Reference lost.
91. Niles National Register.
92. Marvin Meyers, *The Jacksonian Persuasion, Politics and Belief* (New York: Vintage, 1957) pp. 20–21.
93. Ibid., pp. 253–254.
94. [No doubt, some counties of New York should have been included in the first migration.]
95. [States such as Illinois, Missouri and Arkansas partially figured in the second migration, but were omitted. The included states are more likely to yield a representative sample of the second migration. It is possible that the actual peak in the 1840s was greater than 50 percent.]
96. *Economic History of the United States* (New York: Ronald, 1955).
97. Speech on American Industry in the House of Representatives. March 30 and 31 in *State Papers and Speeches on the Tariff*, ed. Frank W. Taussig (Cambridge: Harvard,1893) p. 254.
98. *The Economic Growth of the United States, 1790-1860* (New York: W.W. Norton, 1966) p.190.
99. Alexis de Tocqueville, *Journey to America* (1832; New Haven: Yale, 1962)
100. Ibid.
101. John K. Winkler, *Morgan the Magnificent* (New York: Doubleday, Doran, 1932) p. 311.
102. John Tipple, "The Robber Baron in the Gilded Age, Entrepreneur or Iconoclast?" *The Gilded Age: A Reappraisal*, ed. H.Wayne Morgan (Syracuse: Syracuse, 1963) p. 16.
103. Ibid., p. 403.

104. [See note 68.]
105. *H.S.*
106. "Wealth," *North American Review*, June, 1889.
107. Russell Baker, *The Good Times* (New York: William Morrow, 1989) p.253.
108. [1931-1970,*H.S.*, Series H 972 multiplied by .95 to splice to series on "Murder" in *S.A.* 1977-1986.]
109. [My theory predicts that penturbia's peak share may occur from the socioeconomy's peak integration to the end of its season of prosperity.]
110. Cited by Scott Donaldson, *The Suburban Myth* (New York: Columbia, 1969) p.70.
111. [The description of Levitt's operations is based on William Manchester, *The Glory and the Dream* (New York: Little, Brown, 1973) p. 528.]
112. Ibid.
113. *The Christian Science Monitor*, April 4, 1978.
114. *U.S. News and World Report,* March 12, 1984.
115. *Fortune*, December 15, 1980.
116. *Ladies' Home Journal*, February 1978.
117. *U.S. News*, April 8, 1974.
118. *New York Times Magazine*, March 15, 1980.
119. Ibid.
120. *The Wall Street Journal,* May 14, 1976.
121. Ibid.
122. [While evidence for the theory of socioeconomic cycles is drawn primarily from American experience, it is tempting to note worldwide parallels. The European "revolution" of 1989 was a year crowded with major events—the assassination of a Romanian dictator, the booting out of long-established Communist parties, the tearing down of the Berlin Wall, the unification of Germany, and the end of the Cold War.

Actually, those events culminated a consumer-oriented socioeconomic cycle occuring in the late 1950s at almost precisely the same time a parallel cycle was taking place in America. During the brief Communist "thaw" under Nikita Khruschev, a number of Soviet intellectuals—including Mikhail Gorbachev—worked quietly on dreams and plans for reform. One of the leaders of that group, a young economist named Abel Agenbegyan, began every evening meal with a toast: "We shall outlive them.." According to Tatyana Zaslavskaya, one of Agenbegyan's associates, "We all led double lives, not only scholars but a few progressive-minded politicans like Gorbachev..." (David Remnick, "Gorbachev's Reforms Were Born in the '60s," *The Seattle Times / Seattle Post-Intelligencer*, February 18, 1990.)]

123. Wallace F. Smith, *Urban Development, The Process and Problems (*Berkeley: University of California, 1975) p.1.
124. Calvin L. Beale, *The Revival of Population Growth in Non-metropolitan America* (Economic Development Division, Economic Research Service, U.S. Department of Agriculture, June 1975, ERS-605).
125. C. Jack Tucker, "Changing Patterns of Migration between Metropolitan and Nonmetropolitan Areas in the United States: Recent Evidence," *Demography,* November 1976; Peter A. Morrison, "Rural Renaissance in America? The Revival of Population Growth in Remote Areas," *Population Bulletin (Washington, DC: Population Reference Bureau, 1976);* Peter A. Morrison, *Current Demographic Change in Regions of the United States* (Rand Paper Series, November 1977); George Sternlieb and James W. Hughes, "New Regional and Metropolitan Realities of America," *Journal of the American Institute of Planners,* July 1977, pp. 227–41; Curtis C. Roseman, *Changing Migration Patterns within the United States* (Washington, DC: Association of American Geographers, 1977); John M. Wardell, "Equilibrium and Change in Nonmetropolitan Growth," *Rural Sociology,* Summer 1977, pp. 156-79.
126. *Newsweek,* July 6, 1981, p.26.
127. Leonard Silk, "Economic Scene; Reality's the Thing this Field Needs," *The New York Times*, December 29, 1989.
128. *The New York Times*, June 26, 1990.
129. Michael Cosgrove, "Foreigners Slap $660 Billion into US," *The Christian Science Monitor*, November 21, 1989.

* Deutsche Bank, cited in *The New York Times*, December 21, 1989.

130. Urban C. Lehner, "Japanese May Be Rich, but Are They Satisfied with Quality of Life?" *The Wall Street Journal*, 1990.
131. *The Japan Times Weekly International Edition*, May 28–June 3, 1990, p. 17.
132. James Sterngold, "Well, How Much Golf Is too Much at that Crowded Clubhouse Japan?" *The New York Times International*, April 16, 1990.
133. Floyd Norris, "Market Place; Why Japan Likes Lower U.S. Rates," *The New York Times*, November 10, 1989.
134. Daniel B. Wood, "Television: Is the Audience Shrinking?" *The Christian Science Monitor*, June 4, 1990.
135. Council of Economic Advisors, *Economic Report of the President 1987*, Washington D.C.
136. Takamitsu Sawa, "A Keynes for 1990s Needed," *The Japan Times Weekly International Edition*, May 28–June 3, 1990, p. 9.
137. "Japanese Property," *The Economist*, October 3, 1987.
138. Angus Maddison, *The World Economy in the 20th Century* (OECD, 1989). Cited by Robert L. Bartley, "The Great International Growth Slowdown," *The Wall Street Journal*, July 10, 1990.
139. Manchester, op.cit., p. 91.
140. Ibid.
141. William Fulton, "Can Anything Stop Los Angeles?" *The Wall Street Journal*, May 8, 1990.
142. Nancy Herndon, "Local Land Trusts Flex New Muscle," *The Christian Science Monitor*, June 7, 1989.
143. Land Trust Exchange.
144. Homer Hoyt, *One Hundred Years of Land Values in Chicago* (Chicago: University of Chicago, 1933) Table LXXX, p. 470.
145. Ibid., pp. 345–346.
146. James A. Stone, "Disposition of the Public Domain in Wayne County," M.A. thesis, University of Nebraska, 1952, Table XXIII ("Yearly Average Price of Land Sold by State, Railroads, and Large Land Holders").
147. Richard Jenkyns, *The Victorians and Ancient Greece* (Cambridge: Harvard, 1980).

148. A.R. Radcliffe-Browne, cited in *Social Change: Explorations, Diagnoses and Conjectures*, George K. Zollschan and Walter Hirsch ed. (New York: John Wiley & Sons, 1976) p. 69.
149. ["The economic phenomena of society are not the direct expression of some social force, but are only the resultants of the conduct of individuals, of *wirtschaftende Menschen* (men engaged in economic activity)...," Carl Menger. Cited by Eric Roll, *A History of Economic Thought* (New York: Prentice-Hall, 1946) p. 425.]
150. Kenneth Arrow, cited by Leonard Silk, op. cit.
151. Herbert Simon, cited by Leonard Silk, op. cit.

Appendix A

1990 population* and revised classification of counties**

*Preliminary Census count (in thousands)
** See Chapter 21

Alabama

AUTAUGA	33	V-
BALDWIN	98	V-
BARBOUR	25	III-
BIBB	16	II-
BLOUNT	39	I-
BULLOCK	11	IV+
BUTLER	22	III+
CALHOUN	114	V-
CHAMBERS	37	III-
CHEROKEE	20	II-
CHILTON	32	I-
CHOCTAW	16	III-
CLARKE	27	III-
CLAY	13	III-
CLEBURNE	13	II-
COFFEE	40	III-
COLBERT	51	VII-
CONECUH	14	III-
COOSA	11	III-
COVINGTON	36	III-
CRENSHAW	13	III-
CULLMAN	67	II-
DALE	49	VII-
DALLAS	47	IV-
DE KALB	54	I-
ELMORE	47	I-
ESCAMBIA	35	III-
ETOWAH	99	VII-
FAYETTE	18	II-
FRANKLIN	28	II-
GENEVA	24	III-
GREENE	10	III-
HALE	15	III-
HENRY	15	II-
HOUSTON	80	I-
JACKSON	47	I-
JEFFERSON	643	VII-
LAMAR	15	II-
LAUDERDALE	79	V-
LAWRENCE	31	III-
LEE	85	V-
LIMESTONE	53	III+
LOWNDES	12	III-
MACON	24	III-
MADISON	237	VII+
MARENGO	23	III-
MARION	30	I-
MARSHALL	71	II-
MOBILE	376	V-
MONROE	24	III-
MONTGOMERY	204	V-
MORGAN	98	V-
PERRY	13	III-
PICKENS	20	III-
PIKE	27	II-
RANDOLPH	20	III-
RUSSELL	46	VII-
ST. CLAIR	48	I+
SHELBY	98	I+
SUMTER	16	III-
TALLADEGA	73	V-
TALLAPOOSA	38	II-
TUSCALOOSA	146	V-
WALKER	67	I-
WASHINGTON	17	III-
WILCOX	13	IV+
WINSTON	22	I-

Arizona

APACHE	60	V-
COCHISE	96	V-
COCONINO	96	V-
GILA	40	I-
GRAHAM	26	V-
GREENLEE	8	VII-
MARICOPA	2100	VI-
MOHAVE	90	V-
NAVAJO	75	V-
PIMA	662	V-
PINAL	114	V-
SANTA CRUZ	29	V+
YAVAPAI	106	V+
YUMA	106	V+

Arkansas

ARKANSAS	21	III-
ASHLEY	24	III-
BAXTER	31	I+
BENTON	97	I+
BOONE	28	I-
BRADLEY	12	III-
CALHOUN	6	III-
CARROLL	19	I+
CHICOT	14	III-
CLARK	21	III-
CLAY	18	III-
CLEBURNE	19	I+
CLEVELAND	8	II-
COLUMBIA	25	III-
CONWAY	19	II-
CRAIGHEAD	73	I+

CRAWFORD	43	I+
CRITTENDEN	50	III-
CROSS	19	III-
DALLAS	9	III-
DESHA	17	III-
DREW	17	II-
FAULKNER	60	I+
FRANKLIN	15	I-
FULTON	10	I-
GARLAND	73	V-
GRANT	14	I-
GREENE	32	I-
HEMPSTEAD	21	I-
HOT SPRING	26	I-
HOWARD	13	II-
INDEPENDENCE	31	I-
IZARD	11	I-
JACKSON	19	III-
JEFFERSON	84	III-
JOHNSON	18	I-
LAFAYETTE	9	III-
LAWRENCE	17	II-
LEE	13	IV+
LINCOLN	14	III-
LITTLE RIVER	14	I-
LOGAN	21	II-
LONOKE	39	I+
MADISON	12	II-
MARION	12	I-
MILLER	38	II-
MISSISSIPPI	57	III+
MONROE	11	IV-
MONTGOMERY	8	I-
NEVADA	10	III-
NEWTON	8	I-
OUACHITA	29	III-
PERRY	8	I-
PHILLIPS	29	IV+
PIKE	10	II-
POINSETT	25	VII-
POLK	17	I-
POPE	46	I+
PRAIRIE	10	III-
PULASKI	347	V-
RANDOLPH	17	I-
ST. FRANCIS	28	III-
SALINE	64	V-
SCOTT	10	II-
SEARCY	8	II-
SEBASTIAN	99	II-
SEVIER	14	I-
SHARP	14	I-
STONE	10	I-
UNION	46	III-
VAN BUREN	14	I-
WASHINGTON	114	V-
WHITE	55	I-
WOODRUFF	10	III-
YELL	18	II-

California

ALAMEDA	1255	VII+
ALPINE	1	V-
AMADOR	30	I+
BUTTE	181	V-
CALAVERAS	32	V+
COLUSA	16	IV+
CONTRA COSTA	797	VI+
DEL NORTE	23	V+
EL DORADO	125	V-
FRESNO	659	V+
GLENN	25	V-
HUMBOLDT	118	VII-
IMPERIAL	108	I+
INYO	18	V-
KERN	538	V+
KINGS	101	VII+
LAKE	49	V-
LASSEN	27	V+
LOS ANGELES	8720	VII+
MADERA	86	V-
MARIN	228	VII-
MARIPOSA	14	V-
MENDOCINO	77	V-
MERCED	175	V+
MODOC	10	II+
MONO	10	V-
MONTEREY	326	VI-
NAPA	109	V-
NEVADA	78	V-
ORANGE	2392	VI-
PLACER	171	V+
PLUMAS	20	V-
RIVERSIDE	1144	VI+
SACRAMENTO	1030	VI+
SAN BENITO	35	V+
SAN BERNARDINO	1395	VI+
SAN DIEGO	2466	VI+
SAN FRANCISCO	711	IV+
SAN JOAQUIN	464	V+
SAN LUIS OBISPO	214	V-
SAN MATEO	641	VII-
SANTA BARBARA	366	VI+
SANTA CLARA	1468	VI-
SANTA CRUZ	217	V-
SHASTA	146	V-
SIERRA	3	I-
SISKIYOU	43	II-
SOLANO	332	V+
SONOMA	383	V-
STANISLAUS	367	V+
SUTTER	64	V-
TEHAMA	49	V-
TRINITY	13	V-
TULARE	309	V-
TUOLUMNE	48	V+
VENTURA	651	VI-
YOLO	139	VI+
YUBA	58	V+

Colorado

ADAMS	264	VI-
ALAMOSA	14	IV+
ARAPAHOE	390	V-
ARCHULETA	5	I+
BACA	5	III-
BENT	5	IV-
BOULDER	228	VI-
CHAFFEE	13	V-
CHEYENNE	2	III+
CLEAR CREEK	8	V-
CONEJOS	8	III-
COSTILLA	3	III+
CROWLEY	4	III+
CUSTER	2	I+
DELTA	21	I-
DENVER	460	VII-
DOLORES	2	VII-
DOUGLAS	60	V+
EAGLE	22	V+
ELBERT	10	I+
EL PASO	394	VI-
FREMONT	32	I+
GARFIELD	30	I+
GILPIN	3	V-
GRAND	8	V-
GUNNISON	10	I-
HINSDALE	1	I+
HUERFANO	6	III-
JACKSON	2	VII-
JEFFERSON	436	VI-
KIOWA	2	III-
KIT CARSON	7	III-
LAKE	6	VII-
LA PLATA	32	I+
LARIMER	181	V-
LAS ANIMAS	14	III-
LINCOLN	5	III+
LOGAN	18	III-
MESA	93	V-
MINERAL	1	II-
MOFFAT	11	V-
MONTEZUMA	19	V-
MONTROSE	24	V-
MORGAN	22	II-
OTERO	20	IV-
OURAY	2	I+
PARK	7	I+

PHILLIPS	4	III-
PITKIN	13	VI-
PROWERS	13	III+
PUEBLO	122	VII-
RIO BLANCO	6	V-
RIO GRANDE	11	VII-
ROUTT	14	I-
SAGUACHE	5	III+
SAN JUAN	1	III-
SAN MIGUEL	4	I+
SEDGWICK	3	III-
SUMMIT	13	V-
TELLER	13	I+
WASHINGTON	5	III-
WELD	132	I-
YUMA	9	II-

Connecticut

FAIRFIELD	820	VII-
HARTFORD	850	VII-
LITCHFIELD	168	VII-
MIDDLESEX	142	VI-
NEW HAVEN	801	VII-
NEW LONDON	250	VII-
TOLLAND	128	VII+
WINDHAM	100	VII-

Delaware

KENT	110	VI-
NEW CASTLE	436	VII-
SUSSEX	112	V-
WASHINGTON DC	575	VII-

Florida

ALACHUA	178	V-
BAKER	18	V-
BAY	125	V+
BRADFORD	22	V-
BREVARD	396	VI+
BROWARD	1235	VI-
CALHOUN	11	II+
CHARLOTTE	110	VI+
CITRUS	93	V-
CLAY	104	V-
COLLIER	150	VI+
COLUMBIA	42	V-
DADE	1913	VI-
DE SOTO	24	V-
DIXIE	10	V-
DUVAL	694	VII+
ESCAMBIA	261	VI-
FLAGLER	27	V+
FRANKLIN	9	III+
GADSDEN	40	III-
GILCHRIST	10	I+
GLADES	7	V-
GULF	11	VII-
HAMILTON	11	II+
HARDEE	19	V-
HENDRY	25	V+
HERNANDO	101	V+
HIGHLANDS	68	V-
HILLSBOROUGH	829	V+
HOLMES	16	I-
INDIAN RIVER	89	V+
JACKSON	41	II-
JEFFERSON	11	I-
LAFAYETTE	6	I+
LAKE	150	V+
LEE	331	VI+
LEON	191	V-
LEVY	26	I+
LIBERTY	6	I+
MADISON	16	III+
MANATEE	209	V-
MARION	193	V+
MARTIN	99	V-
MONROE	76	VI+
NASSAU	44	V-
OKALOOSA	142	VI+
OKEECHOBEE	29	V-
ORANGE	670	VI+
OSCEOLA	104	V+
PALM BEACH	849	V+
PASCO	280	V-
PINELLAS	847	VI-
POLK	400	V-
PUTNAM	63	V-
ST. JOHNS	83	V+
ST. LUCIE	144	V+
SANTA ROSA	81	V+
SARASOTA	276	VI-
SEMINOLE	285	V-
SUMTER	31	I+
SUWANNEE	26	I+
TAYLOR	17	I-
UNION	10	I-
VOLUSIA	368	V+
WAKULLA	14	I+
WALTON	28	I+
WASHINGTON	17	I+

Georgia

APPLING	16	I-
ATKINSON	6	III-
BACON	10	V-
BAKER	4	III-
BALDWIN	38	VII-
BANKS	10	I+
BARROW	30	I+
BARTOW	56	I+
BEN HILL	16	I-
BERRIEN	14	II-
BIBB	149	VII-
BLECKLEY	10	III-
BRANTLEY	11	I+
BROOKS	15	III-
BRYAN	15	I+
BULLOCH	43	II+
BURKE	20	III+
BUTTS	15	I-
CALHOUN	5	IV+
CAMDEN	30	V+
CANDLER	8	II-
CARROLL	71	I+
CATOOSA	42	V-
CHARLTON	8	I+
CHATHAM	216	VII-
CHATTAHOOCHEE	17	VII-
CHATTOOGA	22	VII-
CHEROKEE	88	V+
CLARKE	86	VI+
CLAY	3	III-
CLAYTON	179	VI-
CLINCH	6	III-
COBB	446	VI+
COFFEE	29	II-
COLQUITT	36	III-
COLUMBIA	65	V+
COOK	14	III-
COWETA	54	I+
CRAWFORD	9	I+
CRISP	19	III-
DADE	13	V-
DAWSON	9	I+
DECATUR	25	II-
DE KALB	541	VI-
DODGE	17	III-
DOOLY	10	III-
DOUGHERTY	95	VI-
DOUGLAS	70	V-
EARLY	12	III-
ECHOLS	2	II-
EFFINGHAM	26	V+
ELBERT	19	III-
EMANUEL	20	II-
EVANS	9	II-
FANNIN	16	III-
FAYETTE	61	V+
FLOYD	80	VII-
FORSYTH	43	V+
FRANKLIN	17	II-
FULTON	636	VII-
GILMER	13	V-
GLASCOCK	2	III-
GLYNN	62	VII+

GORDON	35 I+
GRADY	20 III-
GREENE	11 III-
GWINNETT	351 V+
HABERSHAM	28 V-
HALL	92 V-
HANCOCK	8 III-
HARALSON	22 II+
HARRIS	18 I+
HART	20 II-
HEARD	9 I+
HENRY	57 V+
HOUSTON	89 VI-
IRWIN	9 III-
JACKSON	29 II+
JASPER	8 I+
JEFF DAVIS	12 I-
JEFFERSON	17 III-
JENKINS	8 III-
JOHNSON	8 II-
JONES	20 V-
LAMAR	13 II-
LANIER	6 II-
LAURENS	40 II-
LEE	16 I+
LIBERTY	52 V-
LINCOLN	7 II-
LONG	6 I+
LOWNDES	75 V-
LUMPKIN	14 V+
McDUFFIE	20 V-
McINTOSH	9 III-
MACON	13 III-
MADISON	21 I+
MARION	6 III+
MERIWETHER	22 III-
MILLER	6 III-
MITCHELL	20 II-
MONROE	17 I+
MONTGOMERY	7 II-
MORGAN	13 II-
MURRAY	26 I+
MUSCOGEE	180 VII-
NEWTON	41 I+
OCONEE	17 I+
OGLETHORPE	10 II-
PAULDING	41 V+
PEACH	21 V-
PICKENS	14 II+
PIERCE	13 I+
PIKE	10 I+
POLK	34 VII-
PULASKI	8 III-
PUTNAM	14 I+
QUITMAN	2 III-
RABUN	11 I-
RANDOLPH	8 III-
RICHMOND	188 VI-
ROCKDALE	52 V-
SCHLEY	3 II-
SCREVEN	14 II-
SEMINOLE	9 I-
SPALDING	53 V-
STEPHENS	23 VII-
STEWART	5 IV+
SUMTER	30 III-
TALBOT	6 III+
TALIAFERRO	2 IV+
TATTNALL	18 III-
TAYLOR	8 III-
TELFAIR	11 III-
TERRELL	10 III-
THOMAS	38 III-
TIFT	34 V-
TOOMBS	24 II-
TOWNS	7 I+
TREUTLEN	6 III-
TROUP	55 V-
TURNER	9 III-
TWIGGS	10 II-
UNION	12 I+
UPSON	26 VII-
WALKER	58 V-
WALTON	38 I+
WARE	35 III-
WARREN	6 III-
WASHINGTON	19 III-
WAYNE	22 V-
WEBSTER	2 III-
WHEELER	5 II-
WHITE	13 I+
WHITFIELD	71 V-
WILCOX	7 III-
WILKES	11 III-
WILKINSON	10 III-
WORTH	19 I-

Idaho

ADA	205 V-
ADAMS	3 II-
BANNOCK	66 V-
BEAR LAKE	6 II-
BENEWAH	8 I-
BINGHAM	37 V-
BLAINE	14 V-
BOISE	4 I+
BONNER	27 I-
BONNEVILLE	72 V-
BOUNDARY	8 V+
BUTTE	3 V-
CAMAS	1 II-
CANYON	90 V-
CARIBOU	7 V-
CASSIA	19 II-
CLARK	1 III-
CLEARWATER	9 VII-
CUSTER	4 II+
ELMORE	21 VI-
FRANKLIN	9 II-
FREMONT	11 I-
GEM	12 I-
GOODING	12 V-
IDAHO	14 II-
JEFFERSON	16 I-
JEROME	15 V-
KOOTENAI	70 V-
LATAH	31 II-
LEMHI	7 V-
LEWIS	4 III-
LINCOLN	3 V-
MADISON	24 V-
MINIDOKA	19 V-
NEZ PERCE	34 VII-
ONEIDA	4 II-
OWYHEE	8 V-
PAYETTE	16 V-
POWER	7 I-
SHOSHONE	14 III-
TETON	3 I+
TWIN FALLS	54 V-
VALLEY	6 I-
WASHINGTON	9 II-

Illinois

ADAMS	66 IV-
ALEXANDER	11 III-
BOND	15 II-
BOONE	30 VI-
BROWN	6 III+
BUREAU	36 III-
CALHOUN	5 III-
CARROLL	17 IV-
CASS	13 III-
CHAMPAIGN	170 VII-
CHRISTIAN	34 III-
CLARK	16 III-
CLAY	14 III-
CLINTON	34 II-
COLES	50 III-
COOK	5037 IV+
CRAWFORD	19 III-
CUMBERLAND	11 II-
DE KALB	77 VII-
DE WITT	16 III-
DOUGLAS	19 IV-
DU PAGE	781 VI-
EDGAR	20 III-
EDWARDS	7 II-
EFFINGHAM	32 I-

FAYETTE	21	III-
FORD	14	IV+
FRANKLIN	40	II-
FULTON	38	III-
GALLATIN	7	III-
GREENE	15	IV-
GRUNDY	32	V-
HAMILTON	9	III-
HANCOCK	21	III-
HARDIN	5	III-
HENDERSON	8	III-
HENRY	51	III-
IROQUOIS	31	IV-
JACKSON	61	VI-
JASPER	11	III-
JEFFERSON	37	II-
JERSEY	20	II-
JO DAVIESS	22	III-
JOHNSON	11	I+
KANE	315	VII+
KANKAKEE	95	VII-
KENDALL	39	V-
KNOX	56	IV-
LAKE	511	VI+
LA SALLE	106	IV-
LAWRENCE	7	III-
LEE	34	IV+
LIVINGSTON	39	IV-
LOGAN	31	IV+
McDONOUGH	35	IV-
McHENRY	181	VI-
McLEAN	128	V-
MACON	117	VII-
MACOUPIN	48	III-
MADISON	247	VII-
MARION	42	II-
MARSHALL	13	III-
MASON	16	II-
MASSAC	15	III-
MENARD	11	I-
MERCER	17	II-
MONROE	22	VII+
MONTGOMERY	31	III-
MORGAN	36	III-
MOULTRIE	14	III-
OGLE	46	IV-
PEORIA	182	VII-
PERRY	21	III-
PIATT	16	III-
PIKE	18	III-
POPE	4	II-
PULASKI	8	III-
PUTNAM	6	II-
RANDOLPH	35	II-
RICHLAND	17	III-
ROCK ISLAND	148	VII-
ST. CLAIR	261	VII-
SALINE	27	III-
SANGAMON	177	III-
SCHUYLER	8	III-
SCOTT	6	III-
SHELBY	22	III-
STARK	7	III-
STEPHENSON	48	IV-
TAZEWELL	123	VII-
UNION	18	IV-
VERMILION	88	IV-
WABASH	13	III-
WARREN	19	III-
WASHINGTON	15	II-
WAYNE	17	III-
WHITE	17	III-
WHITESIDE	60	VII-
WILL	355	V-
WILLIAMSON	58	II-
WINNEBAGO	252	VII-
WOODFORD	33	II-

Indiana

ADAMS	31	III+
ALLEN	299	VII-
BARTHOLOMEW	64	VI-
BENTON	9	IV+
BLACKFORD	14	IV-
BOONE	38	II-
BROWN	14	V-
CARROLL	19	III-
CASS	38	IV-
CLARK	87	VI-
CLAY	24	III-
CLINTON	31	III-
CRAWFORD	10	I-
DAVIESS	27	III-
DEARBORN	39	II+
DECATUR	24	IV-
DE KALB	35	III-
DELAWARE	119	VII-
DUBOIS	36	III-
ELKHART	155	VII+
FAYETTE	26	III-
FLOYD	64	VII-
FOUNTAIN	18	III-
FRANKLIN	19	II-
FULTON	19	II-
GIBSON	32	III-
GRANT	74	VII-
GREENE	30	II-
HAMILTON	108	V-
HANCOCK	45	V-
HARRISON	29	I-
HENDRICKS	75	VI-
HENRY	48	VII-
HOWARD	80	VII-
HUNTINGTON	35	IV-
JACKSON	37	III-
JASPER	25	V-
JAY	21	IV-
JEFFERSON	29	II-
JENNINGS	23	V-
JOHNSON	87	VI-
KNOX	39	III-
KOSCIUSKO	65	V-
LAGRANGE	29	V-
LAKE	471	VII-
LA PORTE	106	VII-
LAWRENCE	42	II-
MADISON	130	VII-
MARION	791	VII-
MARSHALL	42	II-
MARTIN	10	IV-
MIAMI	37	VII-
MONROE	108	VI-
MONTGOMERY	34	IV-
MORGAN	56	VI-
NEWTON	14	I-
NOBLE	38	II-
OHIO	5	I-
ORANGE	18	III-
OWEN	17	I-
PARKE	15	II-
PERRY	19	IV-
PIKE	12	III-
PORTER	128	V-
POSEY	26	I-
PULASKI	13	III-
PUTNAM	30	III-
RANDOLPH	27	III-
RIPLEY	25	II-
RUSH	18	IV-
ST. JOSEPH	246	VII-
SCOTT	21	V-
SHELBY	40	VII-
SPENCER	19	II-
STARKE	23	V-
STEUBEN	27	V-
SULLIVAN	19	III-
SWITZERLAND	8	II-
TIPPECANOE	130	VII-
TIPTON	16	IV-
UNION	7	III-
VANDERBURGH	164	VII-
VERMILLION	17	III-
VIGO	105	IV-
WABASH	35	IV-
WARREN	8	III-
WARRICK	44	I-
WASHINGTON	23	II-
WAYNE	72	VII-
WELLS	26	IV-
WHITE	23	II-

WHITLEY	27	II-

Iowa

ADAIR	8	III-
ADAMS	5	IV-
ALLAMAKEE	14	III-
APPANOOSE	14	III-
AUDUBON	7	IV+
BENTON	22	III-
BLACK HAWK	123	VII-
BOONE	25	IV-
BREMER	23	III-
BUCHANAN	21	III-
BUENA VISTA	20	III-
BUTLER	16	III-
CALHOUN	12	IV-
CARROLL	21	IV-
CASS	15	III-
CEDAR	17	III-
CERRO GORDO	47	IV-
CHEROKEE	14	IV-
CHICKASAW	13	III-
CLARKE	8	II-
CLAY	18	III-
CLAYTON	19	III-
CLINTON	51	IV-
CRAWFORD	17	IV-
DALLAS	30	II-
DAVIS	8	III-
DECATUR	8	III+
DELAWARE	18	IV-
DES MOINES	43	IV-
DICKINSON	15	I-
DUBUQUE	86	IV-
EMMET	12	IV-
FAYETTE	22	IV-
FLOYD	17	III-
FRANKLIN	11	III-
FREMONT	8	III-
GREENE	10	III-
GRUNDY	12	IV-
GUTHRIE	11	III-
HAMILTON	16	IV-
HANCOCK	13	III-
HARDIN	19	IV-
HARRISON	15	III-
HENRY	19	III-
HOWARD	10	III-
HUMBOLDT	11	IV-
IDA	8	III-
IOWA	15	IV-
JACKSON	20	III-
JASPER	35	IV-
JEFFERSON	16	III-
JOHNSON	96	VI+
JONES	19	III-
KEOKUK	12	IV+
KOSSUTH	19	IV-
LEE	39	IV-
LINN	168	VII-
LOUISA	12	II-
LUCAS	9	III-
LYON	12	IV-
MADISON	13	III-
MAHASKA	21	III-
MARION	30	II-
MARSHALL	38	IV-
MILLS	13	II-
MITCHELL	11	IV-
MONONA	10	III-
MONROE	8	III-
MONTGOMERY	12	III-
MUSCATINE	40	III-
O'BRIEN	15	IV-
OSCEOLA	7	III-
PAGE	17	III-
PALO ALTO	11	III-
PLYMOUTH	23	IV-
POCAHONTAS	10	IV-
POLK	326	VII-
POTTAWATTAMIE	82	IV-
POWESHIEK	19	III-
RINGGOLD	5	III-
SAC	12	IV+
SCOTT	150	VI-
SHELBY	13	IV-
SIOUX	30	III-
STORY	73	V-
TAMA	17	IV-
TAYLOR	7	III-
UNION	13	III-
VAN BUREN	8	III-
WAPELLO	36	IV-
WARREN	36	V-
WASHINGTON	20	III-
WAYNE	7	III-
WEBSTER	40	IV-
WINNEBAGO	12	III-
WINNESHIEK	21	IV-
WOODBURY	98	IV+
WORTH	8	III-
WRIGHT	14	IV-

Kansas

ALLEN	15	III-
ANDERSON	8	III-
ATCHISON	17	IV-
BARBER	6	IV-
BARTON	29	VII-
BOURBON	15	III-
BROWN	11	III-
BUTLER	50	II+
CHASE	3	III-
CHAUTAUQUA	4	III-
CHEROKEE	21	III-
CHEYENNE	3	IV+
CLARK	2	IV+
CLAY	9	III-
CLOUD	11	IV-
COFFEY	8	I-
COMANCHE	2	III-
COWLEY	37	III-
CRAWFORD	35	III-
DECATUR	4	IV+
DICKINSON	19	III-
DONIPHAN	8	III-
DOUGLAS	81	VI+
EDWARDS	4	IV-
ELK	3	III-
ELLIS	26	IV-
ELLSWORTH	7	III-
FINNEY	33	V+
FORD	27	III+
FRANKLIN	22	III-
GEARY	35	VII+
GOVE	3	IV-
GRAHAM	4	IV+
GRANT	7	V-
GRAY	5	II-
GREELEY	2	III-
GREENWOOD	8	III-
HAMILTON	2	IV+
HARPER	7	III-
HARVEY	31	II-
HASKELL	4	VII-
HODGEMAN	2	IV+
JACKSON	12	II-
JEFFERSON	16	I-
JEWELL	4	IV+
JOHNSON	354	VI+
KEARNY	4	II+
KINGMAN	8	III-
KIOWA	4	III-
LABETTE	24	III-
LANE	2	IV+
LEAVENWORTH	66	IV+
LINCOLN	4	III+
LINN	8	III-
LOGAN	3	IV+
LYON	34	III-
McPHERSON	27	III-
MARION	13	III+
MARSHALL	12	III-
MEADE	4	IV-
MIAMI	23	II-
MITCHELL	7	III-
MONTGOMERY	39	III-
MORRIS	6	III-
MORTON	4	VII-
NEMAHA	10	IV+

NEOSHO	17	III-
NESS	4	III-
NORTON	6	IV+
OSAGE	15	II-
OSBORNE	5	IV-
OTTAWA	6	III+
PAWNEE	8	III+
PHILLIPS	7	IV-
POTTAWATOMIE	16	I-
PRATT	10	III-
RAWLINS	3	III-
RENO	62	III-
REPUBLIC	7	IV+
RICE	11	III-
RILEY	61	VI-
ROOKS	6	IV-
RUSH	4	IV+
RUSSELL	8	III-
SALINE	59	VII+
SCOTT	5	VII-
SEDGWICK	401	VII-
SEWARD	19	VII-
SHAWNEE	160	VII-
SHERIDAN	3	IV-
SHERMAN	7	IV-
SMITH	5	IV+
STAFFORD	5	III+
STANTON	2	VII-
STEVENS	5	V-
SUMNER	26	III-
THOMAS	8	II-
TREGO	4	IV-
WABAUNSEE	7	III-
WALLACE	2	IV-
WASHINGTON	7	III-
WICHITA	3	IV+
WILSON	10	III-
WOODSON	4	III-
WYANDOTTE	162	IV+

Kentucky

ADAIR	15	II-
ALLEN	15	II-
ANDERSON	15	I+
BALLARD	8	III-
BARREN	34	II-
BATH	10	III-
BELL	31	VII-
BOONE	57	VI-
BOURBON	19	III-
BOYD	51	III-
BOYLE	26	V-
BRACKEN	8	III-
BREATHITT	16	II-
BRECKINRIDGE	16	II-
BULLITT	48	V-
BUTLER	11	II-
CALDWELL	13	III-
CALLOWAY	31	VII-
CAMPBELL	84	IV+
CARLISLE	5	III-
CARROLL	9	III-
CARTER	24	I-
CASEY	14	II-
CHRISTIAN	70	V-
CLARK	29	II-
CLAY	21	V-
CLINTON	9	II-
CRITTENDEN	9	III-
CUMBERLAND	7	III-
DAVIESS	87	VII-
EDMONSON	10	II-
ELLIOTT	6	II-
ESTILL	14	II-
FAYETTE	229	VI-
FLEMING	12	III-
FLOYD	43	V-
FRANKLIN	44	V-
FULTON	8	IV+
GALLATIN	5	II+
GARRARD	11	II-
GRANT	16	I+
GRAVES	34	III-
GRAYSON	21	I-
GREEN	10	III-
GREENUP	37	II-
HANCOCK	8	III-
HARDIN	89	VI-
HARLAN	36	II-
HARRISON	16	III+
HART	15	III-
HENDERSON	43	II-
HENRY	13	II-
HICKMAN	6	III-
HOPKINS	46	II-
JACKSON	12	V-
JEFFERSON	661	VII-
JESSAMINE	3	V-
JOHNSON	23	I-
KENTON	142	IV-
KNOTT	18	V-
KNOX	29	I-
LARUE	12	II-
LAUREL	43	I+
LAWRENCE	14	I-
LEE	7	II-
LESLIE	13	V-
LETCHER	27	I-
LEWIS	13	II-
LINCOLN	20	II-
LIVINGSTON	9	I-
LOGAN	24	III-
LYON	7	II-
McCRACKEN	7	IV-
McCREARY	16	I-
McLEAN	10	III-
MADISON	57	V-
MAGOFFIN	13	I-
MARION	16	III-
MARSHALL	27	V-
MARTIN	13	V-
MASON	17	III-
MEADE	24	VI-
MENIFEE	5	I-
MERCER	19	II-
METCALFE	9	II-
MONROE	11	III-
MONTGOMERY	19	I-
MORGAN	12	II-
MUHLENBERG	31	II-
NELSON	30	II-
NICHOLAS	7	III-
OHIO	21	II-
OLDHAM	33	V-
OWEN	9	II-
OWSLEY	5	II-
PENDLETON	12	III-
PERRY	30	I-
PIKE	72	V-
POWELL	12	I-
PULASKI	49	I-
ROBERTSON	2	III-
ROCKCASTLE	15	II-
ROWAN	20	V-
RUSSELL	15	I-
SCOTT	24	I-
SHELBY	25	I-
SIMPSON	15	II-
SPENCER	7	III+
TAYLOR	21	I-
TODD	11	III-
TRIGG	10	III+
TRIMBLE	6	II-
UNION	16	II-
WARREN	76	V-
WASHINGTON	10	III-
WAYNE	17	II-
WEBSTER	14	II-
WHITLEY	33	I-
WOLFE	7	II-
WOODFORD	20	I+

Louisiana

ACADIA	56	III-
ALLEN	21	VII-
ASCENSION	58	V-
ASSUMPTION	23	II-
AVOYELLES	39	III-
BEAUREGARD	30	I-

BIENVILLE	16	III-
BOSSIER	85	V-
CADDO	245	VII-
CALCASIEU	167	VI-
CALDWELL	10	II-
CAMERON	9	II-
CATAHOULA	11	III-
CLAIBORNE	17	III+
CONCORDIA	21	VII-
DE SOTO	25	II-
EAST BATON ROU(	376	V-
EAST CARROLL	10	IV-
EAST FELICIANA	19	III-
EVANGELINE	33	VII-
FRANKLIN	22	III-
GRANT	17	I-
IBERIA	68	VII-
IBERVILLE	31	IV-
JACKSON	16	III-
JEFFERSON	446	VI-
JEFFERSON DAVIS	31	VII-
LAFAYETTE	164	V-
LAFOURCHE	86	VI-
LA SALLE	14	I-
LINCOLN	42	II-
LIVINGSTON	70	V-
MADISON	12	III-
MOREHOUSE	32	VII-
NATCHITOCHES	36	II-
ORLEANS	488	VII-
OUACHITA	141	V-
PLAQUEMINES	25	VII-
POINTE COUPEE	23	III-
RAPIDES	129	V-
RED RIVER	9	II-
RICHLAND	21	III-
SABINE	23	I-
ST. BERNARD	66	VI-
ST. CHARLES	42	VI-
ST. HELENA	10	IV+
ST. JAMES	21	IV-
ST. JOHN THE BAP'	40	V-
ST. LANDRY	80	VII-
ST. MARTIN	44	I-
ST. MARY	58	VII-
ST. TAMMANY	144	V-
TANGIPAHOA	85	I-
TENSAS	7	IV+
TERREBONNE	96	V-
UNION	21	II-
VERMILION	50	II-
VERNON	61	VII+
WASHINGTON	43	VII-
WEBSTER	42	III-
WEST BATON ROU	19	VI-
WEST CARROLL	12	VII-
WEST FELICIANA	13	II-
WINN	16	III-

Maine

ANDROSCOGGIN	105	III-
AROOSTOOK	84	IV-
CUMBERLAND	242	V+
FRANKLIN	29	II-
HANCOCK	47	II+
KENNEBEC	115	II-
KNOX	36	II-
LINCOLN	30	I+
OXFORD	52	II-
PENOBSCOT	146	III-
PISCATAQUIS	19	III-
SAGADAHOC	33	V-
SOMERSET	50	III-
WALDO	33	I+
WASHINGTON	35	II-
YORK	163	V-

Maryland

ALLEGANY	75	IV-
ANNE ARUNDEL	424	VI-
BALTIMORE	688	VII-
CALVERT	51	V-
CAROLINE	27	II+
CARROLL	123	V-
CECIL	71	VI+
CHARLES	101	V-
DORCHESTER	30	III-
FREDERICK	150	V+
GARRETT	28	I-
HARFORD	181	VI-
HOWARD	186	V+
KENT	17	IV+
MONTGOMERY	751	VII+
PRINCE GEORGE'S	720	VII-
QUEEN ANNE'S	34	I+
ST. MARY'S	75	V+
SOMERSET	23	III+
TALBOT	30	III+
WASHINGTON	121	IV-
WICOMICO	74	V-
WORCESTER	35	I+
BALTIMORE CITY	720	IV+

Massachusetts

BARNSTABLE	184	V-
BERKSHIRE	138	IV-
BRISTOL	502	III-
DUKES	10	I-
ESSEX	648	IV+
FRANKLIN	69	III-
HAMPDEN	453	IV+
HAMPSHIRE	145	VI-
MIDDLESEX	1387	IV-
NANTUCKET	6	I-
NORFOLK	612	VII-
PLYMOUTH	431	VI-
SUFFOLK	671	IV+
WORCESTER	703	IV+

Michigan

ALCONA	10	I-
ALGER	9	III-
ALLEGAN	90	V-
ALPENA	31	VII-
ANTRIM	18	I+
ARENAC	15	I-
BARAGA	8	III-
BARRY	49	V-
BAY	111	VII-
BENZIE	12	V-
BERRIEN	159	VII-
BRANCH	40	VII-
CALHOUN	135	VII-
CASS	48	VI-
CHARLEVOIX	21	II-
CHEBOYGAN	21	I-
CHIPPEWA	34	IV+
CLARE	25	V-
CLINTON	58	VI-
CRAWFORD	12	V-
DELTA	38	III-
DICKINSON	27	III-
EATON	92	V-
EMMET	25	I-
GENESEE	427	VII-
GLADWIN	22	V-
GOGEBIC	18	III-
GRAND TRAVERSE	64	V-
GRATIOT	39	IV-
HILLSDALE	42	II-
HOUGHTON	35	III-
HURON	35	III-
INGHAM	281	VII-
IONIA	57	II-
IOSCO	30	VI-
IRON	13	III-
ISABELLA	54	V-
JACKSON	148	VII-
KALAMAZOO	221	VII-
KALKASKA	13	I+
KENT	497	VII+
KEWEENAW	2	IV+
LAKE	9	V-
LAPEER	74	V-
LEELANAU	16	I+
LENAWEE	90	VII-
LIVINGSTON	115	V-
LUCE	6	VII-
MACKINAC	11	III-
MACOMB	715	VII-
MANISTEE	21	II-
MARQUETTE	71	V-

MASON	25	II-
MECOSTA	37	V-
MENOMINEE	25	III-
MIDLAND	75	VI-
MISSAUKEE	12	I+
MONROE	133	VI-
MONTCALM	53	II+
MONTMORENCY	9	V-
MUSKEGON	158	V+
NEWAYGO	38	V-
OAKLAND	1076	VI-
OCEANA	22	I-
OGEMAW	19	V-
ONTONAGON	9	IV-
OSCEOLA	200	I+
OSCODA	8	V-
OTSEGO	18	V-
OTTAWA	186	VI-
PRESQUE ISLE	14	III-
ROSCOMMON	20	V-
SAGINAW	211	VII-
ST. CLAIR	145	V-
ST. JOSEPH	58	V-
SANILAC	40	II-
SCHOOLCRAFT	8	III-
SHIAWASSEE	69	V-
TUSCOLA	55	II-
VAN BUREN	69	V-
WASHTENAW	28	VI-
WAYNE	2049	VII-
WEXFORD	26	I-

Minnesota

AITKIN	12	II-
ANOKA	243	VI-
BECKER	28	II-
BELTRAMI	34	II-
BENTON	30	II+
BIG STONE	6	III-
BLUE EARTH	54	VII-
BROWN	27	IV-
CARLTON	29	III-
CARVER	48	V+
CASS	22	V-
CHIPPEWA	13	III-
CHISAGO	31	V-
CLAY	50	VII-
CLEARWATER	8	III-
COOK	4	II-
COTTONWOOD	13	III-
CROW WING	44	II-
DAKOTA	274	VI+
DODGE	16	II-
DOUGLAS	29	I-
FARIBAULT	17	IV-
FILLMORE	21	III-
FREEBORN	33	IV-
GOODHUE	41	III-
GRANT	6	III-
HENNEPIN	1028	VII-
HOUSTON	19	IV-
HUBBARD	15	I-
ISANTI	26	V-
ITASCA	41	II-
JACKSON	12	IV-
KANABEC	13	I-
KANDIYOHI	39	II-
KITTSON	6	III-
KOOCHICHING	16	III-
LAC QUI PARLE	9	III-
LAKE	10	VII-
LAKE OF THE WOC	4	III-
LE SUEUR	23	III-
LINCOLN	7	III-
LYON	25	III-
McLEOD	32	IV+
MAHNOMEN	5	III-
MARSHALL	11	III-
MARTIN	23	III-
MEEKER	21	II-
MILLE LACS	19	II-
MORRISON	30	III-
MOWER	37	VII-
MURRAY	10	IV-
NICOLLET	28	VII-
NOBLES	20	IV+
NORMAN	8	IV-
OLMSTED	106	VII+
OTTER TAIL	51	II-
PENNINGTON	13	V-
PINE	21	II-
PIPESTONE	11	IV+
POLK	32	III-
POPE	11	III-
RAMSEY	483	VII-
RED LAKE	5	III-
REDWOOD	17	IV-
RENVILLE	18	IV-
RICE	49	III-
ROCK	10	IV-
ROSEAU	15	III+
ST. LOUIS	198	IV-
SCOTT	58	V+
SHERBURNE	42	V-
SIBLEY	14	IV-
STEARNS	119	V-
STEELE	31	II-
STEVENS	11	IV-
SWIFT	11	III-
TODD	23	II-
TRAVERSE	5	IV-
WABASHA	20	II-
WADENA	13	II-
WASECA	18	III-
WASHINGTON	145	VI-
WATONWAN	12	IV+
WILKIN	8	IV+
WINONA	48	IV-
WRIGHT	69	V-
YELLOW MEDICIN	12	IV-

Mississippi

ADAMS	35	VII-
ALCORN	32	I-
AMITE	13	III+
ATTALA	18	III-
BENTON	8	III-
BOLIVAR	41	IV+
CALHOUN	15	VII-
CARROLL	9	III-
CHICKASAW	18	III-
CHOCTAW	9	III-
CLAIBORNE	11	I-
CLARKE	17	II-
CLAY	21	II-
COAHOMA	31	IV-
COPIAH	27	III-
COVINGTON	16	II-
DE SOTO	67	V-
FORREST	66	V-
FRANKLIN	8	III-
GEORGE	17	V-
GREENE	10	II-
GRENADA	21	III-
HANCOCK	31	V-
HARRISON	162	VI-
HINDS	249	V-
HOLMES	21	III-
HUMPHREYS	12	III-
ISSAQUENA	2	III-
ITAWAMBA	20	I-
JACKSON	113	VI-
JASPER	17	III-
JEFFERSON	8	III-
JEFFERSON DAVIS	14	III-
JONES	61	VII-
KEMPER	10	III+
LAFAYETTE	32	I-
LAMAR	30	I+
LAUDERDALE	75	II-
LAWRENCE	12	II-
LEAKE	18	III-
LEE	65	I+
LEFLORE	37	III-
LINCOLN	30	II-
LOWNDES	59	V-
MADISON	53	I+
MARION	25	II-
MARSHALL	30	I-
MONROE	36	III-
MONTGOMERY	12	III-

NESHOBA	25 II-
NEWTON	20 III-
NOXUBEE	13 III+
OKTIBBEHA	38 V-
PANOLA	30 III+
PEARL RIVER	38 V-
PERRY	11 III+
PIKE	36 II-
PONTOTOC	22 II-
PRENTISS	23 II-
QUITMAN	11 IV+
RANKIN	85 V-
SCOTT	24 II-
SHARKEY	7 IV+
SIMPSON	24 II-
SMITH	15 III-
STONE	11 II-
SUNFLOWER	32 III+
TALLAHATCHIE	15 IV+
TATE	21 III-
TIPPAH	19 II-
TISHOMINGO	18 I-
TUNICA	8 IV+
UNION	22 II-
WALTHALL	14 III-
WARREN	47 II-
WASHINGTON	67 VII-
WAYNE	19 II-
WEBSTER	10 III-
WILKINSON	10 IV+
WINSTON	19 III-
YALOBUSHA	12 III-
YAZOO	25 III-

Missouri

ADAIR	25 III-
ANDREW	14 II-
ATCHISON	7 IV-
AUDRAIN	24 III-
BARRY	28 I+
BARTON	11 III-
BATES	15 III-
BENTON	14 I+
BOLLINGER	11 II-
BOONE	112 V-
BUCHANAN	83 III-
BUTLER	39 V-
CALDWELL	8 III-
CALLAWAY	33 I-
CAMDEN	27 V-
CAPE GIRARDEAU	61 II-
CARROLL	11 III-
CARTER	6 I-
CASS	64 VI-
CEDAR	12 I-
CHARITON	9 III-
CHRISTIAN	32 I+
CLARK	8 III-
CLAY	152 VII+
CLINTON	17 I-
COLE	63 I+
COOPER	15 III+
CRAWFORD	19 I-
DADE	7 III-
DALLAS	12 II-
DAVIESS	8 III-
DE KALB	10 II+
DENT	14 I-
DOUGLAS	12 I-
DUNKLIN	33 VII-
FRANKLIN	80 V-
GASCONADE	14 III-
GENTRY	7 III-
GREENE	206 V-
GRUNDY	11 III-
HARRISON	9 III-
HENRY	20 III-
HICKORY	7 I+
HOLT	6 III-
HOWARD	10 IV+
HOWELL	31 I-
IRON	11 II-
JACKSON	620 IV+
JASPER	89 III-
JEFFERSON	170 VI-
JOHNSON	42 VI-
KNOX	5 III-
LACLEDE	27 I+
LAFAYETTE	31 II-
LAWRENCE	30 II-
LEWIS	10 IV-
LINCOLN	29 V+
LINN	14 III-
LIVINGSTON	15 III-
McDONALD	17 II+
MACON	15 III-
MADISON	11 I-
MARIES	8 III-
MARION	28 III-
MERCER	4 III-
MILLER	21 I+
MISSISSIPPI	14 VII-
MONITEAU	12 II-
MONROE	9 III-
MONTGOMERY	11 III-
MORGAN	16 I+
NEW MADRID	21 VII-
NEWTON	44 I-
NODAWAY	22 IV+
OREGON	9 II-
OSAGE	12 III-
OZARK	9 I-
PEMISCOT	22 III-
PERRY	17 II-
PETTIS	35 III-
PHELPS	35 V-
PIKE	16 VII-
PLATTE	58 V-
POLK	22 I+
PULASKI	40 VII-
PUTNAM	5 III-
RALLS	9 II-
RANDOLPH	24 II-
RAY	22 I-
REYNOLDS	7 II-
RIPLEY	12 I-
ST. CHARLES	211 VI+
ST. CLAIR	8 II-
STE. GENEVIEVE	16 II-
ST. FRANCOIS	49 II+
ST. LOUIS	990 VII-
SALINE	24 III-
SCHUYLER	4 III-
SCOTLAND	5 III-
SCOTT	39 V-
SHANNON	8 III-
SHELBY	7 III-
STODDARD	29 II-
STONE	19 I+
SULLIVAN	6 III-
TANEY	25 I+
TEXAS	21 II-
VERNON	19 III-
WARREN	20 I+
WASHINGTON	20 II+
WAYNE	12 I-
WEBSTER	24 I+
WORTH	2 III-
WRIGHT	17 II-
ST. LOUIS CITY	393 IV+

Montana

BEAVERHEAD	8 IV+
BIG HORN	10 III-
BLAINE	7 III-
BROADWATER	3 I-
CARBON	8 II-
CARTER	2 IV-
CASCADE	77 VII-
CHOUTEAU	5 IV-
CUSTER	12 III-
DANIELS	2 IV-
DAWSON	10 VII-
DEER LODGE	10 VII-
FALLON	3 IV-
FERGUS	12 III-
FLATHEAD	59 V-
GALLATIN	50 V-
GARFIELD	2 IV+

GLACIER	12	VII+
GOLDEN VALLEY	1	III-
GRANITE	3	IV-
HILL	18	VII-
JEFFERSON	8	I+
JUDITH BASIN	2	III-
LAKE	21	V-
LEWIS AND CLARK	47	V-
LIBERTY	2	IV+
LINCOLN	18	VII-
McCONE	2	IV-
MADISON	6	III+
MEAGHER	2	IV-
MINERAL	3	V-
MISSOULA	78	V-
MUSSELSHELL	4	II-
PARK	14	II+
PETROLEUM	1	III-
PHILLIPS	5	III-
PONDERA	6	IV-
POWDER RIVER	2	IV+
POWELL	7	III-
PRAIRIE	1	III-
RAVALLI	25	V-
RICHLAND	11	I-
ROOSEVELT	11	IV+
ROSEBUD	10	I-
SANDERS	9	I-
SHERIDAN	5	IV-
SILVER BOW	34	IV+
STILLWATER	7	II+
SWEET GRASS	3	III-
TETON	6	III-
TOOLE	5	IV-
TREASURE	1	IV+
VALLEY	8	IV-
WHEATLAND	2	IV+
WIBAUX	1	III-
YELLOWSTONE	113	V-
YELLOWSTONE NA	0	I+

Nebraska

ADAMS	30	IV-
ANTELOPE	8	III-
ARTHUR	1	IV+
BANNER	1	IV+
BLAINE	1	III-
BOONE	7	IV+
BOX BUTTE	13	I-
BOYD	3	IV+
BROWN	4	III-
BUFFALO	37	III-
BURT	8	III-
BUTLER	9	III-
CASS	21	II-
CEDAR	10	IV-
CHASE	4	II-
CHERRY	6	III-
CHEYENNE	10	VII-
CLAY	7	IV-
COLFAX	9	III-
CUMING	10	IV-
CUSTER	12	III-
DAKOTA	17	I-
DAWES	9	IV-
DAWSON	20	II-
DEUEL	2	IV+
DIXON	6	III-
DODGE	34	VII-
DOUGLAS	414	VII-
DUNDY	3	III-
FILLMORE	7	III-
FRANKLIN	4	III-
FRONTIER	3	IV-
FURNAS	6	III-
GAGE	23	IV+
GARDEN	3	III-
GARFIELD	2	III-
GOSPER	2	III-
GRANT	1	IV+
GREELEY	3	IV+
HALL	49	IV-
HAMILTON	9	III-
HARLAN	4	III-
HAYES	1	IV+
HITCHCOCK	4	III-
HOLT	13	III-
HOOKER	1	III-
HOWARD	6	IV-
JEFFERSON	9	III-
JOHNSON	5	IV-
KEARNEY	7	III-
KEITH	9	III-
KEYA PAHA	1	III-
KIMBALL	4	VII-
KNOX	10	III-
LANCASTER	213	V-
LINCOLN	33	I-
LOGAN	1	III-
LOUP	1	III-
McPHERSON	1	IV-
MADISON	33	II-
MERRICK	8	III-
MORRILL	5	III-
NANCE	4	IV+
NEMAHA	8	IV+
NUCKOLLS	6	IV-
OTOE	14	IV-
PAWNEE	3	IV+
PERKINS	3	III-
PHELPS	10	IV-
PIERCE	8	III-
PLATTE	30	IV-
POLK	6	III-
RED WILLOW	12	III-
RICHARDSON	10	III-
ROCK	2	III-
SALINE	13	III-
SARPY	102	VI-
SAUNDERS	18	III-
SCOTTS BLUFF	36	III-
SEWARD	15	III-
SHERIDAN	7	III-
SHERMAN	4	IV+
SIOUX	2	III-
STANTON	6	II-
THAYER	7	III-
THOMAS	1	III-
THURSTON	7	III-
VALLEY	5	III-
WASHINGTON	17	II-
WAYNE	9	IV+
WEBSTER	4	IV+
WHEELER	1	III-
YORK	14	III-

Nevada

CHURCHILL	18	V-
CLARK	736	VI+
DOUGLAS	28	V-
ELKO	33	I+
ESMERALDA	1	II+
EUREKA	2	I+
HUMBOLDT	13	V-
LANDER	6	V+
LINCOLN	4	I-
LYON	20	V+
MINERAL	7	VII-
NYE	18	V+
PERSHING	4	I+
STOREY	3	I+
WASHOE	253	V-
WHITE PINE	9	IV+
CARSON CITY	40	V+

New Hampshire

BELKNAP	49	I+
CARROLL	35	I+
CHESHIRE	70	V-
COOS	35	III-
GRAFTON	75	II+
HILLSBOROUGH	334	V-
MERRIMACK	119	I+
ROCKINGHAM	245	V-
STRAFFORD	104	V+
SULLIVAN	38	II-

New Jersey

ATLANTIC	218	IV+
BERGEN	818	VII-
BURLINGTON	394	VI-
CAMDEN	495	VII-
CAPE MAY	94	V-
CUMBERLAND	137	VII-
ESSEX	749	IV+
GLOUCESTER	228	VI-
HUDSON	534	IV-
HUNTERDON	107	V-
MERCER	322	VII-
MIDDLESEX	668	VII+
MONMOUTH	549	VII-
MORRIS	420	VII-
OCEAN	429	VI-
PASSAIC	443	VII-
SALEM	64	VII-
SOMERSET	239	VII+
SUSSEX	130	V-
UNION	490	VII-
WARREN	91	V-

New Mexico

BERNALILLO	475	VI-
CATRON	3	I-
CHAVES	57	V-
COLFAX	13	II-
CURRY	42	VII-
DE BACA	2	III-
DONA ANA	134	V+
EDDY	48	V-
GRANT	27	II-
GUADALUPE	4	IV+
HARDING	1	IV+
HIDALGO	6	I-
LEA	55	VI-
LINCOLN	12	I+
LOS ALAMOS	18	V-
LUNA	18	V-
McKINLEY	56	V-
MORA	4	III+
OTERO	51	VII+
QUAY	11	VII-
RIO ARRIBA	34	II+
ROOSEVELT	17	VII-
SANDOVAL	62	V+
SAN JUAN	89	V-
SAN MIGUEL	25	III+
SANTA FE	96	V-
SIERRA	10	V+
SOCORRO	15	I+
TAOS	23	III+
TORRANCE	10	I+
UNION	4	III-
VALENCIA	45	V+

New York

ALBANY	291	IV+
ALLEGANY	50	II-
BRONX	1223	IV+
BROOME	211	VII-
CATTARAUGUS	84	III-
CAYUGA	81	IV-
CHAUTAUQUA	141	IV-
CHEMUNG	95	IV+
CHENANGO	52	IV-
CLINTON	85	VII-
COLUMBIA	63	II-
CORTLAND	49	IV-
DELAWARE	47	III-
DUTCHESS	258	VII-
ERIE	962	IV+
ESSEX	37	III-
FRANKLIN	46	III+
FULTON	54	III-
GENESEE	60	IV+
GREENE	45	I-
HAMILTON	5	III-
HERKIMER	66	IV+
JEFFERSON	107	IV+
KINGS	2314	IV+
LEWIS	27	III+
LIVINGSTON	62	VII-
MADISON	68	VII-
MONROE	710	VII-
MONTGOMERY	52	IV+
NASSAU	1272	VII-
NEW YORK	1510	IV+
NIAGARA	220	VII-
ONEIDA	249	IV+
ONONDAGA	461	VII-
ONTARIO	95	II-
ORANGE	304	V+
ORLEANS	42	IV+
OSWEGO	121	II-
OTSEGO	60	III-
PUTNAM	84	VI-
QUEENS	1925	VII-
RENSSELAER	153	IV+
RICHMOND	380	V-
ROCKLAND	262	VI-
ST. LAWRENCE	112	IV-
SARATOGA	180	V-
SCHENECTADY	148	IV+
SCHOHARIE	32	II-
SCHUYLER	19	IV-
SENECA	34	IV+
STEUBEN	99	IV+
SUFFOLK	1311	VI-
SULLIVAN	68	I-
TIOGA	52	VII-
TOMPKINS	94	V-
ULSTER	164	VI-
WARREN	59	III-
WASHINGTON	59	IV+
WAYNE	89	VII-
WESTCHESTER	861	VII-
WYOMING	42	III+
YATES	23	III-

North Carolina

ALAMANCE	107	VII-
ALEXANDER	27	V-
ALLEGHANY	10	II-
ANSON	23	III-
ASHE	22	II-
AVERY	15	II-
BEAUFORT	42	II-
BERTIE	20	III-
BLADEN	29	V-
BRUNSWICK	51	I+
BUNCOMBE	174	VII-
BURKE	75	V-
CABARRUS	98	V-
CALDWELL	70	V-
CAMDEN	6	III-
CARTERET	52	V+
CASWELL	21	III-
CATAWBA	117	V-
CHATHAM	38	II+
CHEROKEE	20	II-
CHOWAN	14	II-
CLAY	7	I-
CLEVELAND	83	V-
COLUMBUS	49	VII-
CRAVEN	81	V+
CUMBERLAND	270	VI-
CURRITUCK	14	I+
DARE	23	I+
DAVIDSON	125	V-
DAVIE	27	I+
DUPLIN	40	III-
DURHAM	180	V+
EDGECOMBE	56	III-
FORSYTH	263	VI-
FRANKLIN	36	II+
GASTON	172	VII-
GATES	9	III+
GRAHAM	7	III-
GRANVILLE	38	III+
GREENE	15	III-
GUILFORD	344	VII-
HALIFAX	55	III-
HARNETT	67	V-
HAYWOOD	47	VII-
HENDERSON	69	V-
HERTFORD	23	IV-
HOKE	23	I+
HYDE	5	III-
IREDELL	92	II+

JACKSON	27	II-
JOHNSTON	80	II+
JONES	9	III-
LEE	41	V-
LENOIR	57	VII-
LINCOLN	50	I+
McDOWELL	35	V-
MACON	23	I+
MADISON	17	III-
MARTIN	25	III-
MECKLENBURG	499	VI+
MITCHELL	14	III-
MONTGOMERY	23	II-
MOORE	58	I+
NASH	75	II+
NEW HANOVER	119	V-
NORTHAMPTON	20	III-
ONSLOW	151	VII+
ORANGE	93	V-
PAMLICO	12	III+
PASQUOTANK	31	VII-
PENDER	29	I+
PERQUIMANS	10	II-
PERSON	30	II-
PITT	107	VI-
POLK	14	III+
RANDOLPH	106	V-
RICHMOND	44	II-
ROBESON	104	V-
ROCKINGHAM	86	V-
ROWAN	109	VII-
RUTHERFORD	57	II-
SAMPSON	47	VII-
SCOTLAND	33	V-
STANLY	51	V-
STOKES	37	I+
SURRY	61	II-
SWAIN	11	II-
TRANSYLVANIA	25	V-
TYRRELL	4	III-
UNION	82	I+
VANCE	38	II-
WAKE	417	V+
WARREN	17	III+
WASHINGTON	14	III-
WATAUGA	37	I+
WAYNE	103	V-
WILKES	59	V-
WILSON	65	III-
YADKIN	30	V-
YANCEY	15	II-

North Dakota

ADAMS	3	IV-
BARNES	12	IV-
BENSON	7	III-
BILLINGS	1	III+
BOTTINEAU	8	III-
BOWMAN	4	III-
BURKE	3	IV+
BURLEIGH	60	V-
CASS	102	II+
CAVALIER	6	III-
DICKEY	6	III-
DIVIDE	3	IV+
DUNN	4	III-
EDDY	3	IV+
EMMONS	5	IV+
FOSTER	4	IV-
GOLDEN VALLEY	2	IV-
GRAND FORKS	70	VII-
GRANT	4	IV+
GRIGGS	3	IV+
HETTINGER	3	IV+
KIDDER	3	IV+
LA MOURE	5	IV-
LOGAN	3	IV+
McHENRY	7	IV+
McINTOSH	4	IV+
McKENZIE	6	II-
McLEAN	10	III-
MERCER	10	I-
MORTON	24	I-
MOUNTRAIL	7	IV+
NELSON	4	IV-
OLIVER	2	III-
PEMBINA	9	III-
PIERCE	5	III-
RAMSEY	13	III-
RANSOM	6	IV-
RENVILLE	3	III-
RICHLAND	18	III-
ROLETTE	13	III-
SARGENT	5	IV-
SHERIDAN	2	IV-
SIOUX	4	IV+
SLOPE	1	IV+
STARK	23	II-
STEELE	2	IV+
STUTSMAN	22	III-
TOWNER	4	IV+
TRAILL	9	III-
WALSH	14	IV-
WARD	58	VII-
WELLS	6	IV+
WILLIAMS	21	II-

Ohio

ADAMS	25	I-
ALLEN	109	VII-
ASHLAND	47	VII-
ASHTABULA	99	VII-
ATHENS	59	IV+
AUGLAIZE	44	III-
BELMONT	71	III-
BROWN	35	II-
BUTLER	289	VI-
CARROLL	26	II-
CHAMPAIGN	36	III-
CLARK	147	VII-
CLERMONT	149	VI-
CLINTON	35	III-
COLUMBIANA	108	III-
COSHOCTON	35	III-
CRAWFORD	48	IV-
CUYAHOGA	1404	VII-
DARKE	53	II-
DEFIANCE	39	VII-
DELAWARE	67	V+
ERIE	77	VII-
FAIRFIELD	103	V-
FAYETTE	27	III-
FRANKLIN	953	VII-
FULTON	38	II-
GALLIA	31	II-
GEAUGA	81	VI-
GREENE	136	VII-
GUERNSEY	39	II-
HAMILTON	853	VII-
HANCOCK	65	VII-
HARDIN	31	III-
HARRISON	16	III-
HENRY	29	IV+
HIGHLAND	35	II-
HOCKING	25	II-
HOLMES	33	I+
HURON	56	VII-
JACKSON	30	II-
JEFFERSON	80	IV-
KNOX	47	III-
LAKE	215	VII-
LAWRENCE	61	II-
LICKING	128	VI-
LOGAN	42	II-
LORAIN	270	VII-
LUCAS	459	IV+
MADISON	37	II+
MAHONING	264	IV-
MARION	64	IV-
MEDINA	122	V-
MEIGS	23	II-
MERCER	39	IV-
MIAMI	93	VII-
MONROE	15	III-
MONTGOMERY	568	VII-
MORGAN	14	II-
MORROW	28	I-
MUSKINGUM	82	III-
NOBLE	11	III-

OTTAWA	40	VII-
PAULDING	20	III-
PERRY	31	II-
PICKAWAY	48	VII-
PIKE	24	II-
PORTAGE	142	VII-
PREBLE	40	VII-
PUTNAM	34	IV-
RICHLAND	126	VII-
ROSS	69	III+
SANDUSKY	62	VII-
SCIOTO	80	III-
SENECA	60	IV-
SHELBY	45	II-
STARK	366	VII-
SUMMIT	514	VII-
TRUMBULL	227	VII-
TUSCARAWAS	84	III-
UNION	32	I-
VAN WERT	30	III-
VINTON	11	I-
WARREN	113	VI-
WASHINGTON	62	II-
WAYNE	101	VI-
WILLIAMS	37	IV-
WOOD	113	V-
WYANDOT	22	IV-

Oklahoma

ADAIR	18	I-
ALFALFA	6	III-
ATOKA	13	II-
BEAVER	6	III-
BECKHAM	19	I-
BLAINE	11	II-
BRYAN	32	II-
CADDO	29	III-
CANADIAN	74	I+
CARTER	43	II-
CHEROKEE	34	I+
CHOCTAW	15	II-
CIMARRON	3	IV+
CLEVELAND	173	V-
COAL	6	III-
COMANCHE	108	VII-
COTTON	7	III-
CRAIG	14	III-
CREEK	61	I-
CUSTER	27	II-
DELAWARE	28	I+
DEWEY	6	III-
ELLIS	5	III-
GARFIELD	57	II-
GARVIN	27	II-
GRADY	42	I-
GRANT	6	III-
GREER	7	IV+
HARMON	4	IV+
HARPER	4	IV+
HASKELL	11	II-
HUGHES	13	III-
JACKSON	29	VII-
JEFFERSON	7	II-
JOHNSTON	10	I-
KAY	48	III-
KINGFISHER	13	III-
KIOWA	11	III-
LATIMER	10	II-
LE FLORE	43	I-
LINCOLN	29	I-
LOGAN	28	I-
LOVE	8	I-
McCLAIN	23	I+
McCURTAIN	33	I-
McINTOSH	17	I-
MAJOR	8	II-
MARSHALL	11	I-
MAYES	33	I-
MURRAY	12	II-
MUSKOGEE	67	II-
NOBLE	11	II-
NOWATA	10	II-
OKFUSKEE	12	III+
OKLAHOMA	595	VII-
OKMULGEE	36	III-
OSAGE	41	I-
OTTAWA	30	III-
PAWNEE	16	I-
PAYNE	61	V-
PITTSBURG	41	III-
PONTOTOC	34	II-
POTTAWATOMIE	58	I-
PUSHMATAHA	11	I-
ROGER MILLS	4	III-
ROGERS	55	V-
SEMINOLE	25	III-
SEQUOYAH	34	I-
STEPHENS	42	II-
TEXAS	16	VII-
TILLMAN	10	III-
TULSA	500	VI-
WAGONER	48	I+
WASHINGTON	48	V-
WASHITA	11	II-
WOODS	9	IV-
WOODWARD	19	I-

Oregon

BAKER	15	III-
BENTON	71	V-
CLACKAMAS	278	V-
CLATSOP	33	V-
COLUMBIA	38	I-
COOS	60	V-
CROOK	14	V-
CURRY	19	VI-
DESCHUTES	75	V-
DOUGLAS	94	V-
GILLIAM	2	IV-
GRANT	8	V-
HARNEY	7	II-
HOOD RIVER	17	V-
JACKSON	146	V-
JEFFERSON	14	V-
JOSEPHINE	62	V-
KLAMATH	58	V-
LAKE	7	V-
LANE	282	V-
LINCOLN	39	V-
LINN	91	V-
MALHEUR	26	V-
MARION	227	V-
MORROW	8	I-
MULTNOMAH	580	VII-
POLK	49	V-
SHERMAN	2	III-
TILLAMOOK	21	V-
UMATILLA	59	V-
UNION	24	I-
WALLOWA	7	II-
WASCO	22	VII-
WASHINGTON	310	V-
WHEELER	1	IV+
YAMHILL	65	V-

Pennsylvania

ADAMS	78	II+
ALLEGHENY	1324	IV+
ARMSTRONG	73	III-
BEAVER	185	IV-
BEDFORD	48	III-
BERKS	335	IV+
BLAIR	130	III-
BRADFORD	61	III-
BUCKS	539	VI-
BUTLER	151	II-
CAMBRIA	162	III-
CAMERON	6	VII-
CARBON	57	III+
CENTRE	122	VI-
CHESTER	371	VI+
CLARION	42	II-
CLEARFIELD	78	II-
CLINTON	37	III-
COLUMBIA	62	II-
CRAWFORD	86	VII-
CUMBERLAND	194	VI-
DAUPHIN	236	IV-

DELAWARE	542	VII-
ELK	35	IV-
ERIE	274	VII-
FAYETTE	145	III-
FOREST	5	III-
FRANKLIN	121	II-
FULTON	14	II-
GREENE	39	II-
HUNTINGDON	44	III-
INDIANA	90	II-
JEFFERSON	46	III-
JUNIATA	21	II-
LACKAWANNA	217	IV+
LANCASTER	421	V+
LAWRENCE	96	IV-
LEBANON	114	III-
LEHIGH	290	IV+
LUZERNE	322	III-
LYCOMING	117	III-
McKEAN	47	IV-
MERCER	120	IV-
MIFFLIN	46	III-
MONROE	94	V-
MONTGOMERY	673	VII-
MONTOUR	18	IV+
NORTHAMPTON	246	IV+
NORTHUMBERLAN	97	III-
PERRY	41	I+
PHILADELPHIA	1543	IV+
PIKE	28	V+
POTTER	17	III-
SCHUYLKILL	151	III-
SNYDER	37	II-
SOMERSET	78	III-
SULLIVAN	6	III-
SUSQUEHANNA	40	III-
TIOGA	41	IV-
UNION	36	V-
VENANGO	59	III-
WARREN	45	IV-
WASHINGTON	204	III-
WAYNE	40	II+
WESTMORELAND	369	IV-
WYOMING	28	I-
YORK	338	V-

Rhode Island

BRISTOL	48	VII-
KENT	163	VII-
NEWPORT	85	VII-
PROVIDENCE	601	IV+
WASHINGTON	107	VII+

South Carolina

ABBEVILLE	24	III-
AIKEN	118	VI-
ALLENDALE	11	III-
ANDERSON	144	I-
BAMBERG	17	II-
BARNWELL	20	II-
BEAUFORT	85	V+
BERKELEY	126	V-
CALHOUN	12	II-
CHARLESTON	281	VI-
CHEROKEE	43	II-
CHESTER	31	III+
CHESTERFIELD	37	II-
CLARENDON	28	III-
COLLETON	34	II-
DARLINGTON	61	II-
DILLON	29	III-
DORCHESTER	81	V-
EDGEFIELD	18	II-
FAIRFIELD	22	III+
FLORENCE	112	V-
GEORGETOWN	46	V-
GREENVILLE	316	V-
GREENWOOD	59	II-
HAMPTON	18	II-
HORRY	143	V+
JASPER	15	I-
KERSHAW	41	II-
LANCASTER	53	V-
LAURENS	56	III+
LEE	18	III-
LEXINGTON	164	V-
McCORMICK	9	III+
MARION	34	II-
MARLBORO	29	II-
NEWBERRY	33	III-
OCONEE	57	II+
ORANGEBURG	83	II-
PICKENS	92	V-
RICHLAND	282	VI-
SALUDA	16	III-
SPARTANBURG	219	V-
SUMTER	100	VII+
UNION	30	III-
WILLIAMSBURG	36	V-
YORK	128	V-

South Dakota

AURORA	3	IV+
BEADLE	18	IV+
BENNETT	3	III+
BON HOMME	7	IV-
BROOKINGS	25	III-
BROWN	36	IV-
BRULE	6	IV+
BUFFALO	2	IV-
BUTTE	8	III-
CAMPBELL	2	IV+
CHARLES MIX	9	III-
CLARK	4	IV+
CLAY	13	IV-
CODINGTON	23	III-
CORSON	4	III-
CUSTER	6	I-
DAVISON	17	III-
DAY	7	III-
DEUEL	5	III-
DEWEY	6	III+
DOUGLAS	4	IV+
EDMUNDS	4	IV-
FALL RIVER	7	II-
FAULK	3	IV+
GRANT	8	III-
GREGORY	5	IV+
HAAKON	3	IV-
HAMLIN	5	III-
HAND	4	IV+
HANSON	3	IV+
HARDING	2	IV+
HUGHES	15	V-
HUTCHINSON	8	IV+
HYDE	2	IV+
JACKSON	3	VI-
JERAULD	2	IV-
JONES	1	IV+
KINGSBURY	6	IV+
LAKE	11	IV+
LAWRENCE	21	III+
LINCOLN	15	II+
LYMAN	4	IV+
McCOOK	6	IV+
McPHERSON	3	IV+
MARSHALL	5	IV+
MEADE	22	V-
MELLETTE	2	IV+
MINER	3	IV+
MINNEHAHA	123	V-
MOODY	7	IV+
PENNINGTON	81	VI-
PERKINS	4	III-
POTTER	3	IV+
ROBERTS	10	III+
SANBORN	3	IV+
SHANNON	10	V-
SPINK	8	IV+
STANLEY	3	VII-
SULLY	2	IV+
TODD	8	VII+
TRIPP	7	IV+
TURNER	9	IV+
UNION	10	II-
WALWORTH	6	IV+
YANKTON	19	IV+
ZIEBACH	2	III-

Tennessee

ANDERSON	68	V-
BEDFORD	30	II-
BENTON	14	I-
BLEDSOE	10	I-
BLOUNT	86	V-
BRADLEY	73	V-
CAMPBELL	35	V-
CANNON	10	I-
CARROLL	27	III-
CARTER	51	V-
CHEATHAM	27	V-
CHESTER	13	I-
CLAIBORNE	26	I-
CLAY	7	II-
COCKE	29	II-
COFFEE	40	V-
CROCKETT	13	III-
CUMBERLAND	35	V-
DAVIDSON	515	VII-
DECATUR	10	II-
DE KALB	14	I-
DICKSON	35	I+
DYER	35	II-
FAYETTE	24	II-
FENTRESS	15	V-
FRANKLIN	35	II-
GIBSON	46	III-
GILES	26	III-
GRAINGER	17	II-
GREENE	56	II-
GRUNDY	13	V-
HAMBLEN	50	V-
HAMILTON	282	V-
HANCOCK	7	III-
HARDEMAN	23	III-
HARDIN	23	I-
HAWKINS	44	V-
HAYWOOD	19	III-
HENDERSON	22	I-
HENRY	28	II-
HICKMAN	17	I+
HOUSTON	7	II-
HUMPHREYS	16	II-
JACKSON	9	II-
JEFFERSON	33	I-
JOHNSON	14	II-
KNOX	329	V-
LAKE	7	III-
LAUDERDALE	23	I-
LAWRENCE	35	II-
LEWIS	9	I-
LINCOLN	28	III-
LOUDON	31	V-
McMINN	42	II-
McNAIRY	22	I-
MACON	16	I-
MADISON	77	II-
MARION	24	II-
MARSHALL	22	II-
MAURY	54	II-
MEIGS	8	I-
MONROE	31	I-
MONTGOMERY	92	V-
MOORE	4	I-
MORGAN	17	I-
OBION	32	III-
OVERTON	18	II-
PERRY	7	II-
PICKETT	5	II-
POLK	14	II-
PUTNAM	51	V-
RHEA	24	I-
ROANE	47	V-
ROBERTSON	41	I+
RUTHERFORD	118	V+
SCOTT	18	V-
SEQUATCHIE	9	V-
SEVIER	51	I+
SHELBY	815	VII-
SMITH	14	II-
STEWART	9	II-
SULLIVAN	143	V-
SUMNER	102	V-
TIPTON	37	II+
TROUSDALE	6	II-
UNICOI	17	VII-
UNION	14	I+
VAN BUREN	5	I-
WARREN	33	II-
WASHINGTON	91	V-
WAYNE	14	II-
WEAKLEY	32	II-
WHITE	20	II-
WILLIAMSON	80	V-
WILSON	67	V-

Texas

ANDERSON	48	I+
ANDREWS	14	VI-
ANGELINA	70	V-
ARANSAS	18	V-
ARCHER	8	I-
ARMSTRONG	2	III-
ATASCOSA	30	V-
AUSTIN	20	I+
BAILEY	7	VII-
BANDERA	11	I+
BASTROP	38	I+
BAYLOR	4	III-
BEE	25	V-
BELL	188	V+
BEXAR	1177	VI+
BLANCO	6	I+
BORDEN	1	III+
BOSQUE	15	I+
BOWIE	81	VII-
BRAZORIA	191	V-
BRAZOS	121	V-
BREWSTER	9	IV+
BRISCOE	2	IV-
BROOKS	8	VII-
BROWN	34	I-
BURLESON	14	I-
BURNET	23	I+
CALDWELL	26	II+
CALHOUN	19	VII-
CALLAHAN	12	I-
CAMERON	252	V-
CAMP	10	II-
CARSON	7	III-
CASS	30	I-
CASTRO	9	VII-
CHAMBERS	20	V-
CHEROKEE	41	II-
CHILDRESS	6	III-
CLAY	10	II-
COCHRAN	4	VII-
COKE	3	III+
COLEMAN	10	III-
COLLIN	262	V+
COLLINGSWORTH	4	III-
COLORADO	18	III-
COMAL	52	V+
COMANCHE	13	III-
CONCHO	3	III+
COOKE	31	II+
CORYELL	63	V-
COTTLE	2	III-
CRANE	5	V-
CROCKETT	4	V-
CROSBY	7	IV-
CULBERSON	3	VII-
DALLAM	5	III-
DALLAS	1837	VI+
DAWSON	14	VII-
DEAF SMITH	19	VI-
DELTA	5	III+
DENTON	270	V+
DE WITT	19	III-
DICKENS	3	III-
DIMMIT	10	I-
DONLEY	4	III-
DUVAL	13	VII-
EASTLAND	19	III-
ECTOR	118	VI-
EDWARDS	2	III+
ELLIS	85	I+
EL PASO	578	V-

ERATH	28	I+
FALLS	18	III-
FANNIN	25	III-
FAYETTE	20	III+
FISHER	5	III-
FLOYD	8	IV+
FOARD	2	III-
FORT BEND	225	V-
FRANKLIN	8	I+
FREESTONE	16	I-
FRIO	13	I-
GAINES	14	V-
GALVESTON	216	VI-
GARZA	5	III-
GILLESPIE	17	I+
GLASSCOCK	1	II-
GOLIAD	6	III+
GONZALES	17	III-
GRAY	24	IV-
GRAYSON	94	III-
GREGG	104	V-
GRIMES	19	II+
GUADALUPE	64	I+
HALE	35	VII-
HALL	4	III-
HAMILTON	8	II-
HANSFORD	6	VII-
HARDEMAN	5	III-
HARDIN	41	V-
HARRIS	2791	V-
HARRISON	57	II-
HARTLEY	4	V-
HASKELL	7	III+
HAYS	65	V+
HEMPHILL	4	I-
HENDERSON	58	I+
HIDALGO	368	V-
HILL	27	III-
HOCKLEY	24	V-
HOOD	29	I+
HOPKINS	29	I+
HOUSTON	21	I-
HOWARD	32	VII-
HUDSPETH	3	II-
HUNT	64	II+
HUTCHINSON	26	VII-
IRION	2	I+
JACK	7	III-
JACKSON	13	III-
JASPER	31	I-
JEFF DAVIS	2	III+
JEFFERSON	237	VII-
JIM HOGG	5	III-
JIM WELLS	37	VII-
JOHNSON	97	V+
JONES	17	III-
KARNES	12	III-
KAUFMAN	52	II+
KENDALL	15	I+
KENEDY	1	IV+
KENT	1	IV+
KERR	36	V-
KIMBLE	4	III-
KING	0	III+
KINNEY	3	III+
KLEBERG	31	VII-
KNOX	5	III+
LAMAR	44	II-
LAMB	15	III-
LAMPASAS	13	I+
LA SALLE	5	III-
LAVACA	19	III-
LEE	13	I+
LEON	13	III+
LIBERTY	52	V-
LIMESTONE	21	II-
LIPSCOMB	3	III-
LIVE OAK	10	I-
LLANO	12	I+
LOVING	0	IV+
LUBBOCK	218	VI-
LYNN	7	IV-
McCULLOCH	9	III-
McLENNAN	188	V-
McMULLEN	1	IV+
MADISON	11	I-
MARION	10	II-
MARTIN	5	III+
MASON	3	III-
MATAGORDA	37	I-
MAVERICK	36	V-
MEDINA	27	II+
MENARD	2	IV+
MIDLAND	106	VI+
MILAM	23	II-
MILLS	5	III-
MITCHELL	8	III-
MONTAGUE	17	II-
MONTGOMERY	180	V-
MOORE	18	V-
MORRIS	13	II-
MOTLEY	2	VII-
NACOGDOCHES	55	I+
NAVARRO	40	II+
NEWTON	14	II-
NOLAN	17	III-
NUECES	290	VI-
OCHILTREE	9	VII-
OLDHAM	2	VII-
ORANGE	80	VI-
PALO PINTO	25	VII-
PANOLA	22	I-
PARKER	64	V+
PARMER	10	VII-
PECOS	15	VII-
POLK	30	I+
POTTER	97	VII-
PRESIDIO	6	III+
RAINS	7	I+
RANDALL	89	VI-
REAGAN	5	V-
REAL	2	II-
RED RIVER	14	II-
REEVES	16	VII-
REFUGIO	8	VII-
ROBERTS	1	I-
ROBERTSON	15	III+
ROCKWALL	25	I+
RUNNELS	11	III-
RUSK	44	V-
SABINE	10	I+
SAN AUGUSTINE	8	II-
SAN JACINTO	16	I+
SAN PATRICIO	58	V-
SAN SABA	5	II-
SCHLEICHER	3	I-
SCURRY	19	V-
SHACKELFORD	3	II-
SHELBY	22	II-
SHERMAN	3	VII-
SMITH	150	V-
SOMERVELL	5	I+
STARR	39	I+
STEPHENS	9	II-
STERLING	2	II+
STONEWALL	2	III-
SUTTON	4	V-
SWISHER	8	VII-
TARRANT	1162	VI+
TAYLOR	119	VI-
TERRELL	1	IV+
TERRY	13	VII-
THROCKMORTON	2	III+
TITUS	24	I+
TOM GREEN	98	V-
TRAVIS	572	V+
TRINITY	11	I+
TYLER	17	I-
UPSHUR	31	I-
UPTON	4	VII-
UVALDE	23	V-
VAL VERDE	38	V-
VAN ZANDT	38	I+
VICTORIA	74	V-
WALKER	51	V-
WALLER	23	I+
WARD	13	VII-
WASHINGTON	26	II+
WEBB	131	V+
WHARTON	40	III-
WHEELER	6	III-

WICHITA	122	VII-
WILBARGER	15	III-
WILLACY	17	V-
WILLIAMSON	139	I+
WILSON	23	I+
WINKLER	9	VII-
WISE	34	I+
WOOD	29	I+
YOAKUM	9	VI-
YOUNG	17	I-
ZAPATA	9	V-
ZAVALA	12	III+

Utah

BEAVER	5	II-
BOX ELDER	36	V-
CACHE	70	I+
CARBON	20	V-
DAGGETT	1	VI-
DAVIS	187	VI-
DUCHESNE	13	I-
EMERY	10	I-
GARFIELD	4	II-
GRAND	7	VI-
IRON	21	V-
JUAB	6	I-
KANE	5	I+
MILLARD	11	I+
MORGAN	6	V-
PIUTE	1	II-
RICH	2	I-
SALT LAKE	721	V-
SAN JUAN	12	V-
SANPETE	16	I-
SEVIER	15	I-
SUMMIT	16	I+
TOOELE	26	V-
UINTAH	22	I-
UTAH	261	V-
WASATCH	10	I+
WASHINGTON	48	V+
WAYNE	2	I+
WEBER	158	VI-

Vermont

ADDISON	33	I+
BENNINGTON	36	II-
CALEDONIA	28	II-
CHITTENDEN	131	VI-
ESSEX	6	II-
FRANKLIN	40	III+
GRAND ISLE	5	I+
LAMOILLE	20	I+
ORANGE	26	I+
ORLEANS	24	II-
RUTLAND	62	III-
WASHINGTON	55	III-
WINDHAM	41	III+
WINDSOR	54	II-

Virginia

ACCOMACK	32	III-
ALBEMARLE	67	V-
ALLEGHANY	13	II-
AMELIA	9	II-
AMHERST	29	II-
APPOMATTOX	12	I-
ARLINGTON	170	VII+
AUGUSTA	54	I+
BATH	5	II-
BEDFORD	45	I+
BLAND	7	II-
BOTETOURT	25	I-
BRUNSWICK	16	III+
BUCHANAN	31	V-
BUCKINGHAM	13	II-
CAMPBELL	48	VII-
CAROLINE	19	I-
CARROLL	27	II-
CHARLES CITY	6	IV-
CHARLOTTE	12	III-
CHESTERFIELD	207	V-
CLARKE	11	I+
CRAIG	4	II+
CULPEPER	28	V-
CUMBERLAND	8	I-
DICKENSON	18	V-
DINWIDDIE	21	IV-
ESSEX	9	I-
FAIRFAX	815	VI+
FAUQUIER	48	I+
FLOYD	12	II-
FLUVANNA	12	I+
FRANKLIN	39	I-
FREDERICK	45	VI-
GILES	16	VII-
GLOUCESTER	30	V+
GOOCHLAND	14	II+
GRAYSON	16	III-
GREENE	10	I+
GREENSVILLE	9	II-
HALIFAX	29	III-
HANOVER	62	V-
HENRICO	217	V+
HENRY	57	VI-
HIGHLAND	3	II-
ISLE OF WIGHT	25	II+
JAMES CITY	35	VI+
KING AND QUEEN	6	III-
KING GEORGE	14	V+
KING WILLIAM	11	I+
LANCASTER	11	III-
LEE	24	I-
LOUDOUN	86	V-
LOUISA	20	I+
LUNENBURG	11	III-
MADISON	11	II+
MATHEWS	8	III-
MECKLENBURG	29	III+
MIDDLESEX	9	I+
MONTGOMERY	73	V-
NELSON	13	III+
NEW KENT	10	V-
NORTHAMPTON	13	III-
NORTHUMBERLAN	11	III+
NOTTOWAY	15	III+
ORANGE	21	I+
PAGE	21	II-
PATRICK	17	II-
PITTSYLVANIA	55	II-
POWHATAN	15	V-
PRINCE EDWARD	17	II-
PRINCE GEORGE	27	VII-
PRINCE WILLIAM	216	VI+
PULASKI	34	V-
RAPPAHANNOCK	7	II-
RICHMOND	7	III-
ROANOKE	78	VII-
ROCKBRIDGE	18	III-
ROCKINGHAM	57	V+
RUSSELL	29	I-
SCOTT	23	III-
SHENANDOAH	31	II+
SMYTH	32	III-
SOUTHAMPTON	18	III-
SPOTSYLVANIA	57	V+
STAFFORD	59	V-
SURRY	6	III-
SUSSEX	10	IV+
TAZEWELL	46	V-
WARREN	26	V-
WASHINGTON	45	II-
WESTMORELAND	15	II-
WISE	39	I-
WYTHE	25	II-
YORK	41	VI+
ALEXANDRIA	112	VII-
BRISTOL	18	V-
CHARLOTTESVILLI	40	VII-
CHESAPEAKE	150	I+
COLONIAL HEIGHT	16	VII-
COVINGTON	7	VII-
DANVILLE	52	VII+
FAIRFAX	20	VII-
FALLS CHURCH	10	VII-
FREDERICKSBURG	19	VII-
HAMPTON	133	VII-
HARRISONBURG	28	V-
HOPEWELL	23	VII-
LYNCHBURG	63	I-

MARTINSVILLE	16	VII-
NEWPORT NEWS	168	VII+
NORFOLK	230	VII-
PETERSBURG	38	V-
PORTSMOUTH	103	VII-
RADFORD	16	V+
RICHMOND	201	VII-
ROANOKE	95	VII-
SALEM	22	VII-
STAUNTON	24	VII-
SUFFOLK	51	VII-
VIRGINIA BEACH	389	VI+
WAYNESBORO	19	VII-
WINCHESTER	22	V-

Washington

ADAMS	14	VII-
ASOTIN	18	V-
BENTON	112	V-
CHELAN	52	VII+
CLALLAM	56	V-
CLARK	237	V-
COLUMBIA	4	IV+
COWLITZ	82	V-
DOUGLAS	26	V-
FERRY	6	I-
FRANKLIN	37	V-
GARFIELD	2	IV+
GRANT	54	VI-
GRAYS HARBOR	64	II-
ISLAND	59	V-
JEFFERSON	20	V-
KING	1500	VII+
KITSAP	186	V-
KITTITAS	27	IV+
KLICKITAT	16	I-
LEWIS	59	I-
LINCOLN	9	III-
MASON	38	V-
OKANOGAN	33	V-
PACIFIC	19	III+
PEND OREILLE	9	I-
PIERCE	576	V+
SAN JUAN	10	I+
SKAGIT	79	V+
SKAMANIA	8	V-
SNOHOMISH	461	VI+
SPOKANE	359	V-
STEVENS	31	I-
THURSTON	160	V-
WAHKIAKUM	3	III-
WALLA WALLA	48	V-
WHATCOM	127	I+
WHITMAN	39	IV-
YAKIMA	187	V-

West Virginia

BARBOUR	16	II-
BERKELEY	59	I+
BOONE	26	V-
BRAXTON	13	III-
BROOKE	27	IV-
CABELL	96	IV-
CALHOUN	8	II-
CLAY	10	II-
DODDRIDGE	7	II-
FAYETTE	48	II-
GILMER	8	III-
GRANT	10	II-
GREENBRIER	35	II-
HAMPSHIRE	16	I+
HANCOCK	35	IV-
HARDY	11	II-
HARRISON	69	III-
JACKSON	26	V-
JEFFERSON	36	I+
KANAWHA	205	VII-
LEWIS	17	III-
LINCOLN	21	I-
LOGAN	43	VII-
McDOWELL	35	III-
MARION	57	III-
MARSHALL	37	III-
MASON	25	III-
MERCER	65	II-
MINERAL	27	II-
MINGO	34	V-
MONONGALIA	75	II-
MONROE	12	II-
MORGAN	12	I+
NICHOLAS	27	V-
OHIO	51	IV-
PENDLETON	8	II-
PLEASANTS	8	II-
POCAHONTAS	9	II-
PRESTON	29	II-
PUTNAM	43	V-
RALEIGH	76	V-
RANDOLPH	28	II-
RITCHIE	10	II-
ROANE	15	II-
SUMMERS	14	II-
TAYLOR	15	II-
TUCKER	8	II-
TYLER	10	II-
UPSHUR	23	I-
WAYNE	42	V-
WEBSTER	11	V-
WETZEL	19	III-
WIRT	5	II-
WOOD	86	IV-
WYOMING	29	V-

Wisconsin

ADAMS	16	I+
ASHLAND	16	III-
BARRON	41	II-
BAYFIELD	14	II-
BROWN	194	VII+
BUFFALO	14	III-
BURNETT	13	I-
CALUMET	34	VI-
CHIPPEWA	52	III-
CLARK	32	III-
COLUMBIA	45	III-
CRAWFORD	16	III-
DANE	366	VI+
DODGE	77	III-
DOOR	26	I-
DOUGLAS	42	III-
DUNN	36	II-
EAU CLAIRE	85	V-
FLORENCE	5	I+
FOND DU LAC	90	IV-
FOREST	9	II-
GRANT	48	III-
GREEN	30	II-
GREEN LAKE	19	III-
IOWA	20	III-
IRON	6	III-
JACKSON	17	III-
JEFFERSON	66	VII-
JUNEAU	22	II-
KENOSHA	128	VII-
KEWAUNEE	19	IV-
LA CROSSE	98	V-
LAFAYETTE	16	III-
LANGLADE	19	III-
LINCOLN	27	II-
MANITOWOC	80	IV-
MARATHON	115	II-
MARINETTE	41	III-
MARQUETTE	12	I-
MENOMINEE	3	I-
MILWAUKEE	951	VII-
MONROE	36	III-
OCONTO	30	II-
ONEIDA	32	V-
OUTAGAMIE	140	VII-
OZAUKEE	73	V-
PEPIN	7	III-
PIERCE	33	II-
POLK	35	I-
PORTAGE	61	V-
PRICE	16	III-
RACINE	175	VII-
RICHLAND	17	III-
ROCK	139	VII-
RUSK	15	III-

ST. CROIX	50 I+
SAUK	47 III-
SAWYER	14 I+
SHAWANO	37 III-
SHEBOYGAN	104 IV-
TAYLOR	19 III-
TREMPEALEAU	25 II-
VERNON	26 III-
VILAS	18 V-
WALWORTH	75 VI-
WASHBURN	14 I-
WASHINGTON	95 V-
WAUKESHA	304 VI-
WAUPACA	46 II-
WAUSHARA	19 I-
WINNEBAGO	140 VII-
WOOD	74 VII-

Wyoming

ALBANY	31 VII-
BIG HORN	11 II-
CAMPBELL	29 V-
CARBON	17 V-
CONVERSE	11 I-
CROOK	5 II-
FREMONT	33 V-
GOSHEN	12 III-
HOT SPRINGS	5 V-
JOHNSON	6 I-
LARAMIE	72 V-
LINCOLN	13 I-
NATRONA	61 V-
NIOBRARA	3 III-
PARK	23 V-
PLATTE	8 I-
SHERIDAN	24 I-
SUBLETTE	5 V-
SWEETWATER	39 I-
TETON	11 V-
UINTA	19 I+
WASHAKIE	8 V-
WESTON	7 V-

Appendix B

Maps: Penturban counties, by seven regions of the U.S.
(Revised classifications)

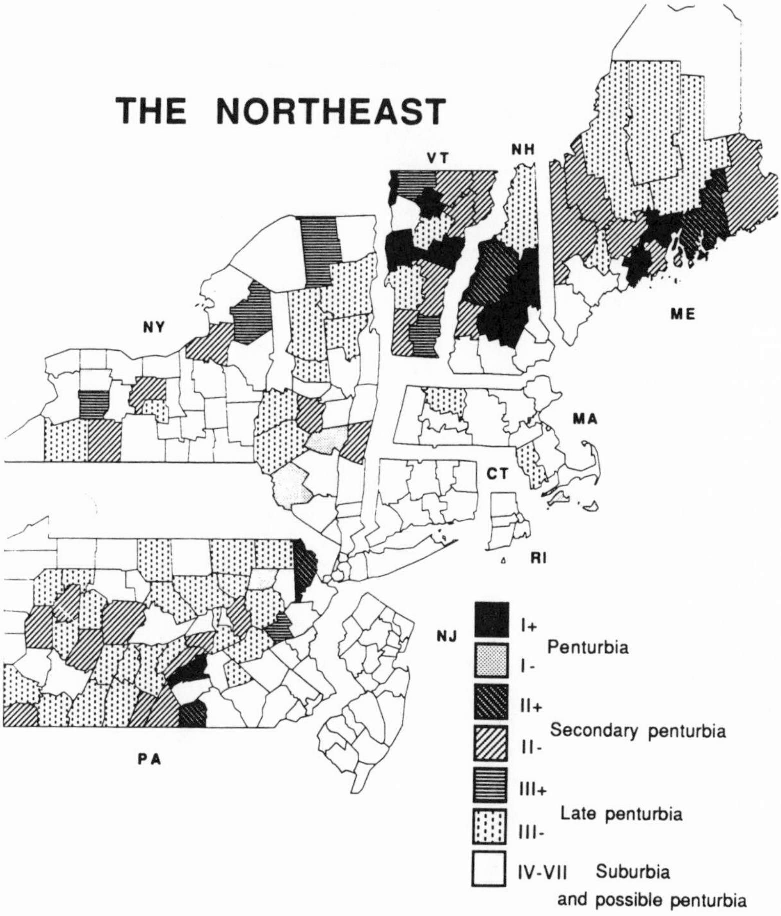

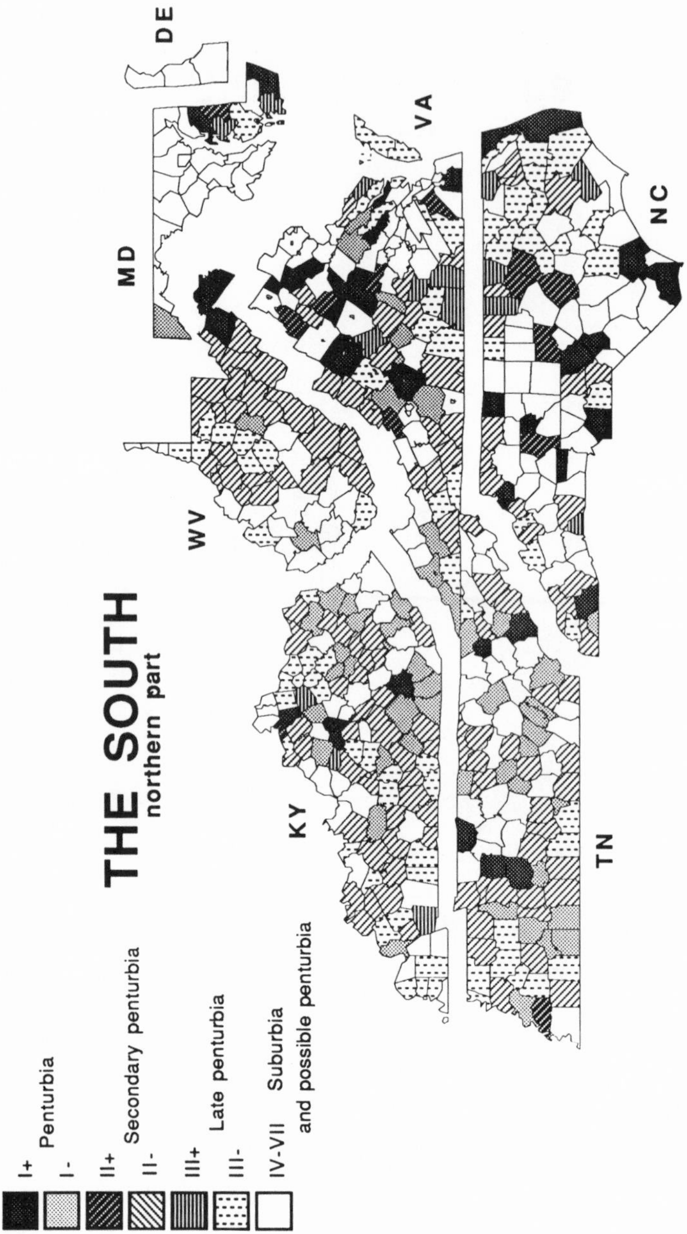
THE SOUTH
northern part
I+ Penturbia
I-
II+ Secondary penturbia
II-
III+ Late penturbia
III-
IV-VII Suburbia and possible penturbia
MD
DE
VA
WV
KY
NC
TN

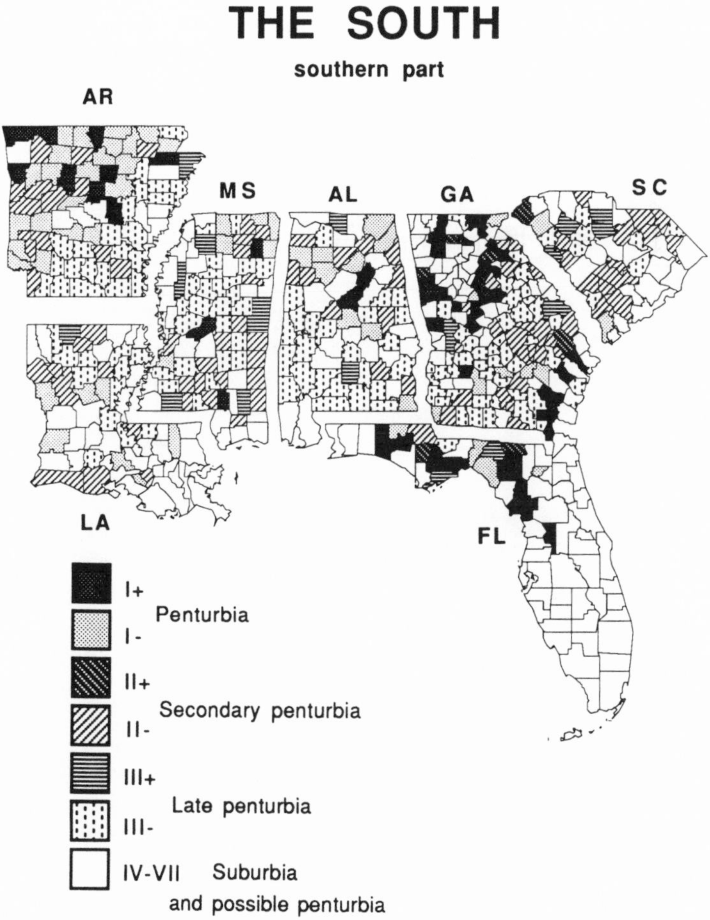
THE SOUTH
southern part
AR
MS
AL
GA
SC
LA
FL
I+
Penturbia
I-
II+
Secondary penturbia
II-
III+
Late penturbia
III-
IV-VII Suburbia
and possible penturbia

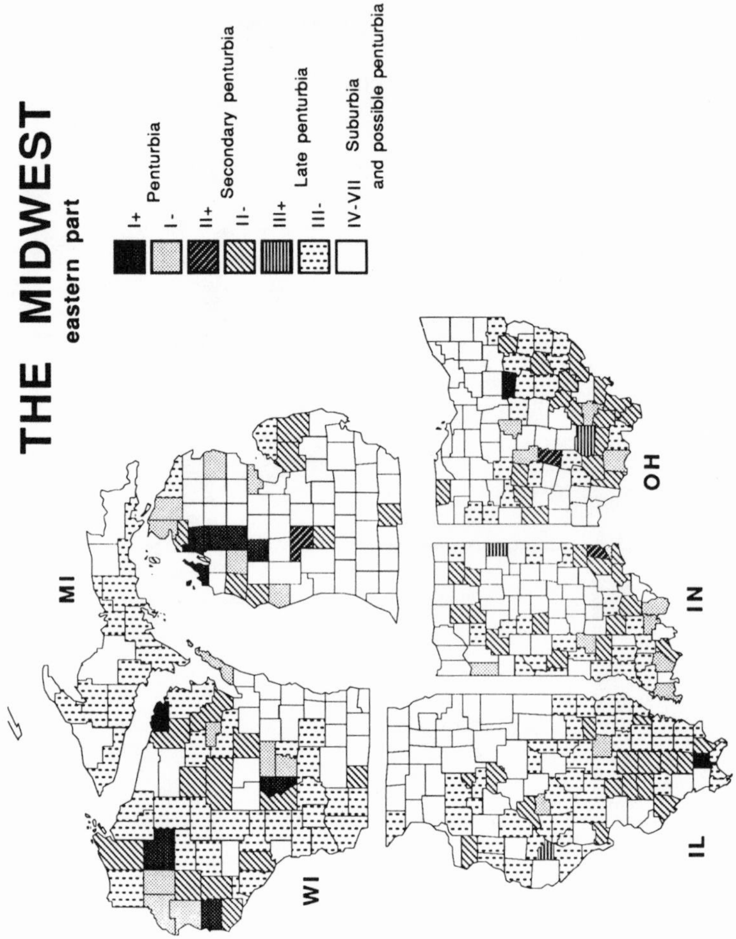
THE MIDWEST
eastern part
I+
Penturbia
I-
II+
Secondary penturbia
II-
III+
Late penturbia
III-
IV-VII
Suburbia
and possible penturbia
MI
WI
OH
IN
IL

THE MIDWEST

western part

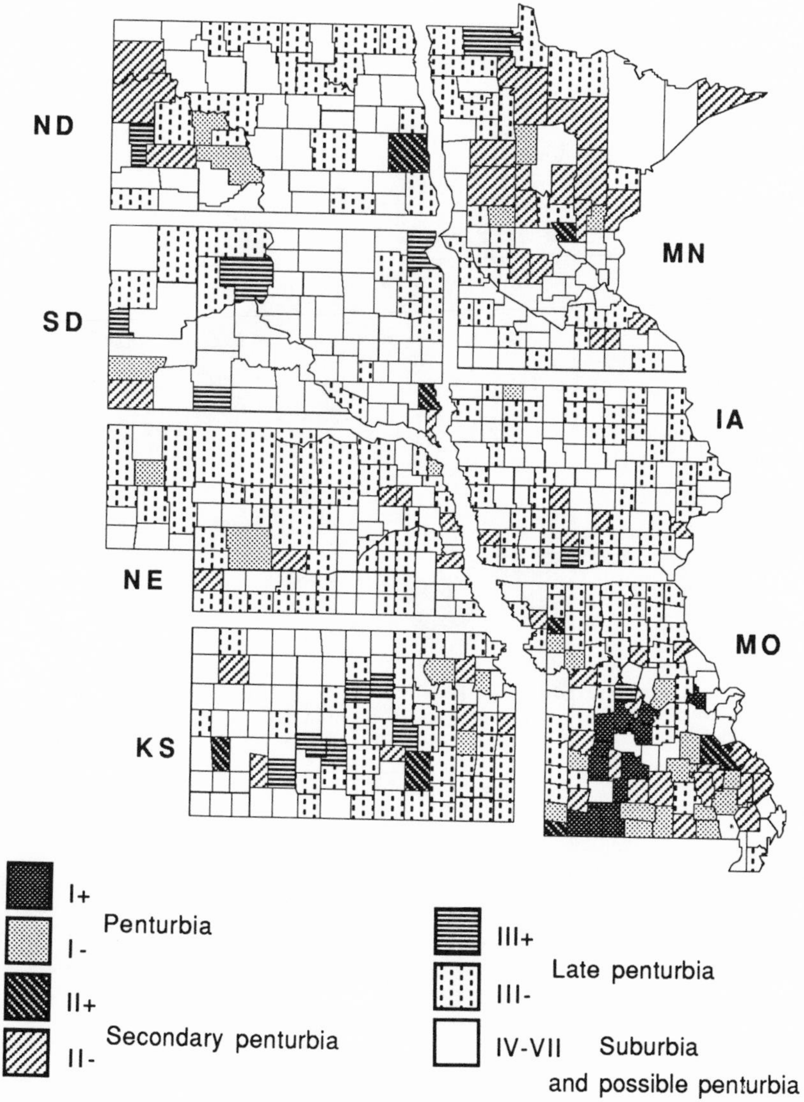

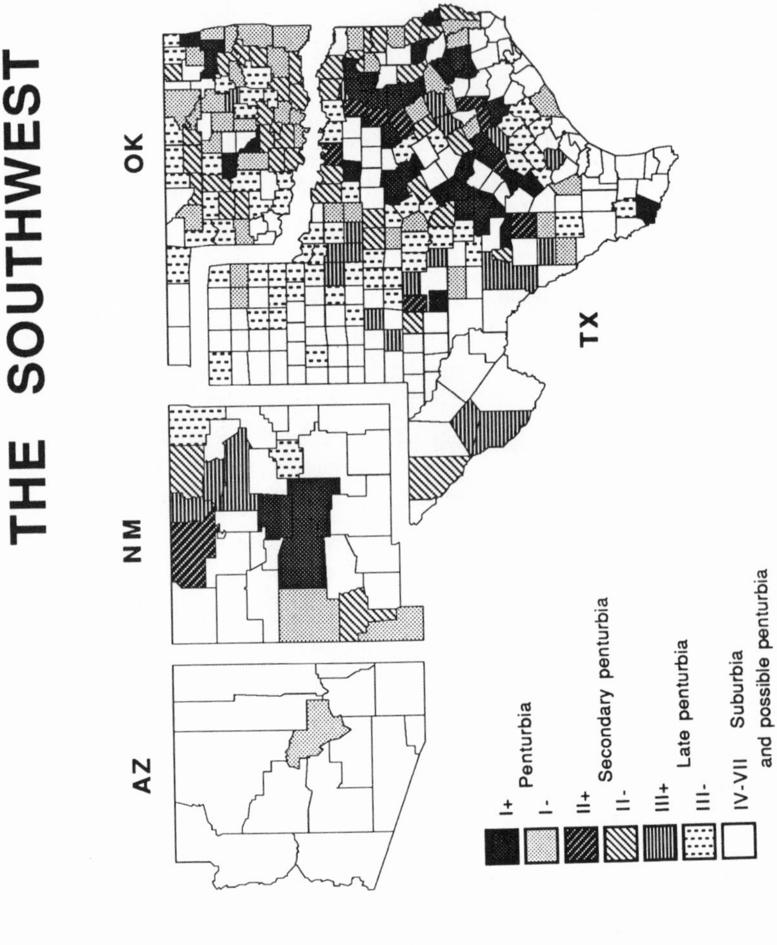
THE SOUTHWEST
OK
NM
AZ
TX
I+ Penturbia
I-
II+ Secondary penturbia
II-
III+ Late penturbia
III-
IV-VII Suburbia and possible penturbia

THE WEST

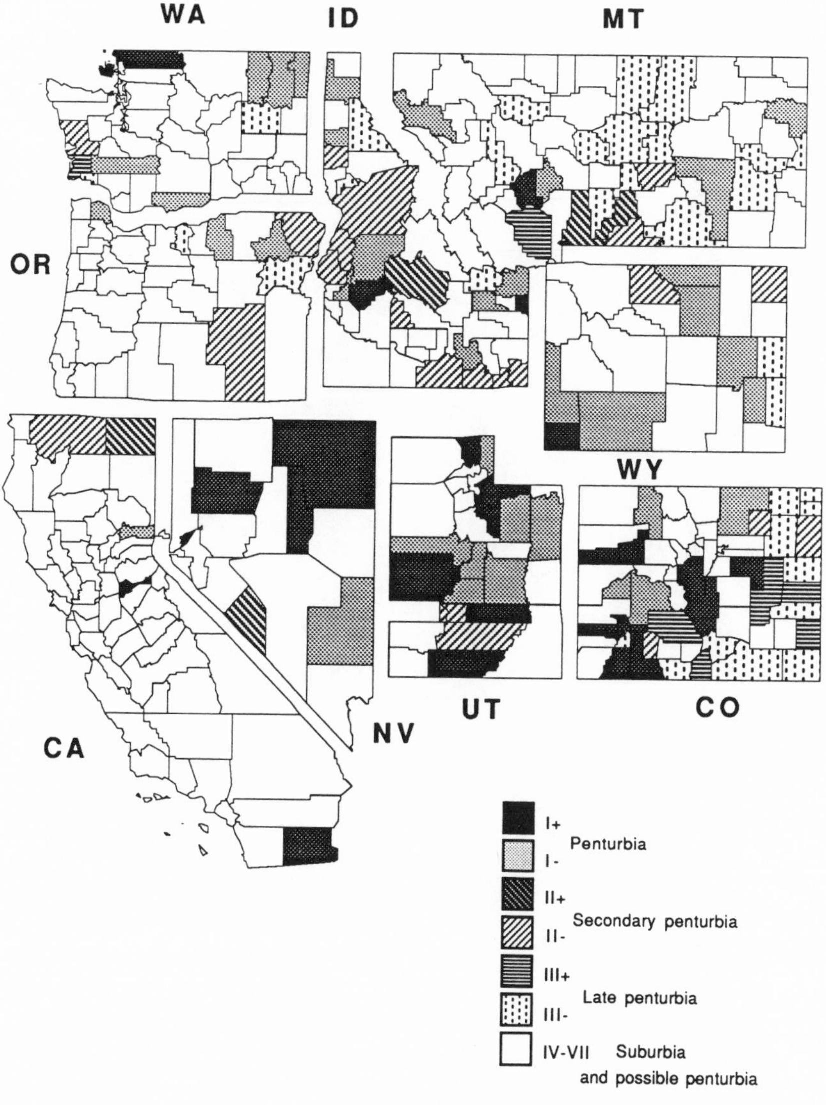
WA
ID
MT
OR
WY
UT
CO
NV
CA
I+
Penturbia
I-
II+
Secondary penturbia
II-
III+
Late penturbia
III-
IV-VII Suburbia
and possible penturbia

Appendix C

Maps: All other counties, by seven regions of the U.S.

(Revised classifications)

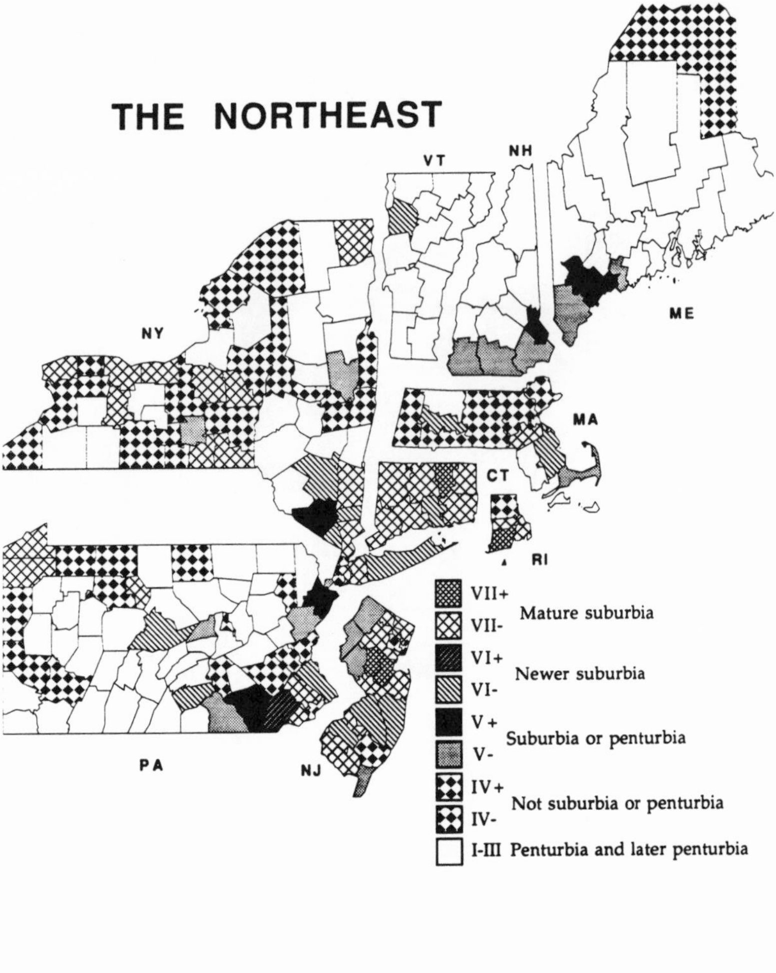

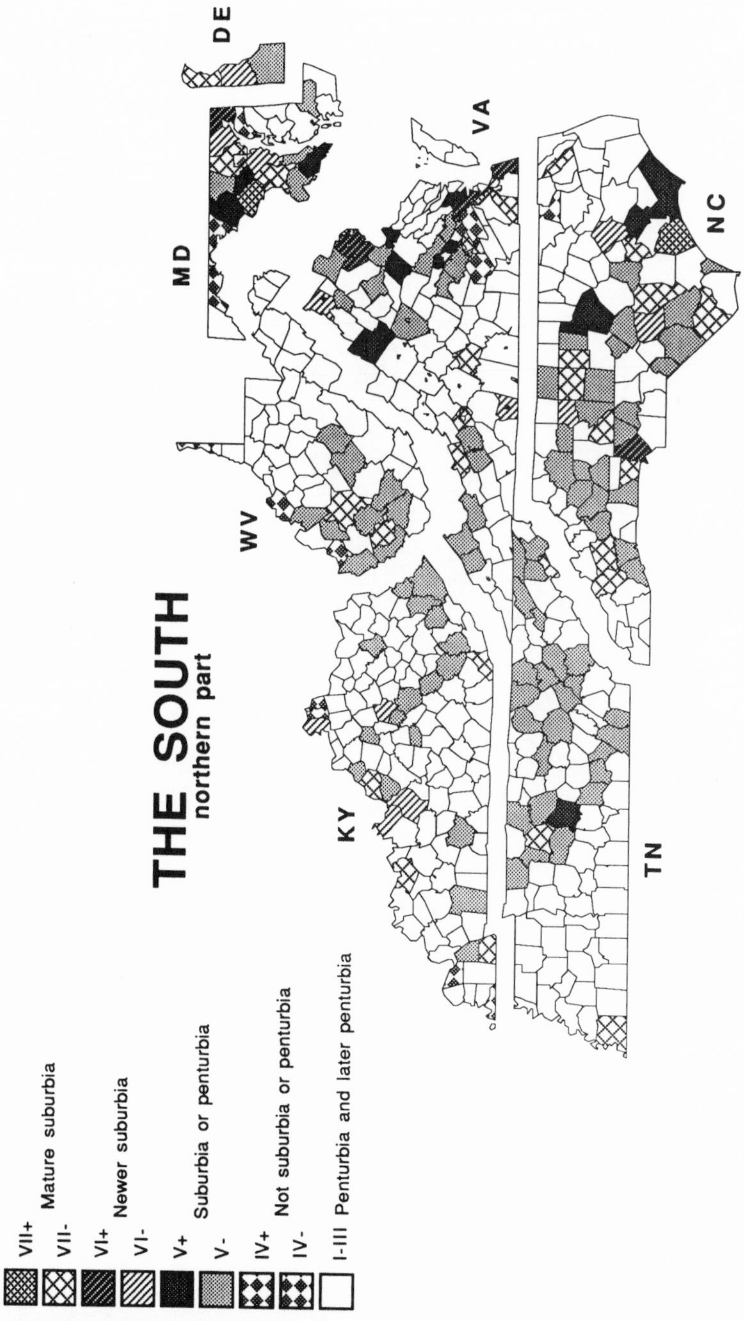
THE SOUTH
northern part
MD
DE
VA
WV
NC
KY
TN
VII+ Mature suburbia
VII-
VI+ Newer suburbia
VI-
V+ Suburbia or penturbia
V-
IV+ Not suburbia or penturbia
IV-
I-III Penturbia and later penturbia

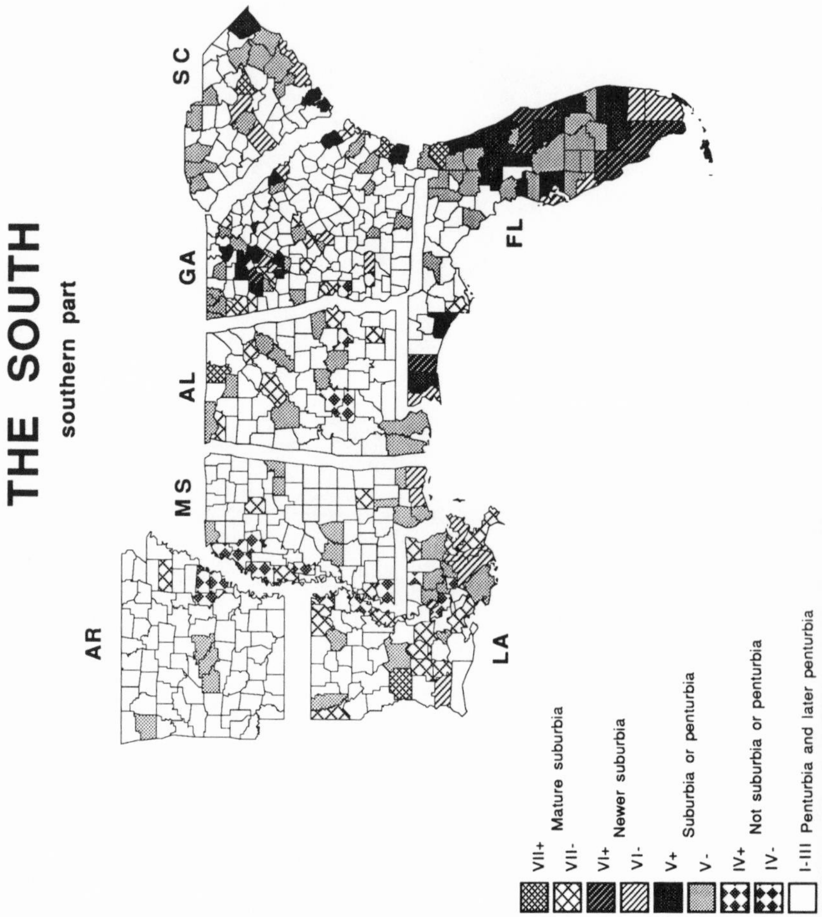
THE SOUTH
southern part
AR
MS
AL
GA
SC
FL
LA
VII+ Mature suburbia
VII-
VI+ Newer suburbia
VI-
V+ Suburbia or penturbia
V-
IV+ Not suburbia or penturbia
IV-
I-III Penturbia and later penturbia

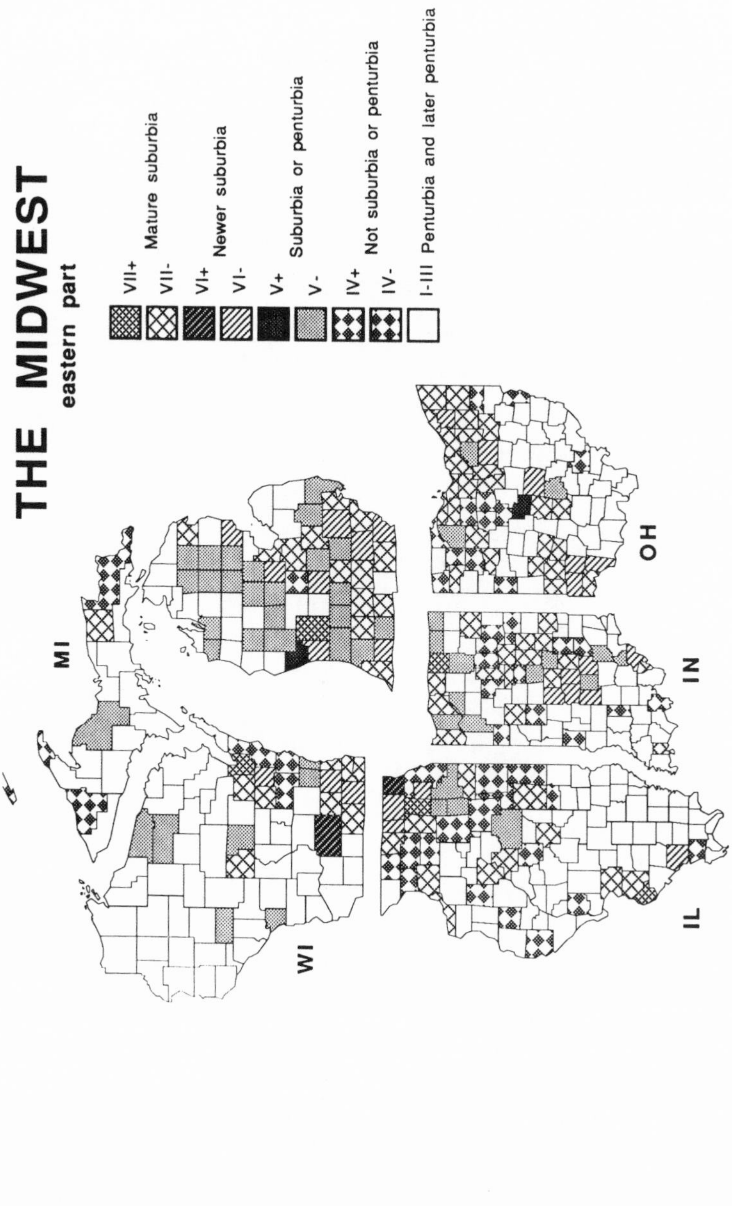
THE MIDWEST
eastern part
VII+ Mature suburbia
VII-
VI+ Newer suburbia
VI-
V+ Suburbia or penturbia
V-
IV+ Not suburbia or penturbia
IV-
I-III Penturbia and later penturbia
MI
WI
IL
IN
OH

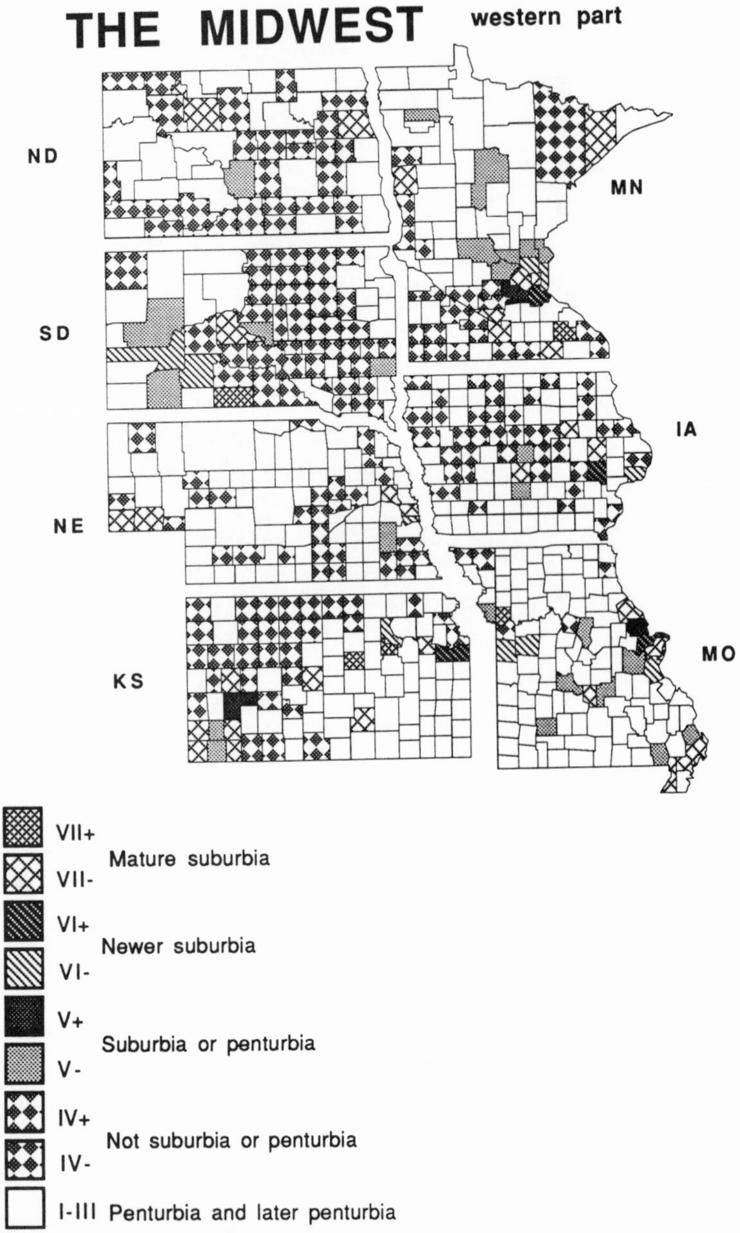
THE MIDWEST western part
ND
MN
SD
IA
NE
MO
KS
VII+
VII-
Mature suburbia
VI+
VI-
Newer suburbia
V+
V-
Suburbia or penturbia
IV+
IV-
Not suburbia or penturbia
I-III Penturbia and later penturbia

THE SOUTHWEST

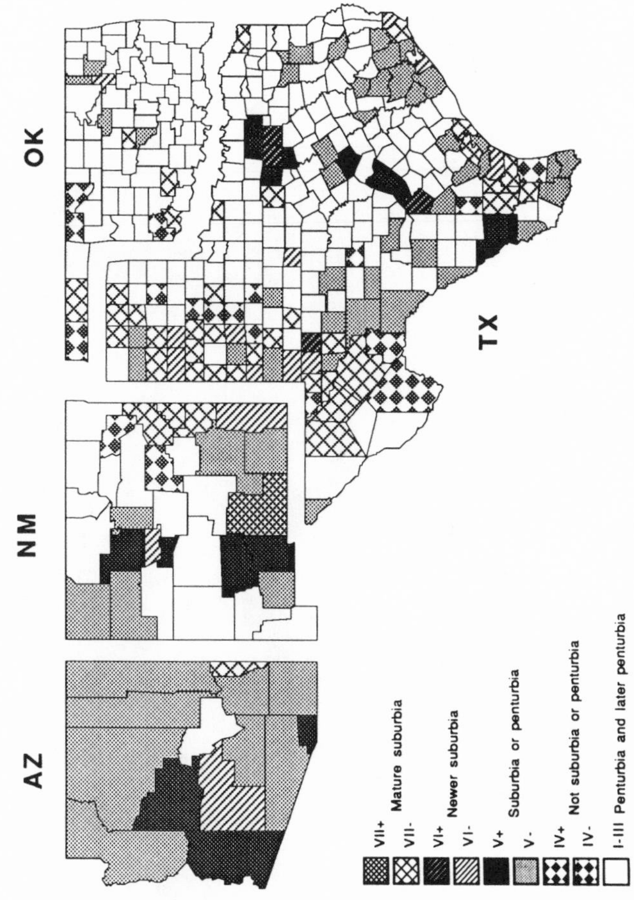
OK
NM
AZ
TX
VII+ Mature suburbia
VII-
VI+ Newer suburbia
VI-
V+ Suburbia or penturbia
V-
IV+ Not suburbia or penturbia
IV-
I-III Penturbia and later penturbia

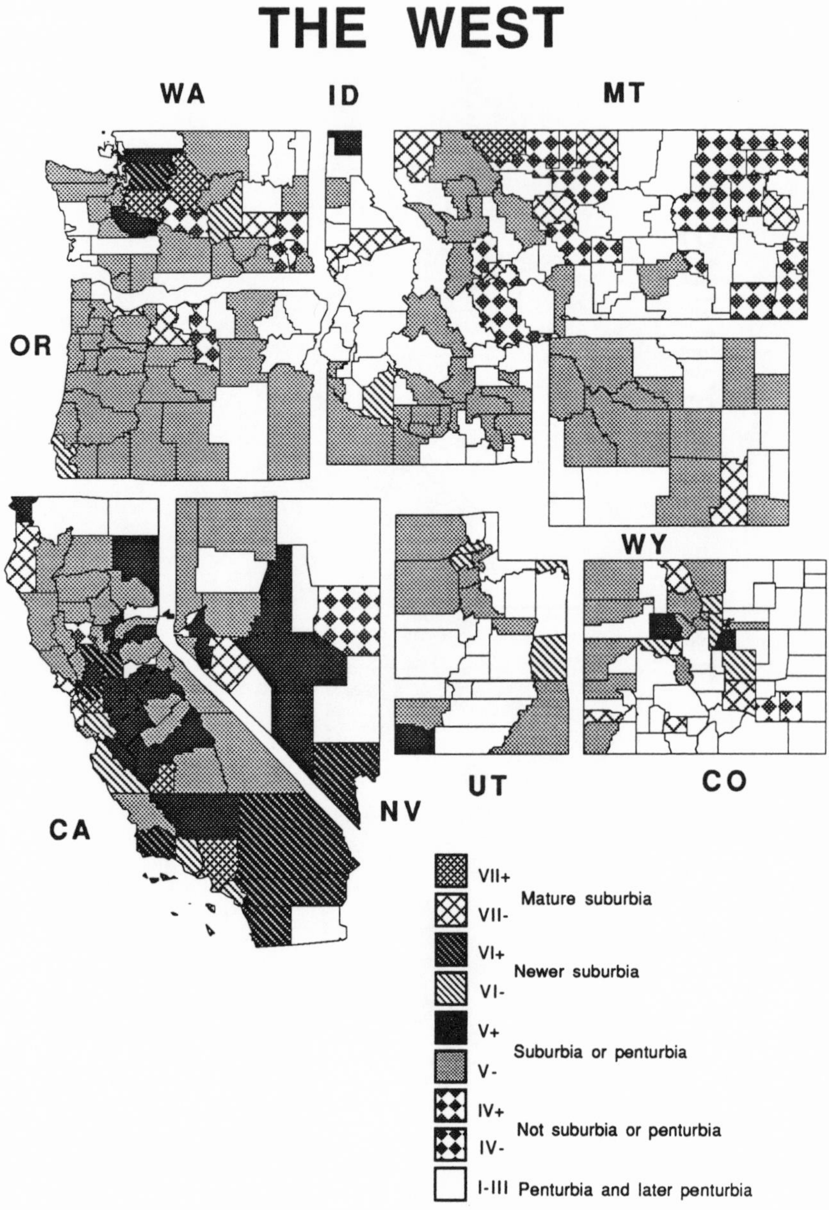
THE WEST
WA
ID
MT
OR
WY
CA
NV
UT
CO
VII+
VII-
Mature suburbia
VI+
VI-
Newer suburbia
V+
V-
Suburbia or penturbia
IV+
IV-
Not suburbia or penturbia
I-III Penturbia and later penturbia

Appendix D

Maps: Growth counties of the 1990s. (Classes I+, I-, II+, V+, V-), by six regions of the U.S.

(For the West see p. ii.)

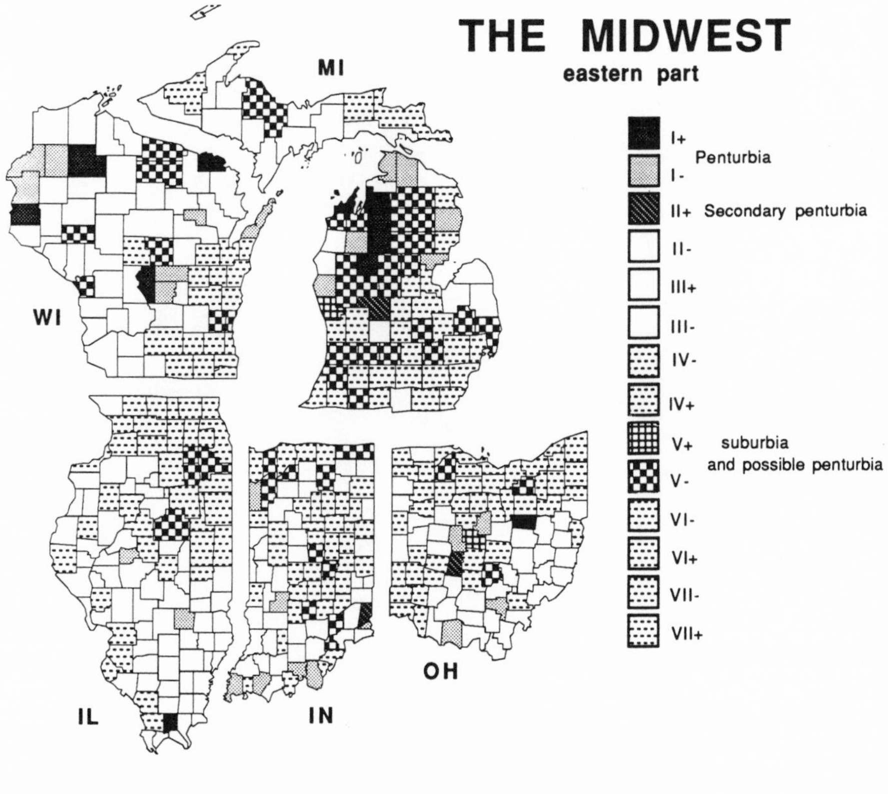

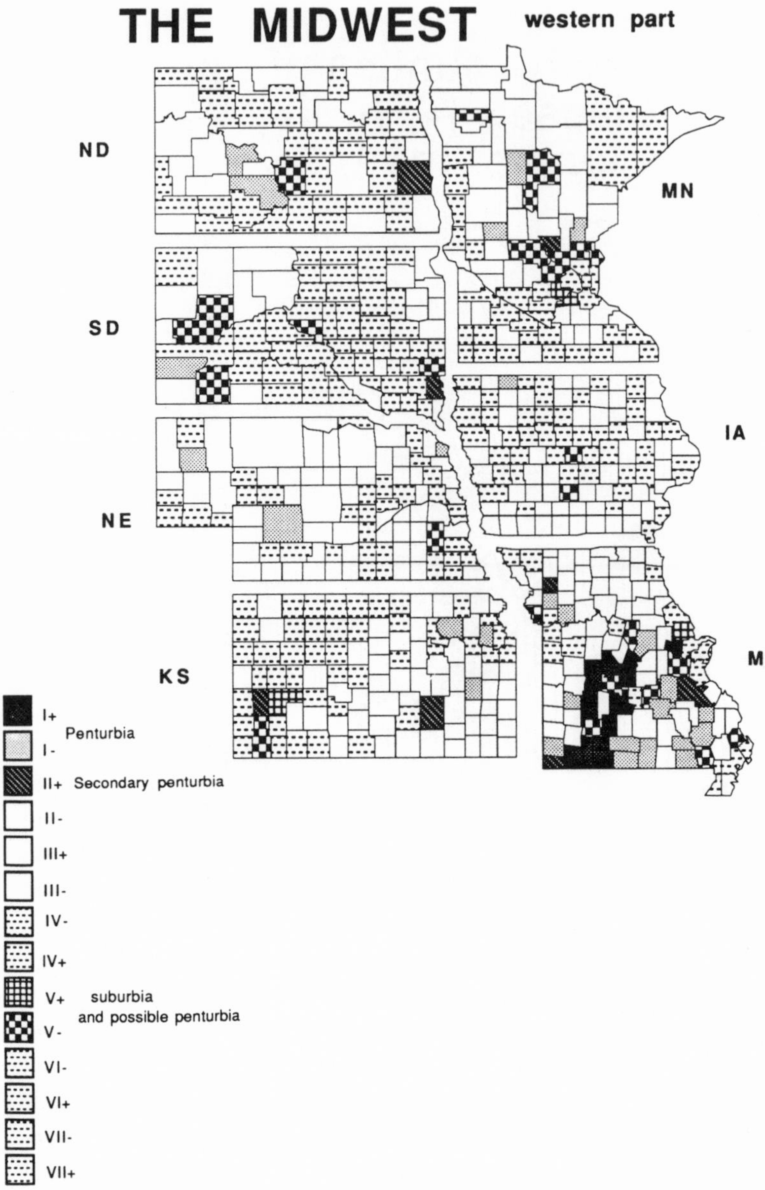
THE MIDWEST western part
ND
MN
SD
IA
NE
KS
MO
I+
Penturbia
I-
II+ Secondary penturbia
II-
III+
III-
IV-
IV+
V+ suburbia
and possible penturbia
V-
VI-
VI+
VII-
VII+

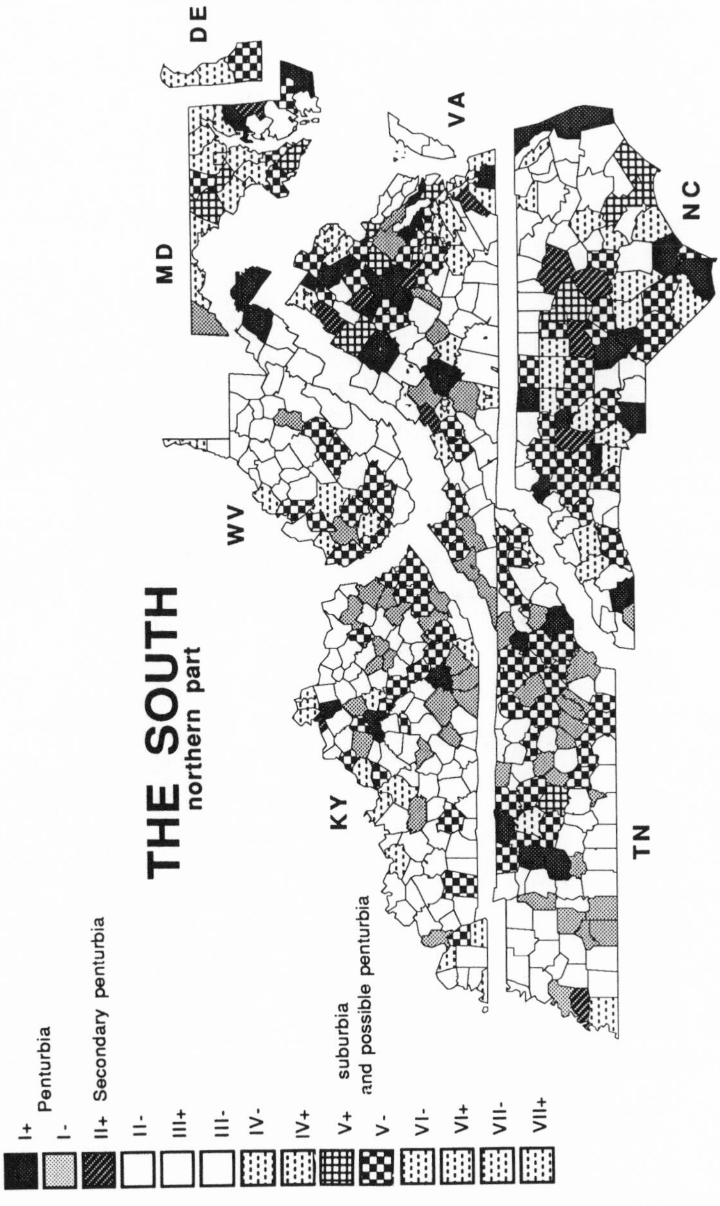
THE SOUTH
northern part
I+ Penturbia
I-
II+ Secondary penturbia
II-
III+
III-
IV-
IV+
V+ suburbia and possible penturbia
V-
VI-
VI+
VII-
VII+
KY
WV
MD
DE
VA
NC
TN

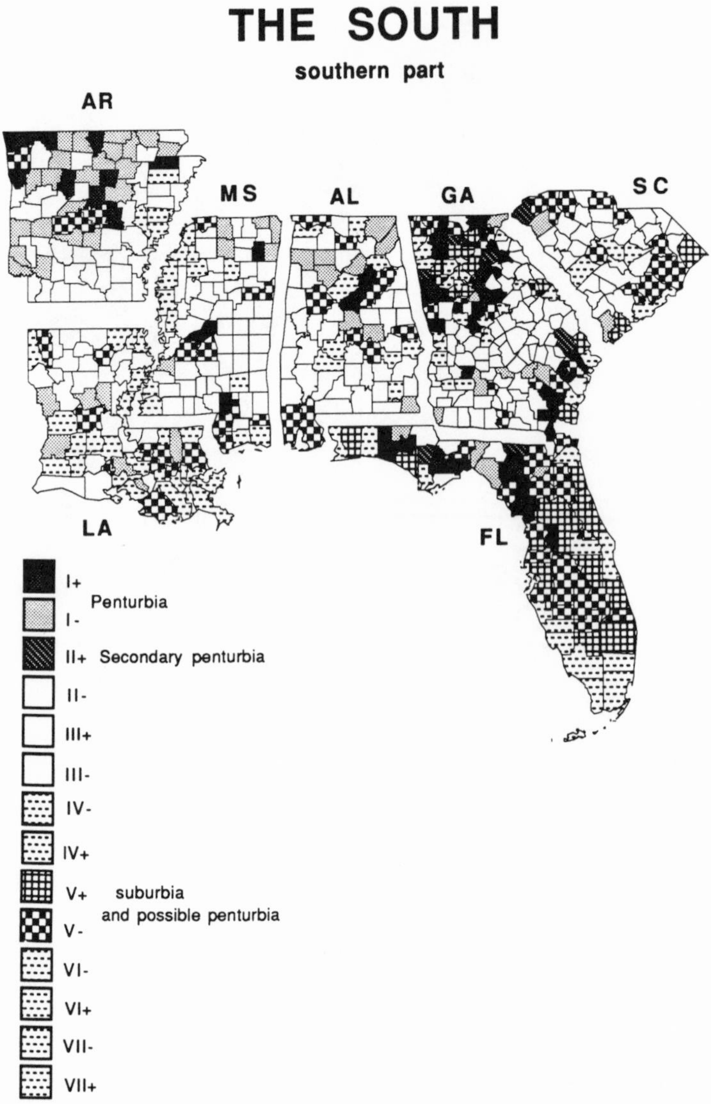
THE SOUTH
southern part
AR
MS
AL
GA
SC
LA
FL
I+
Penturbia
I-
II+ Secondary penturbia
II-
III+
III-
IV-
IV+
V+ suburbia
and possible penturbia
V-
VI-
VI+
VII-
VII+

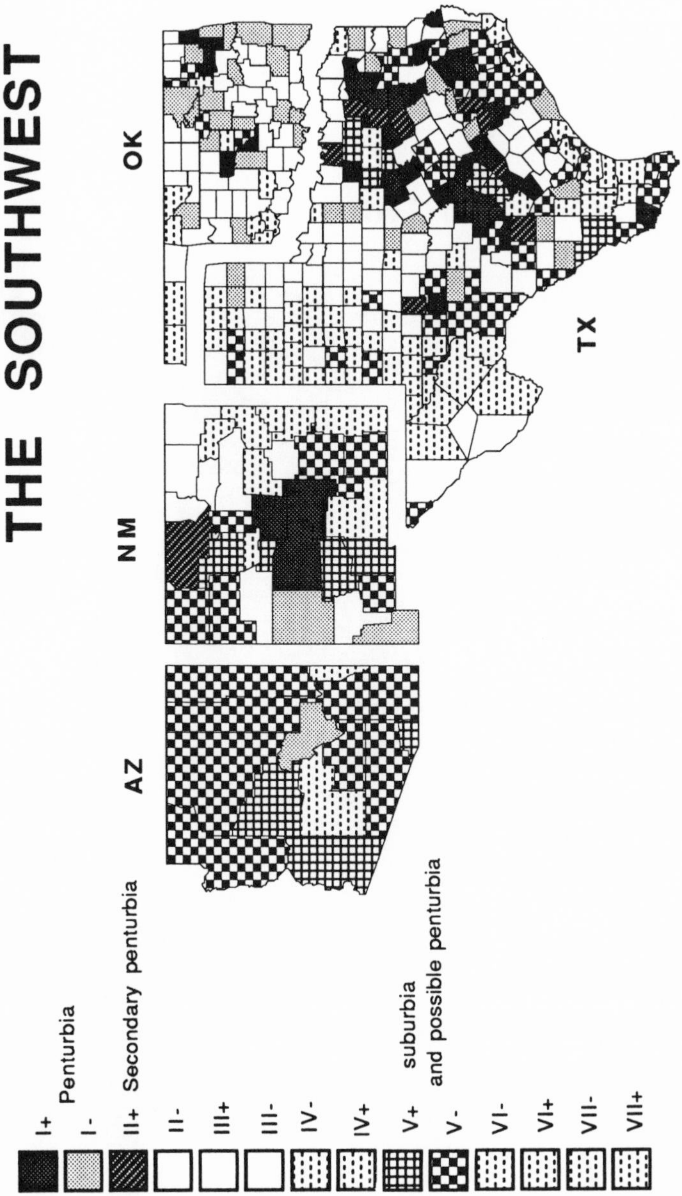
THE SOUTHWEST
AZ
NM
OK
TX
I+
I- Penturbia
II+ Secondary penturbia
II-
III+
III-
IV-
IV+
V+ suburbia
V- and possible penturbia
VI-
VI+
VII-
VII+

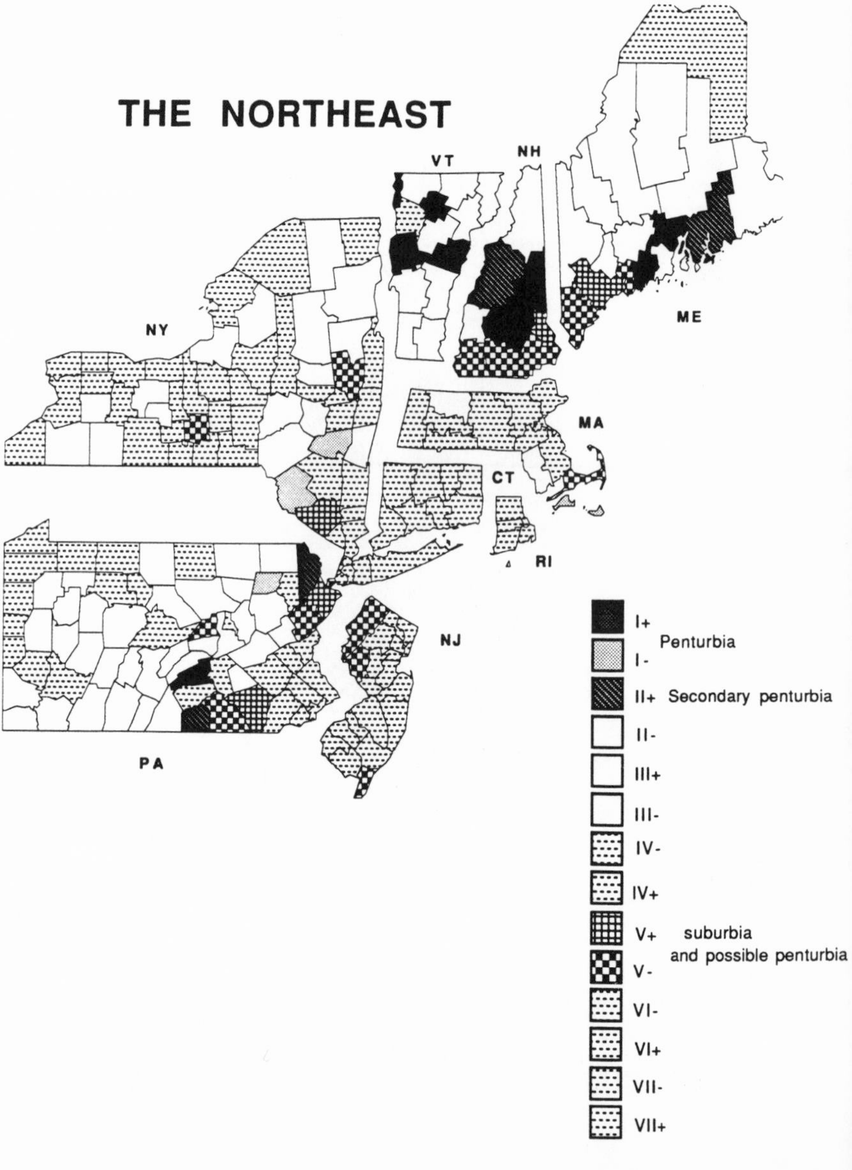
THE NORTHEAST
VT
NH
NY
ME
MA
CT
RI
NJ
PA
I+
I-
Penturbia
II+ Secondary penturbia
II-
III+
III-
IV-
IV+
V+
V-
suburbia
and possible penturbia
VI-
VI+
VII-
VII+

Appendix E

Classification by age of structures (See pages 205-6)

ALABAMA

Bibb	IIA
Blount	IB
Cherokee	IIA
Chilton	IB
Cleburne	IIA
Cullman	IIB
De Kalb	IB
Elmore	IB
Fayette	IIA
Franklin	IIB
Henry	IIA
Houston	IB
Jackson	IB
Lamar	IIA
Marion	IB
Marshall	IIB
Pike	IIA
St. Clair	IB
Shelby	IB
Tallapoosa	IIB
Walker	IB
Winston	IB

ARIZONA

Gila	IB

ARKANSAS

Baxter	IB
Benton	IB
Boone	IB
Carroll	IA
Cleburne	IA
Cleveland	IIA
Conway	IIA
Craighead	IB
Crawford	IB
Drew	IIA
Faulkner	IB
Franklin	IA
Fulton	IA
Grant	IA
Greene	IB
Hempstead	IA
Hot Spring	IB
Howard	IIA
Independence	IB
Izard	IA
Johnson	IA
Lawrence	IIA
Little River	IA
Logan	IIA
Lonoke	IA
Madison	IIA
Marion	IA
Miller	IIB
Montgomery	IA
Newton	IA
Perry	IA
Pike	IIA
Polk	IA
Pope	IB
Randolph	IA
Scott	IIA
Searcy	IIA
Sebastian	IIB
Sevier	IA
Sharp	IA
Stone	IA
Van Buren	IA
White	IB
Yell	IIA

CALIFORNIA

Amador	IB
Imperial	IB
Modoc	IIB
Sierra	IA
Siskiyou	IIB

COLORADO

Archuleta	IA
Custer	IA
Delta	IB
Elbert	IA
Fremont	IB
Garfield	IB
Gunnison	IB
Hinsdale	IA
La Plata	IA
Mineral	IIA
Morgan	IIB
Ouray	IA
Park	IA
Routt	IA
San Miguel	IA
Teller	IA
Weld	IB
Yuma	IIA

FLORIDA

Calhoun	IIA
Gilchrist	IA
Hamilton	IIA
Holmes	IA
Jackson	IIB
Jefferson	IA
Lafayette	IA
Levy	IB
Liberty	IA
Sumter	IB
Suwannee	IA
Taylor	IB
Union	IB
Wakulla	IB
Walton	IB
Washington	IA

GEORGIA

Appling	IB
Banks	IA
Barrow	IB
Bartow	IB
Ben Hill	IA
Berrien	IIA
Brantley	IA
Bryan	IB
Bulloch	IIB
Butts	IA
Candler	IIA
Carroll	IB
Charlton	IB
Coffee	IIB
Coweta	IB
Crawford	IA
Dawson	IA
Decatur	IIA
Echols	IIA
Emanuel	IIA
Evans	IIB
Franklin	IIA
Gordon	IB
Haralson	IIB
Harris	IA
Hart	IIA
Heard	IA
Jackson	IIA
Jasper	IA
Jeff Davis	IB
Johnson	IIA
Lamar	IIB
Lanier	IIB
Laurens	IIA
Lee	IA
Lincoln	IIA
Long	IA
Madison	IA
Mitchell	IIA
Monroe	IA
Montgomery	IIA
Morgan	IIA
Murray	IA
Newton	IB
Oconee	IA
Oglethorpe	IIA

Pickens	IIB
Pierce	IA
Pike	IA
Putnam	IA
Rabun	IB
Schley	IIA
Screven	IIA
Seminole	IB
Toombs	IIB
Towns	IB
Twiggs	IIA
Union	IA
Walton	IB
Wheeler	IIA
White	IB
Worth	IA

IDAHO

Adams	IIB
Bear Lake	IIA
Benewah	IA
Boise	IA
Bonner	IB
Camas	IIA
Cassia	IIB
Custer	IIA
Franklin	IIA
Fremont	IA
Gem	IB
Idaho	IIB
Jefferson	IB
Latah	IIB
Oneida	IIA
Boger	IB
Teton	IA
Valley	IB
Washington	IIA

ILLINOIS

Bond	IIA
Clinton	IIB
Cumberland	IIA
Edwards	IIA
Effingham	IB
Franklin	IIA
Jefferson	IIB
Jersey	IIB
Johnson	IA
Marion	IIB
Mason	IIB
Menard	IA
Mercer	IIA
Pope	IIA
Putnam	IIA
Randolph	IIB
Washington	IIA
Williamson	IIA
Woodford	IIB

INDIANA

Boone	IIB
Crawford	IA
Dearborn	IIB
Franklin	IIA
Fulton	IIB
Greene	IIA
Harrison	IB
Jefferson	IIB
Lawrence	IIB
Marshall	IIB
Newton	IB
Noble	IIB
Ohio	IA
Owen	IA
Parke	IIA
Posey	IB
Ripley	IIB
Spencer	IIA
Switzerland	IIA
Warrick	IB
Washington	IIB
White	IIB
Whitley	IIB

IOWA

Clarke	IIA
Dallas	IIB
Dickinson	IB
Louisa	IIA
Marion	IIB
Mills	IIA

KANSAS

Butler	IIA
Coffey	IA
Gray	IIA
Harvey	IIB
Jackson	IIA
Jefferson	IA
Kearny	IIB
Miami	IIA
Osage	IIA
Pottawatomie	IA
Thomas	IIB

KENTUCKY

Adair	IIA
Allen	IIA
Anderson	IA
Barren	IIB
Breathitt	IIA
Breckinridge	IIA
Butler	IIA
Carter	IA
Casey	IIA
Clark	IIB
Clinton	IIA
Edmonson	IIA
Elliott	IIA
Estill	IIA
Gallatin	IIA
Garrard	IIA
Grant	IA
Grayson	IA
Greenup	IIB
Harlan	IIA
Henderson	IIB
Henry	IIA
Hopkins	IIB
Johnson	IA
Knox	IA
Larue	IIB
Laure	IIB
Lawrence	IA
Lee	IIA
Letcher	IA
Lewis	IIA
Lincoln	IIB
Livingston	IA
Lyon	IIA
McCreary	IA
Magoffin	IA
Menifee	IA
Mercer	IIA
Metcalfe	IIA
Montgomery	IB
Morgan	IIA
Muhlenberg	IIA
Nelson	IIB
Ohio	IIA
Owen	IIA
Owsley	IIA
Perry	IA
Powell	IB
Pulaski	IB
Rockcastle	IIA
Russell	IA
Scott	IB
Shelby	IA
Simpson	IIB
Taylor	IB
Trimble	IIA
Union	IIA
Wayne	IIA
Webster	IIA
Whitley	IA
Wolfe	IIA
Woodford	IB

LOUISIANA

Assumption	IIA
Beauregard	IB
Caldwell	IIA
Cameron	IIB
De Soto	IIA
Grant	IA
La Salle	IB
Lincoln	IIB
Natchitoches	IIB
Red River	IIA
Sabine	IA
St. Martin	IB
Tangipahoa	IB
Union	IIA
Vermilion	IIB
West Feliciana	IIA

MAINE

Franklin	IIB
Hancock	IIA
Kennebec	IIB
Knox	IIA
Lincoln	IA
Oxford	IIB
Waldo	IA
Washington	IIA

MARYLAND

Caroline	IIB
Garrett	IB
Queen Annes	IB
Worcester	IB

MASSACHUSETTS

Dukes	IB
Nantucket	IA

MICHIGAN

Alcona	IB
Antrim	IA
Arenac	IB
Charlevoix	IIA
Cheboygan	IB
Emmet	IB
Hillsdale	IIB
Ionia	IIB
Kalkaska	IA
Leelanau	IB
Manistee	IIA
Mason	IIB
Missaukee	IA
Montcalm	IIB
Oceana	IB
Osceola	IA
Sanilac	IIB
Tuscola	IIB
Wexford	IB

MINNESOTA

Aitkin	IIA
Becker	IIB
Beltrami	IIB
Benton	IIB
Cook	IIB
Crow Wing	IIB
Dodge	IIB
Douglas	IB
Hubbard	IB
Itasca	IIB
Kanabec	IB
Kandiyohi	IIB
Meeker	IIB
Mille Lacs	IIB
Otter Tail	IIA
Pine	IIA
Steele	IIB
Todd	IIA
Wabasha	IIB
Wadena	IIB

MISSISSIPPI

Alcorn	IB
Claiborne	IA
Clarke	IIA
Clay	IIB
Covington	IIA
Greene	IIA
Itawamba	IB
Lafayette	IB
Lamar	IB
Lauderdale	IIB
Lawrence	IIA
Lee	IB
Lincoln	IIB
Madison	IA
Marion	IIB
Marshall	IA
Neshoba	IIA
Pike	IIA
Pontotoc	IIA
Prentiss	IIB
Scott	IIB
Simpson	IIB
Stone	IIB
Tippah	IIA
Tishomingo	IA
Union	IIA
Warren	IIB
Wayne	IIB

MISSOURI

Andrew	IIA
Barry	IA
Benton	IA
Bollinger	IIA
Callaway	IB
Cape Girardeau	IIB
Carter	IA
Cedar	IA
Christian	IA
Clinton	IA
Cole	IB
Crawford	IB
Dallas	IIA
De Kalb	IIA
Dent	IA
Douglas	IA
Hickory	IA
Howe	IIB
Iron	IIB
Laclede	IB
Lafayette	IIA
Lawrence	IIA
McDonald	IIA
Madison	IA
Miller	IA
Moniteau	IIA
Morgan	IA
Newton	IB
Oregon	IIA
Ozark	IA
Perry	IIB
Polk	IA
Ralls	IIA
Randolph	IIA
Ray	IA
Reynolds	IIA
Ripley	IA
St. Clair	IIA
St. Francois	IIB
Ste. Genevieve	IIB
Stoddard	IIA
Stone	IA
Taney	IB
Texas	IIA
Warren	IA
Washington	IIB
Wayne	IA
Webster	IA
Wright	IIA

MONTANA

Broadwater	IA
Carbon	IIA
Jefferson	IA
Musselshell	IIA
Park	IIB
Richland	IB
Rosebud	IA
Sanders	IB
Stillwater	IIA
Yellowstone	IB

NEBRASKA

Box Butte	IA
Cass	IIA
Chase	IIA
Dakota	IB
Dawson	IIB
Lincoln	IB
Madison	IIB
Stanton	IIA
Washington	IIB

NEVADA

Elko	IB
Esmeralda	IIA
Eureka	IA
Lincoln	IA
Pershing	IB
Storey	IA

NEW HAMPSHIRE

Belknap	IB
Carroll	IA
Grafton	IIB
Merrimack	IB
Sullivan	IIB

NEW MEXICO

Catron	IA
Colfax	IIA
Grant	IIB
Hidalgo	IB
Lincoln	IB
Rio Arriba	IIB
Socorro	IA
Torrance	IA

NEW YORK

Allegany	IIB
Columbia	IIB
Greene	IB
Ontario	IIA
Oswego	IIB
Schoharie	IIA
Sullivan	IB

NORTH CAROLINA

Alleghany	IIB
Ashe	IIB
Avery	IIB
Beaufort	IIB
Brunswick	IB
Chatham	IIB
Cherokee	IIB
Chowan	IIB
Clay	IB
Currituck	IA
Dare	IB
Davie	IB

Franklin	IIB
Hoke	IB
Iredell	IIB
Jackson	IIB
Johnston	IIB
Lincoln	IB
Macon	IB
Montgomery	IIB
Moore	IB
Nash	IIB
Pender	IB
Perquimans	IIA
Person	IIB
Richmond	IIB
Rutherford	IIB
Stokes	IB
Surry	IIB
Swain	IIA
Union	IB
Vance	IIB
Watauga	IB
Yancey	IIA

NORTH DAKOTA

Cass	IIB
McKenzie	IIA
Mercer	IA
Morton	IA
Stark	IIB
Williams	IIB

OHIO

Adams	IA
Brown	IIA
Carroll	IIB
Darke	IIB
Fulton	IIB
Gallia	IIA
Guernsey	IIA
Highland	IIB
Hocking	IIA
Holmes	IB
Jackson	IIA
Lawrence	IIB
Logan	IIB
Madison	IIB
Meigs	IIA
Morgan	IIA
Morrow	IB
Perry	IIA
Pike	IIB
Shelby	IIB
Union	IB
Vinton	IA
Washington	IIB

OKLAHOMA

Adair	IB
Atoka	IIA
Beckham	IA
Blaine	IIA
Bryan	IIA
Canadian	IB
Carter	IIA
Cherokee	IB
Choctaw	IIA
Creek	IA
Custer	IIA
Delaware	IB
Garfield	IIB
Garvin	IIA
Grady	IA
Haskell	IIA
Jefferson	IIA
Johnston	IA
Latimer	IIA
Le Flore	IA
Lincoln	IA
Logan	IA
Love	IA
McClain	IA
McCurtain	IA
McIntosh	IA
Major	IIA
Marshall	IA
Mayes	IB
Murray	IIA
Muskogee	IIA
Noble	IIA
Nowata	IIA
Osage	IA
Pawnee	IA
Pontotoc	IIA
Pottawatomie	IA
Pushmataha	IA
Sequoyah	IA
Stephens	IIB
Wagoner	IB
Washita	IIA
Woodward	IB

OREGON

Columbia	IB
Harney	IIB
Morrow	IA
Union	IB
Wallowa	IIA

PENNSYLVANIA

Adams	IIB
Butler	IIB
Clarion	IIB
Clearfield	IIA
Columbia	IIB
Franklin	IIB
Fulton	IIB
Greene	IIA
Indiana	IIB
Juniata	IIB
Perry	IB
Snyder	IIB
Wayne	IIA
Wyoming	IB

SOUTH CAROLINA

Anderson	IB
Bamberg	IIA
Barnwell	IIA
Calhoun	IIA
Cherokee	IIB
Chesterfield	IIB
Colleton	IIA
Darlington	IIB
Edgefield	IIA
Greenwood	IIB
Hampton	IIA
Jasper	IB
Kershaw	IIB
Marion	IIA
Marlboro	IIA
Oconee	IIB
Orangeburg	IIB

SOUTH DAKOTA

Custer	IA
Fall River	IIA
Lincoln	IIA
Union	IIA

TENNESSEE

Bedford	IIA
Benton	IB
Bledsoe	IB
Cannon	IA
Chester	IB
Claiborne	IA
Clay	IIA
Cocke	IIB
Decatur	IIA
De Kalb	IA
Dickson	IB
Dyer	IIB
Fayette	IIA
Franklin	IIB
Grainger	IIA
Greene	IIB
Hardin	IB
Henderson	IB
Henry	IIA
Hickman	IA
Houston	IIA
Humphreys	IIB
Jackson	IIA
Jefferson	IB
Johnson	IIA
Lauderdale	IA
Lawrence	IIA
Lewis	IB
McMinn	IIB
McNairy	IB
Macon	IA
Madison	IIB
Marion	IIB
Marshall	IIA
Maury	IIB
Meigs	IA
Monroe	IB
Moore	IA
Morgan	IB
Overton	IIA
Perry	IIA
Pickett	IIA
Polk	IIA
Rhea	IB
Robertson	IB
Sevier	IB
Smith	IIA
Stewart	IIA
Tipton	IIB
Trousdale	IIA
Union	IA

Van Buren	IB
Warren	IIB
Wayne	IIB
Weakley	IIA
White	IIB

TEXAS

Anderson	IA
Archer	IA
Austin	IA
Bandera	IA
Bastrop	IA
Blanco	IA
Bosque	IA
Brown	IB
Burleson	IA
Burnet	IB
Caldwell	IIA
Callahan	IA
Camp	IIA
Cass	IA
Cherokee	IIA
Clay	IIA
Cooke	IIA
Dimmit	IB
Ellis	IA
Erath	IA
Franklin	IA
Freestone	IA
Frio	IB
Gillespie	IB
Glasscock	IIA
Grimes	IIA
Guadalupe	IB
Hamilton	IIA
Harrison	IIB
Hemphill	IA
Henderson	IA
Hood	IA
Hopkins	IA
Houston	IA
Hudspeth	IIA
Hunt	IIB
Irion	IA
Jasper	IB
Kaufman	IIA
Kendall	IB
Lamar	IIA
Lampasas	IB
Lee	IA
Limestone	IIA
Live Oak	IA
Llano	IB
Madison	IA
Marion	IIA
Matagorda	IB
Medina	IIB
Milam	IIA
Montague	IIA
Morris	IIB
Nacogdoches	IB
Navarro	IIA
Newton	IIB
Panola	IA
Polk	IA
Rains	IA
Real	IIB
Red River	IIA
Roberts	IA
Rockwell	IA
Sabine	IA
San Augustin	IIA
San Jacinto	IA
San Saba	IIA
Schleicher	IA
Shackelford	IIA
Shelby	IIA
Somervell	IA
Starr	IB
Stephens	IIA
Sterling	IIA
Titus	IB
Trinity	IA
Tyler	IB
Upshur	IB
Van Zandt	IA
Waller	IB
Washington	IIA
Williamson	IA
Wilson	IA
Wise	IA
Wood	IA
Young	IA

UTAH

Beaver	IIA
Cache	IB
Duchesne	IA
Emery	IA
Garfield	IIA
Juab	IA
Kane	IA
Millard	IA
Piute	IIA
Rich	IA
Sanpete	IA
Sevier	IA
Summit	IA
Uintah	IB
Wasatch	IA
Wayne	IA

VERMONT

Addison	IB
Bennington	IIB
Caledonia	IIA
Essex	IIA
Grand Isle	IA
Lamoille	IB
Orange	IA
Orleans	IIA
Windsor	IIB

VIRGINIA

Alleghany	IIA
Amelia	IIA
Amherst	IIB
Appomattox	IB
Augusta	IB
Bath	IIA
Bedford	IA
Bland	IIA
Botetourt	IB
Buckingham	IIA
Caroline	IA
Carroll	IIB
Clarke	IB
Craig	IIA
Cumberland	IA
Essex	IA
Fauquier	IB
Floyd	IIA
Fluvanna	IA
Franklin	IB
Goochland	IIB
Greene	IA
Greensville	IIA
Highland	IIA
Isle of Wigh	IIB
King William	IA
Lee	IA
Louisa	IA
Madison	IIA
Middlesex	IA
Orange	IB
Page	IIB
Patrick	IIA
Pittsylvania	IIB
Prince Edwar	IIB
Rappahannock	IIA
Russell	IB
Shenandoah	IIB
Washington	IIB
Westmoreland	IIB
Wise	IA
Wythe	IIB
Chesapeake	IB
Lynchburg	IB
Manassas	IB
Norton	IIB
Poquoson	IB

WASHINGTON

Ferry	IA
Grays Harbor	IIB
Klickitat	IB
Lewis	IB
Pend Oreille	IA
San Juan	IB
Stevens	IA
Whatcom	IB

WEST VIRGINIA

Barbour	IIA
Berkeley	IB
Calhoun	IIA
Clay	IIA
Doddridge	IIA
Fayette	IIA
Grant	IIB
Greenbrier	IIA
Hampshire	IA
Hardy	IIA
Jefferson	IB
Lincoln	IB
Mercer	IIB
Mineral	IIB
Monongalia	IIB
Monroe	IIA
Morgan	IB
Pendleton	IIA
Pleasants	IIA
Pocahontas	IIA
Preston	IIA

Randolph	IIB
Ritchie	IIA
Roane	IIA
Summers	IIA
Taylor	IIA
Tucker	IIA
Tyler	IIA
Upshur	IB
Wirt	IIA

WISCONSIN

Adams	IB
Barron	IIB
Bayfield	IIA
Burnett	IA
Door	IB
Dunn	IIB
Florence	IA
Forest	IIA
Green	IIB
Juneau	IIA
Lincoln	IIB
Marathon	IIB
Marquette	IA
Menominee	IB
Oconto	IIB
Pierce	IIB
Polk	IB
St. Croix	IB
Sawyer	IB
Trempealeau	IIB
Washburn	IB
Waupaca	IIB
Waushara	IA

WYOMING

Big Horn	IIA
Converse	IA
Crook	IIA
Johnson	IB
Lincoln	IA
Platte	IA
Sheridan	IB
Sweetwater	IB
Uinta	IA

Bibliography

Berger, Peter L. *Invitation to Sociology: A Humanistic Perspective.* Garden City, N.Y.: Doubleday, 1963.

Carneiro, Robert L. Ed. *The Evolution of Society, Selections from Herbert Spencer's Principles of Sociology.* Chicago: University of Chicago, 1967.

Cochran, Thomas C. *Basic History of American Business.* Princeton, N.J.: D. Van Nostrand, 1957.

Colley, Leland F. and Lee M. Colley. *The Simple Truth About Western Land Investment,* revised edition. Garden City, N.Y.: Doubleday, 1968.

Coolidge, Olivia. *The Statesmanship of Abraham Lincoln.* New York: Charles Scribner's Sons, 1976.

Croce, Benedetto. *History of Europe in the Nineteenth Century.* Henry Furst, Trans. New York: Harcourt, Brace & World, 1933.

Cutler, Richard L. *The Liberal Middle Class: Maker of Radicals.* New Rochelle, N.Y.: Arlington House, 1973.

Darwin, Charles R. *On the Origin of Species by Means of Natural Selection, or, The Preservation of Favoured Races in the Struggle for Life.* London: G. Richards, 1902.

deVoto, Bernard. *The Year of Decision, 1846.* Boston: Houghton-Mifflin, 1942.

Easterlin, Richard A. "Economic-Demographic Interactions and Long Swings in Economic Growth." *The American Economic Review* Dec. 1966.

Freud, Sigmund. *"Civilized" Sexual Morality and Modern Nervousness*. Collected papers, Vol. 2. Authorized translation under the supervision of Joan Riviere. New York: Basic, 1959.

Friedman, Saul. "The Dismal Religion." *Harpers Magazine* Jul. 1975.

Furnas, J.C. *The Americans, A Social History, 1587–1914*. New York: Capricorn, 1969.

Garvy, George. "Kondratieff's Theory of Long Cycles." *The Review of Economic Statistics* 1943.

Geyl, Pieter. *Debates with Historians*. New York: Meridian, 1958.

Geyl, Pieter. "Toynbee's System of Civilization." *The Pattern of the Past, Can We Determine It?* Boston: Beacon, 1949.

Hamlin, Talbot. Greek *Revival Architecture in America: Being an Account of Important Trends in American Architecture and American Life Prior to the War Between the States*. New York: Oxford University, 1944.

Hartmann, William E. and Donald Johnson. *Nudist Society, An Authoritative, Complete Study of Nudism in America*. New York: Crown, 1970.

Heilbroner, Robert L. *The Worldly Philosophers, The Lives, Times and Ideas of the Great Economic Thinkers*. New York: Simon and Schuster, 1953.

Herbers, John. *The New Heartland, America's Flight Beyond*

the Suburbs and How It Is Changing Our Future. New York: Times Books, 1986.

Hicks, John D. et al. *A History of American Democracy*, 3rd edition. Boston: Houghton Mifflin, 1966.

Hofstadter, Richard. *Social Darwinism in American Thought*. Boston: Beacon, 1945.

Holt, Henry. Ed. *Garrulities of an Octogenarian*. Boston: Houghton Mifflin, 1923.

Hoyt, Homer. *One Hundred Years of Land Values in Chicago, 1833—1933*. Chicago: University of Chicago, 1933.

Kafker, Frank A. and James M. Laux, Ed. *The French Revolution: Conflicting Interpretations*, 3rd edition. Malabar, FL: Robert E. Krieger, 1983.

Kondratieff, Nicolai D. "The Long Waves in Economic Life." *The Review of Economic Statistics* Nov. 1935.

Kuznets, Simon. *Secular Movements in Production and Prices*. New York: Houghton Mifflin, 1930.

Lessinger, Jack. *Regions of Opportunity*. New York: Times Books, 1986.

Lippmann, Walter. *The Good Society*. Boston: Little Brown, 1946.

Manchester, William. *The Glory and the Dream, A Narrative History of America 1932—1972*. Boston: Little Brown, 1974.

Marx, Karl and Frederick Engels. *Selected Correspondence, 1846–1895*. Dona Torr, Trans. New York: International, 1942.

Mowry, George E. *The Era of Theodore Roosevelt, and the Birth of Modern America, 1900–1912*. New York: Harper and Row, 1958.

Naisbitt, John and Patricia Aburdene. *Megatrends 2000, Ten New Directions For the 1990s*. New York: William Morrow, 1990.

Okun, Arthur. *The Political Economy of Prosperity*. Washington, D.C.: The Brookings Institution, 1970.

Riegel, Robert E. *Young America, 1830—1840*. Norman: University of Oklahoma , 1949.

Rosen, Charles. "The Controversial Schoenberg." *High Fidelity, and Musical America* Sept. 1974.

Schlesinger, Arthur M. Jr. *The Age of Jackson*. Boston: Little Brown, 1945.

Schumpeter, Joseph A. Business Cycles; *A Theoretical, Historical and Statistical Analysis of the Capitalist Process*. New York: McGraw-Hill, 1939.

Spencer, Herbert. *Social Statics*. New York: D. Appleton, 1896.

Spengler, Oswald. *The Decline of the West*, translated with notes by Charles F. Atkinson. New York: Alfred A. Knopf, 1932.

Stampp, Kenneth M. *The Era of Reconstruction, 1865–1877*. New York: Vintage, 1965.

Steel, Ronald. *Walter Lippmann and the American Century*. Boston: Little Brown, 1980.

Wallbank, Walter T. et al. *Civilization, Past and Present.* Glenview, IL: Scott, Foresman, 1967.

Warner, Sam Bass , Jr. *The Urban Wilderness, A History of the American City*. New York: Harper and Row, 1972.

Wiltse, Charles M. *The New Nation, 1800–1845*. New York: Hill and Wang, 1961.

Index (The index has been planned for review of important concepts after an initial reading.)

142 Nancy Herndon, "Local land trusts flex new muscle," *The Christian Science Monitor*, 6/7/89. p. 13.
143 Land Trust Exchange
144 Homer Hoyt, *One Hundred Years of Land Values in Chicago* (Chicago, University of Chicago Press, 1933), Table LXXX, p. 470.
145 Ibid., pp. 345,346.
146 James A. Stone, "Disposition of the Public Domain in Wayne County" (M.A. thesis, University of Nebraska, 1952), Table XXIII ("Yearly Average Price of Land Sold by State, Railroads, and Large Land Holders").
147 *The Victorians and ancient Greece*, Cambridge MA: Harvard University Press, 1980.
148 A.R. Radcliffe-Browne, cited in *Social change: explorations, diagnoses and conjectures*, George K. Zollschan and Walter Hirsch ed., New York, John Wiley &Sons, 1976. p. 69.
149 "The economic phenomena of society are not the direct expression of some social force, but are only the resultants of the conduct of individuals, of *wirtschaftende Menschen* (men engaged in economic activity)..." Carl Menger. Cited in Eric Roll, *A history of economic thought*, New York, Prentice-Hall, Inc. 1946, p 425.
150 Kenneth Arrow, as reported by Leonard Silk, "Economic scene; reality's the thing this field needs," *The New York Times*, December 29, 1989..
151 Herbert Simon, cited by Leonard Silk, op. cit.

FREE INVESTMENT TOOL

THE LESSINGER SOCIOECONOMIC EVALUATION TECHNIQUE

For a free investment tool to help you select prospective investments, send us a self-addressed, stamped envelope ($.52 in the U.S.). We will also put you on our mailing list for coming books, articles, conferences, and newsletters on penturbia

Name____
Title____
Company_____________________________________
Street Address________________________________
____
City_______________________State____Zip__________
Daytime phone (   )_____________________________

To serve you better in the future please give us a few details about yourself.

Type of business activity:
Lending? (bank, insurance, etc.) ____________________
Real estate? (sales, construction, etc.) _______________
Investing? (personal residence, comm'l, etc.) __________
Other? (manufacturing, retailing, etc.) _______________
____

Country of interest__________Region of interest_______
Comments or questions_______________________________
____
____
____

SocioEconomics, Inc.

P.O. Box 25062
Seattle, WA 98125-1962